READING

CSI

Crime TV
Under the
Microscope

EDITED BY

MICHAEL ALLEN

I.B. TAURIS

LONDON · NEW YORK

Published in 2007 by I.B.Tauris & Co Ltd
6 Salem Road, London W2 4BU
175 Fifth Avenue, New York NY 10010
www.ibtauris.com

In the United States of America and in Canada distributed by
Palgrave Macmillan, a division of St Martin's Press
175 Fifth Avenue, New York NY 10010

ISBN 978 1 84511 428 2

A full CIP record for this book is available from the British Library
A full CIP record for this book is available from the Library of Congress

Library of Congress catalog card: available

Typeset in Goudy Old Style by Steve Tribe, Andover
Printed and bound in the United States

CONTENTS

ACKNOWLEDGEMENTS

The editor would first like to thank the contributors to this collection – Sue Turnbull, Roberta Pearson, Kim Akass, Deborah Jermyn, Elke Weissmann, Karen Boyle, Anna König, Lury, Lucia Rahilly, Charlie Gere, Patrick West, Janet McCabe, Simone Knox, Dermot Horan, Shelley Robinson, Daryl Vinall, Matt Hills, Amy Luther, and David Bianculli. Together, they have produced a wonderfully incisive, funny, stylish and thought-provoking collection, which they have written and rewritten to tight deadlines with good humour. This collection bears the quality it does because of them.

Special thanks go to Philippa Brewster, not only for her calm professionalism and sage advice, but also for her great patience in dealing with several delays to submission. Gratitude to Adrian Wootton, for his generous time in responding to Kim Akass's question about the Crime Scene weekend he organised at the NFT in 2005 as well as his helpful advice during the project. Additional thanks go to Sue Turnbull for generously making the time to talk to me about *CSI* as well as for securing Shelley Robinson's contribution to the collection. I would like to acknowledge the *Guardian* Newspaper Group for giving permission to reprint the review of *CSI:Miami* from *The Observer*, and the Billy Rose Theater Collection at the New York Public Library for Performing Arts for providing photocopies of articles and reviews on *CSI*.

Love and thanks to Kim Akass, not only for her sterling work in helping to edit the collection, but also just for being a great friend.

All my love and gratitude also to Janet, who has offered her own love and support throughout the length of the project, not only giving me sound advice and guidance but also, in the final days of work, great shoulder-to-shoulder editing to get the collection into the best of shapes. I cannot thank her enough.

And finally, my love to Olivia, our new daughter, who has transformed both our personal and our working lives, so that we now juggle teaching, writing and editing with disturbed nights, nappies and playtime.

CONTRIBUTORS

KIM AKASS has co-edited and contributed to *Reading* Sex and the City (I.B.Tauris, 2004), *Reading* Six Feet Under: *TV To Die For* (I.B.Tauris, 2005), *Reading* The L Word: *Outing Contemporary Television* (I.B.Tauris, 2006) and *Reading* Desperate Housewives: *Beyond The White Picket Fence* (I.B.Tauris, 2006). She is currently researching the representation of motherhood on American TV and is co-editor of the new television journal *Critical Studies in Television* (MUP) as well as (with McCabe) series editor of 'Reading Contemporary Television' for I.B.Tauris.

MICHAEL ALLEN is a Lecturer in Film and Electronic Media at Birkbeck College, University of London. His publications include the books *Family Secrets: The Feature Films of D.W. Griffith* (BFI, 1999) and *Contemporary US Cinema* (Pearson, 2003), as well as numerous articles on the history of media technologies. He is currently completing a book detailing the relationship between film, television and the Space Race of the 1960s.

ANDREW ANTHONY is a television critic for *The Observer*.

DAVID BIANCULLI is a television critic for the *New York Daily News* and National Public Radio's *Fresh Air*.

KAREN BOYLE is a Lecturer in Film and Television Studies at the University of Glasgow. She is the author of *Media and Violence: Gendering the Debates* (Sage, 2004) and has published a number of articles on feminism, violence and pornography.

CHARLIE GERE is a Reader in New Media Research at the Institute for Cultural Research, Lancaster University. He is the Chair of Computers and the History of Art (CHArt) and author of *Digital Culture* (Reaktion, 2002), *Art, Time and Technology* (Berg, 2006), co-editor of *White Heat, Cold Logic* (MIT, forthcoming 2008) as well as many articles and papers on aspects of the relation between new media and culture. He lives in a village in North Yorkshire with his family.

MATT HILLS is the author of *Fan Cultures* (Routledge, 2002), *The Pleasures of Horror* (Continuum, 2005) and *How To Do Things With Cultural Theory* (Hodder Arnold, 2005). A Senior Lecturer at the Cardiff School of Journalism, Media and Cultural Studies, Matt is currently researching and writing a book for I.B.Tauris about the BBC Wales' series of *Doctor Who*, as well as a textbook for Sage introducing Key Concepts in Cultural Studies.

DERMOT HORAN is the Director of Broadcast and Acquisitions for RTE, the Irish public broadcaster. As such he sits on the board of the Television division of RTE, and is responsible for the following areas: Programme Acquisitions, Scheduling, On Air Presentation and Promotion, Press and Publicity, Marketing, Programme Sales, Merchandising and Licensing. His high profile acquisitions for RTE include *ER*, *The Sopranos*, *Desperate Housewives*, *Lost*, *Ally McBeal*, *24*, *The West Wing* and *Friends*.

DEBORAH JERMYN is a Senior Lecturer in Film and TV at Roehampton University. She has co-edited *The Audience Studies Reader* (with Will Brooker) (Routledge, 2002), *The Cinema of Kathryn Bigelow: Hollywood Transgressor* (with Sean Redmond) (Wallflower, 2002) and *Understanding Reality TV* (with Su Holmes) (Routledge, 2003). She has published widely on women, feminism and popular culture, and is the author of *Crime Watching: Investigating Real Crime TV* (I.B.Tauris, 2006).

ANNA KÖNIG is a Lecturer at the London College of Fashion. She has written for publications including *The Times* and *The Guardian*, and research interests include the language of fashion journalism and ethical consumption within the fashion industry.

KAREN LURY is a Reader in Film and Television Studies in the Department of Theatre, Film and Television Studies at the University of Glasgow, Scotland. She is the author of *Interpreting Television* (Hodder

Arnold, 2005) and *British Youth Television: Cynicism and Enchantment* (Oxford University Press, 2001). Her current research concentrates on the figure of the child in cinema. She is an editor of the journal *Screen*.

AMY LUTHER is a PhD candidate at the Cardiff School of Journalism, Media and Cultural Studies. Her PhD analyses the discursive gender identity of male fiction readers and is in the process of completion. Recently Amy has worked on research projects for Mediawise investigating levels of PR reliance in British national newspapers and for INSI researching deaths of journalists and media workers.

JANET McCABE is a Research Associate (TV Drama) at Manchester Metropolitan University. She is the author of *Feminist Film Studies: Writing the Woman into Cinema* (Wallflower, 2004), and co-editor of and contributor to *Reading* Sex and the City (I.B.Tauris, 2004), *Reading* Six Feet Under: *TV To Die For* (I.B.Tauris, 2005), *Reading* The L Word: *Outing Contemporary Television* (I.B.Tauris, 2006) and *Reading* Desperate Housewives: *Beyond The White Picket Fence* (I.B.Tauris, 2006). She is managing editor of the new television journal *Critical Studies in Television* (MUP) as well as (with Akass) series editor of 'Reading Contemporary Television' for I.B.Tauris.

SILKE PANSE wrote on self-reflexivity in documentary for her doctoral thesis. Her research explores the tensions between documentary subjectivity and objectivity in different cultural, conceptual and political contexts. Her article 'The Film-maker as Rückenfigur: Documentary as Painting in Alexandr Sokurov's *Elegy of a Voyage*' has been published by Third Text, and she contributed to the *Encyclopedia of the Documentary Film*. She organised the conference 'Werner Herzog's Cinema: Between the Visionary and the Documentary', and is editing the conference collection. She is an Associate Lecturer at the University of Kent, Chelsea College of Art and Design and the University College for the Creative Arts.

ROBERTA PEARSON is Director of the Institute of Film and Television Studies at the University of Nottingham. She is the co-editor of *Cult Television* (University of Minnesota Press, 2004) and the co-author of *Small Screen, Big Universe: Star Trek as Television* (University of California Press, forthcoming).

LUCIA RAHILLY has done graduate work in film, TV and literature, and holds an MA from the Cinema Studies Department at New York University. Her other TV-related criticism includes 'WWF Wrestling as Popular Sadomasochism' in *No Holds Barred* (2004). A freelance writer and editor, she lives in New York City.

SHELLEY ROBINSON is a doctor and pathologist. She has been awarded Fellowships from the Royal College of Pathologists of Australasia and the Royal College of Physicians, and is a Fellow of the Australian College of Legal Medicine, and obtained a post-graduate Diploma of Medical Jurisprudence in Pathology (DMJ) from the Society of Apothecaries, London in 1996. She has trained in blood spatter analysis in the USA, and teaches at the University of Monash, Melbourne. She is a keen reader of crime fiction and true crime, is a member of 'Sisters-in-Crime', and has published her own short crime fiction.

SUE TURNBULL is an Associate Professor in Media Studies at La Trobe University, Melbourne where she teaches about audiences, television and aesthetics in popular culture. She also reviews crime fiction for the *Age*, and is chief crime fiction reviewer for the *Sydney Morning Herald*. She has been a co-convenor of the writers and readership network 'Sisters-in-Crime Australia' since 1992 and has published widely on crime fiction and its readerships. Her current research project with Dr Felicity Collins at La Trobe is concerned with the history of Australian screen comedy, and is funded by an Australian Research Council Discovery Grant.

DARYL VINALL is a BTEC student of forensic science at City & Islington College. He hopes to pursue a career in forensic science, either as a Scene of Crime Officer or in ballistics.

ELKE WEISSMANN recently submitted her PhD on *CSI* and the shift towards forensics in television crime drama. She is a post-doctoral researcher for the project 'British TV Drama & Acquired US Programmes' at the University of Reading.

PATRICK WEST is Senior Lecturer in Writing in the School of Arts at Griffith University, Brisbane. His research interests span television studies, psychoanalytic theory, Australian and New Zealand literature and creative writing. His academic output is supplemented by publications in the short story, creative non-fiction and literary journalism genres.

REGULAR CAST LIST

CSI: CRIME SCENE INVESTIGATION

Capt. Jim Brass — Paul Guilfoyle
Warrick Brown — Gary Dourdan
Gil Grissom — William L. Petersen
David Phillips — David Berman
Dr Al Robbins — Robert David Hall
Greg Sanders — Eric Szmanda
Sara Sidle — Jorja Fox
Nick Stokes — George Eads
Catherine Willows — Marg Helgenberger
Sofia Curtis — Louise Lombard

CSI: MIAMI

Natalia Boa Vista — Eva La Rue
Lieut. Horatio Caine — David Caruso
Eric Delko — Adam Rodriguez
Megan Donner — Kim Delaney
Calleigh Duquesne — Emily Procter
Det. Yelina Salas — Sofia Milos
Tim Speedle — Rory Cochrane
Det. Frank Tripp — Rex Linn
Ryan Wolfe — Jonathan Togo
Dr Alexx Woods — Khandi Alexander

CSI: NY

Det. Stella Bonasera	Melina Kanakaredes
Aiden Burn	Vanessa Ferlito
Det. Don Flack	Eddie Cahill
Dr Sid Hammerback	Robert Joy
Dr Sheldon Hawkes	Hill Harper
Danny Messer	Carmine Giovinazzo
Lindsay Monroe	Anna Belknap
Det. Mac Taylor	Gary Sinise

:I:

THIS MUCH WE KNOW
Introductions and Contexts

∶ ∶
Introduction
THIS MUCH I KNOW...
MICHAEL ALLEN

In America's *TV Guide* of 23 February 2002, Janet Weeks reported that:

> *Variety*, the entertainment industry's premier trade publication,
> has at last published a story detailing [*CSI: Crime Scene
> Investigation*'s] rise to No.2 television drama (behind *ER*) and
> its membership in the select '25 million viewer club'. Without
> adoring critics or sweeping awards-show wins, the dark drama
> (CBS, Thursdays, 9P.M./ET) about the unseemly sides of
> science, law enforcement and Las Vegas has become a megahit
> (2002: 16).

Four-and-a-half years later, in *TV Guide*'s British equivalent, *Radio Times*,
Jenny Eden reported that:

> *CSI: Miami* is the most popular programme in the world. This
> startling fact was unearthed by a study of global viewing trends
> earlier this year ... Although trashed in the US ratings by its
> older sibling *CSI: Crime Scene Investigation*, Jerry Bruckheimer's
> *CSI: Miami* has, within four seasons, established itself as the
> greater success in foreign territories (2006: 11).

As these two quotations amply demonstrate, the *CSI* franchise – *CSI:
Crime Scene Investigation*, *CSI: Miami* and *CSI: NY* – has, as a series of
procedural dramas about forensic scientists in different locations, become
a worldwide television phenomenon.

Why?

Perhaps the clues are in the two quotes above: the showing of the 'unseemly side' of criminal life from a fresh angle; the importance of location (location, location) as the 'scene' in 'Crime Scene Investigation'; the foreign appeal; and a Hollywood producer behind the show, (in)famous for the excessive visual quality of his blockbuster movie hits. Such factors have enabled the original show, *CSI: Crime Scene Investigation*, and its two spin-offs to rejuvenate the over-familiar crime-based television drama genre.

And yet...

On the downside are several other elements: the formulaic structure, repeated week-in week-out, which focuses on the painstaking scientific analysis of evidence rather than the exciting confrontation with criminals; the enigmatic characters about whom we learn virtually nothing, at least about their private lives. (Assuming, dedicated professionals that they are, they have private lives.) Why would such a drama capture such huge global attention and a loyal fan following?

CSI: Crime Scene Investigation first aired in America on 6 October 2000. It was to have been made as a partnership between CBS and Touchstone Pictures, the Disney offshoot, but Touchstone pulled out of the deal because it 'didn't believe that producing *CSI* made financial sense, given the inability of its international sales force to generate sizeable deals for the show overseas' (Schneider and Adalian 2000: 13). Touchstone was replaced by Alliance Atlantis, an eclectic Canadian film and television production company whose previous notable works included *Due South* (with CBS), the Neil LaBute independent feature *In the Company of Men* (1997) and David Cronenberg's *eXistenZ* (1999). Quirky crime-solving television dramedy; revenge drama driven by characters damaged by love; and a director noted for his focus on the visceral physicality of the human body: these are the origins of the elements that would make *CSI: Crime Scene Investigation* and its two offspring so distinctive and so compelling as original television.

The main creative personnel on the show had had mixed degrees of previous success in film and television production. Original creator Anthony E. Zuiker's only prior credit was as the writer of the low-budget feature, *The Runner* (1999), starring Courtney Cox, while Carol Mendelsohn's most notable earlier credit was as a writer on *Melrose Place*. Director Danny Cannon's relatively short career had been responsible for such box-office failures as the Sylvester Stallone vehicle, *Judge Dredd* (1995), and the unremarkable (and appallingly titled) slasher-movie sequel, *I Still Know What You Did Last Summer* (1998). Little here to reassure nervous television executives.

Perhaps unsurprisingly, therefore, CBS's uncertainty about the show caused it to place it after what it thought would be a sure-fire hit: a remake of the 1960s television drama *The Fugitive* (already remade in 1993 as a Harrison Ford vehicle), in the hope that the latter show would capture the audience who would then stay with CBS to see what *CSI* was all about. Much to the surprise of CBS, *CSI* was a hit, overshadowing its much more vaunted 'protector' which received mixed reviews. Before the end of Season One, CBS had moved the show to 9 p.m. on Thursdays, a timeslot in which NBC had held sway since the early 1980s. In its 2000–2001 season it gained eleventh place in the ratings. The following season it climbed to second before attaining pole position in the 2002–2003 season. *CSI: Miami* subsequently aired on 23 September 2002, and *CSI: NY* on 22 September 2004, compounding the growing presence that the CSI franchise commanded on American prime-time television.

The franchise concept is certainly not new to television. *Star Trek*, originally created in 1966 by Gene Roddenberry, had generated several strands, all with the *Star Trek* prefix, including *Next Generation*, *Deep Space Nine* and *Voyager*. Closer to home, generically speaking, the crime drama *Law & Order* and its offshoots, *Special Victims Unit* and *Criminal Intent*, all of which are still in production, enjoy continued success in the ratings. Another reason for this replication is obviously television's endless voracious need for product to fill its schedules along with its inherent fragility, with ever more costly productions surviving or being cancelled within the first few episodes, depending on audience and critic reaction. But drama costs. It is the most expensive form of television and this is why development executives like the franchise. When you have a success like *CSI* the race is on to repeat it. In sum, networks like to play it safe, and 'Franchising is perfectly suited to network television, which loathes risk to begin with' (James 2002: E5).

What has helped the *CSI* shows stand out from the televisual crowd is their casting. All three are headed by actors with notable, if occasionally chequered, Hollywood careers. William Petersen, star of the original *CSI: Crime Scene Investigation*, has gained a reputation for artistic integrity, both by appearing with the respected theatre company Steppenwolf and for the films he has made (*Manhunter* [1986]) and those he has not (*Platoon* [1986]). David Caruso, star of *CSI: Miami*, had controversially walked away after the first season of *NYPD Blue* in a bid to become a film star; an attempt that was famously curtailed with the relative failure of films such as the prophetically titled *Kiss of Death* (1995) and *Proof of Life* (2000). Gary Sinise, star of *CSI: NY*, has perhaps the most notable feature-film curriculum vitae of the three leads. Before making his first foray into television, he received an Academy Award nomination for his portrayal of Lt. Dan Taylor in *Forrest Gump* (1994) in 1995, won a Golden Globe for his role in *Truman* (1996) as well as numerous film appearances, including *Of Mice and Men* (1992), *Apollo 13* (1995) and *The Green Mile* (1999). Each are backed up by strong supporting casts with solid television credentials: Jorja Fox (*ER*, *The West Wing*), Marg Helgenberger (*China Beach*, *ER*) and Emily Procter (*The West Wing*). The history of quality American television informs the three shows, and strengthens their ability to extend the *CSI* franchise into new strands. 'Although the revolving door of *Law & Order* suggests that franchises are actor-proof, they're not; they just rely on smart casting' (James 2002: E5).

Actors are not solely responsible for the success of a television show. Writers, directors and producers are as, perhaps even more, important creatively, and the *CSI* franchise boasts strength in these areas too. Writers Anthony E. Zuiker, Carol Mendelsohn and Ann Donahue have ensured that the narrative quality of each episode remains high. Director Danny Cannon has been instrumental in creating and maintaining a distinctive look for all three *CSI* strands. Standing over the production process is executive producer Jerry Bruckheimer, responsible for having produced many of the biggest Hollywood blockbusters of the 1980s and 1990s such as *Beverley Hills Cop* (1984) and *The Rock* (1996). Bruckheimer's trademark use of bombastic action and excessive visual effects have, at least in the latter case, had a marked influence on the *CSI* visual aesthetic, especially in the so-called 'CSI-shot' – the dynamic and visceral zooming into and through human bodies as they are punctured by knives and bullets.

But it cannot just be about the star names, actors, directors or producers, who are responsible for one or other of the franchise strands, important though these figures are. What else does *CSI* offer the television networks and companies who spend huge sums of money for the privilege of screening it and, indeed, its ever-increasing global audience? For CBS, as noted earlier, it provided a show which could capture a coveted weekly evening schedule from a rival who had come to assume it as its own. In Britain, as Simone Knox details in her chapter in this collection, Five bought it as one of the means by which it planned to reinvent itself as a serious terrestrial channel after several years as a provider of notoriously low-culture product, as Jeff Ford, the channel's Director of Acquisitions has admitted:

We'd been trying to make a statement, trying to find a show
to make a change in terms of what we buy, and this was that
sort of show. OK, some people have said it's not pushing the
envelope, but what it does do is tell a story extremely well with
style. It is a far more upmarket piece than we have been going
for in the past (Morris 2001: 8).

An added attraction, noted by many of those responsible for buying and
scheduling the shows, including RTÉ buyer/scheduler Dermot Horan in
this volume, is that, because of a number of elements for which they were
often criticised – lack of character development, formulaic repetition, etc
– the shows have little narrative or character continuity. The consequence
of this is that audiences don't feel forced to watch week after week or
risk missing vital plot information (as is the case, for example, with 24,
where missing an episode necessitates a great deal of effort to catch up
with the plot). Episodes can therefore easily be seen out of sequence, an
'attribute' of particular attraction to schedulers who often have spare,
unpredictable, hours to fill in their weekly schedules.

For its audiences it offered, as Ford indicates, a show that told its
stories 'extremely well and with style'. And, although its repetitive
structure and format, and its reluctance to expand upon the private lives
of principal characters has been criticised, it is perhaps this very coyness
that has helped to make the franchise a growing success. Audiences
perhaps feel the need to return each week to watch the next episode, to
be given another fragment of backstory that will help them piece together
their knowledge of the CSI teams and, especially, their idiosyncratic and
mysterious leaders.

This need can be witnessed in the plethora of websites, official and
unofficial, which has grown in support of the franchise. Matt Hills and
Amy Luther in this anthology investigate the often strange and nuanced
world of the CSI web-fan, but it is worth saying a few words here about
the traffic on these websites. Everything about the CSI-world is discussed
in exhaustive detail: the ins and outs of each episode; the likes and
dislikes of every fan; interpretations of characters' motives and actions,
especially the ongoing 'are they/aren't they?' relationship between Gil
Grissom and Sara Sidle in CSI: Crime Scene Investigation. This discussion
forum adds emotional weight and substance to the enigmatic framework
offered by the show itself; a circuit of debate that often feeds back into
the series, as the programme's creative personnel add themselves to the
mix. Mendelsohn has noted that, 'For a show that's a procedural, with

very few windows into the characters' intimate private lives, people are so into character. Are Grissom and Sara meant to be together? Is Grissom meant to be with Catherine?' (Holston date unknown: D14)

One additional element is worth considering; to return to the 'location, location, location' theme posited at the head of this Introduction: the importance of the cities themselves. Las Vegas (absent from the title of the original series – CSI: Crime Scene Investigation – but retrospectively allowed to 're-brand' it in light of subsequent spin-offs); Miami; New York. These are specific sites of American culture and identity. Las Vegas: the embodiment of the American Dream – instant fortune, immediate gratification, wonderful living – and its inverse – failure, tragedy, death; Miami: sunshine and wealth, racial melting-pot, illegal immigration and infiltration of national security and borders; New York: the Big Apple, another racial melting-pot and site of legal immigration, globally iconic, the city that never sleeps, epicentre of the nation's worst nightmare of the 9/11 terrorist attacks. The three cities, together, present the best and worst of America and, in so doing, offer their CSI teams an inexhaustible (for inexhaustible investigators) supply of dead bodies and cases to solve. But the differences between the three also informs the style and tone of the shows that bear their names:

> In New York, of course, some of the criminals will be single-minded – in part because of the harsher conditions of the city. When you have to bundle up and fight to get into Manhattan to get to your job, that makes you different than the girl that's in Miami, which is peaceful and placid,' Ms. Donahue said. 'That's the kind of girl you'll be able to break really quickly' (Levine 2004: 25).

Therefore, although they are cut from the same franchise cloth, the three CSI shows have their distinctive personalities, figured in colour scheme, character, accent, and type of victim and culprit.

Ultimately, in a vulnerable, permanently threatened (if you believe the scaremongers headed by President George W. Bush) post-9/11 America, CSI offers certainty and unrelenting professionalism in the search for truth and justice.

If CSI came along at the right scientific moment, it also coincided with a moment of anxiety. It premiered 11 months before the terrorist attacks on New York and Washington, and far from being undone by its graphic depiction of charred or mutilated human bodies, the series climbed even higher in the Nielsen ratings after the world experienced a new level of vulnerability.

> 'From people's back yards all the way to Afghanistan and
> Iraq, there is a clear sense of uncertainty that CSI addresses
> cleanly, clinically and satisfyingly to many viewers,' says John
> Rash, senior vice president of Minneapolis' Campbell-Mithun
> Advertising (Holston date unknown: D14).

America currently needs reassuring, and the über-professional teams that head the three *CSI* shows are unrelenting in their investigation of the minutiae of criminal evidence. Indeed, the scale of their work – tiny fragments of hair, bodily fluid, skin – connects all too fundamentally with the terrorist attacks. Not only to the reality of post-9/11 rescue work, which continues to identify victims' remains from their smallest traces, but also, inversely, on a massive scale, to the enormity of the event itself – the biggest structure in Manhattan razed to the ground. *CSI*'s task is to understand its huge tragedies and human complexities from the smallest of remains. This is, of course, a dynamic that *CSI: NY*, inevitably, confronts head on (and a subject which Janet McCabe addresses in her chapter), while *CSI: Crime Scene Investigation* and *CSI: Miami* address obliquely, acknowledging the national agenda of fear and paranoia through more distanced and localised referents.

Diffusion, thereby, lends common cause to America's battle against crime and, specifically, terrorist threats. New York we can understand: it happened, horrifically, there and was globally witnessed. But *New York* is the third of the current stable of *CSI* shows, airing two years after *Miami*, three after the 9/11 event itself and four after the very beginning of *CSI: Crime Scene Investigation*. Therefore, it is not a direct response to the terrorism but, rather, a considered culmination that confirms the agendas staked by its previous two incarnations. In a fundamental sense *CSI: NY*, the most derided of the three strands (by critics and even by members of *CSI*'s own production team – William Petersen rejected *Miami*, and *New York* even more so) comes to represent the most; a lurking fear amongst Americans (and not just Americans; people across the globe) that life has become more untenable. Not just because of terrorism, but because of global warming, greenhouse gases, pollution and unseeable threats (AIDS on the grand scale, obviously, but also, more immediately, house mites causing chronic asthma, and unidentified chemicals causing who-knows-what), as well as the impossible-to-understand complexity of human relationships, has prompted a driving need to understand: why, how, when, where. *CSI* answers the need while prolonging the quest. Its weekly solving of the crime provides temporary resolution and comfort, while also gesturing towards the insurmountable caseload that is both the marker of the crime-ridden modern age and the ensurer of the continuance, and perhaps further expansion, of the *CSI* franchise.

The essays in this volume explore the varied and complex meanings of the continuity and difference that is embodied in the *CSI* franchise. They acknowledge both *CSI*'s unique form and contemporary global appeal while always ensuring that this phenomenal success is carefully situated within multiple television histories: of industrial practice, relations with its 'big brother' cinema, multiple-media forms and the specifics of the crime drama genre. It also offers an exploration of *CSI* within a theoretical framework, considering its significance in terms of television and film aesthetics, notably spectacle and realism, narrative and character, and notions of Derridean trace, Lacanian lack and Mulveyian to-be-looked-at-ness. Together, these essays seek to understand *CSI* in the fullness of its significance for contemporary television, both as an industrial business and as a site for cultural meditation and debate.

Following the survey of the general *CSI* context outlined by this Introduction, Sue Turnbull offers a valuable history of the crime and pathology genre on television. Drawing on significant television crime dramas of the past fifty years, she situates *CSI* at the end of this history, imbued with its values and terms of reference while seeking to offer something new and different. A contemporary response to this is the witty and pithy review from *The Observer* of *CSI: Miami*. Responding to the recent poll that *CSI: Miami* was the most watched TV show on the planet, Andrew Anthony mixes humorous parody with pseudo-reluctant liking for the show which perfectly captures its position in the contemporary televisual landscape: an inherently derided generic product that has become the world's most popularly viewed programme.

Part Two begins with Roberta Pearson's investigation into the restrictions on character development. Primarily focusing on the original *CSI: Crime Scene Investigation*, she uses the show as a means of understanding narrative in general and television (and film) narrative in particular. Hers is a significant contribution in two major, and related, ways: understanding how character development and narrative arcs operate across television drama generally and how they operate in *CSI* specifically. In this double investigation, Pearson succeeds in situating *CSI*'s distinctiveness within the broad spectrum of television drama, identifying CSI's reticence in terms of its character development within a longer history of serial form.

Following on from Pearson's lead, I then explore the expansion of our knowledge of the world of CSI and its principal characters through the range of additional CSI narratives made available in non-televisual form: in the written and graphic novels and video games manufactured as tie-ins to the television shows. I argue that these extra-narrative accounts provide us with knowledge of the CSI teams, and especially their leaders, denied us in the shows themselves. Through the differing demands they make on their reader/player, these extra-diegetic narratives echo aspects both of the operations performed by members of the CSI teams and the viewing experience of watching the shows.

Kim Akass completes this section with her account of the Crime Scene Weekend event hosted at London's National Film Theatre in July 2006. In her analysis of the event, she offers another layer of narrative for the CSI franchise as she explores the cultural and intellectual significance of a 'low-culture' television programme occupying centre stage at a national cinema venue.

Part Three deals with the formal aesthetic qualities of the CSI franchise. Deborah Jermyn considers the relationship between realism and spectacle in relation to the celebrated CSI special effects and offers an historical perspective on the depiction and dissection of the corpse in the shows. Elke Weissmann and Karen Boyle take this consideration of the aesthetic presentation of the body in CSI within the purview of pornography. They analyse the graphic qualities of the special effects, and especially the celebrated 'CSI-shot' showing violent and garish penetration of human flesh and inner organs, in terms of revealing and making visible truth, especially as it relates to the 'maleness' both of many of the dead victims and of their CSI investigators.

Anna König offers a take on the fashion aesthetic operating throughout the CSI franchise; a perspective that partly cuts against the ostensible image of the CSI-ers as science geeks rather than cool dudes. All three CSI strands are revealed as high-fashion, cutting a dash and an image. CSI: Miami is all about being seen. CSI: NY has attitude in general and certainly one specifically about its looks. But even the original CSI is peopled by characters who consider their wardrobe and respect their image... well, perhaps not Grissom, but certainly his team.

Karen Lury's contribution concerns itself with the qualities of the soundtrack of CSI. Sound is an habitually under-investigated and considered element of the audio-visual text, filmic or televisual, and

Lury's exploration of the complex layers of meaning carried by the sonic layer of the *CSI* text is an invaluable addition to our understanding of both sound in media generally and, more importantly in the present instance, its function in carrying meaning within the *CSI* context. Her movement from the diegetically and the extra-diegetically audible to the spiritually profound, especially in terms of Grissom's encroaching deafness, is elegant and illuminating. Finally, in this section, Lucia Rahilly explores the relationship between appearance and reality in Las Vegas in relation to *CSI*'s search for objective truth through scientific rationale and method.

Part Four explores a number of theoretical approaches to *CSI*. Charlie Gere's interest lies in teasing out the implications of Derridean terms of trace and writing in relation to the procedural framework of *CSI* analysis. He explores notions of the law as they relate both to the business of policing and to the rules of genre. He then explores the idea of the ghostly process of writing as a trace of the absent writer, tying this in with the forensic procedures of the *CSI* teams in revealing invisible traces of absent bodies and events.

Patrick West offers a complex argument founded upon a seemingly simple and obvious trope: that of Horatio Caine/David Caruso's almost obsessive taking off/putting on of his sunglasses (the character and actor are conflated because the character tic is generated out of the actor's need for a hook to hang his characterisation upon). While, superficially (so redolent of Miami) just a pretentious mannerism (of character, or actor, take your pick), West builds the gesture into a complex system of looks which draws upon a wealth of theoretical material surrounding subject and identity formation operating around the power of the gaze.

Offering another perspective on this theme of looking and the gaze, Silke Panse explores the role of the visible and invisible, and the deficiencies of the eye and vision in determining truth. She discusses these in relation to various theoretical positions, including psychoanalysis and cognitive science.

Concluding this section is Janet McCabe with her chapter on *CSI: NY*. Fascinated why we get to know so much about Detective Mac Taylor so soon, she argues that the latest *CSI* franchise is based on the founding trauma of an absent body. She views the series as a melancholic text – formulaic narrative, generic patterns, aesthetic forms, thematic concerns, cultural politics, industrial conditions – which participates in rituals of re-remembering and forgetting 9/11 while providing a space verbosely concerned with trauma and recovery.

Part Five, the concluding section, explores questions of reception and industry. Simone Knox opens with a specific case of how *CSI* was used by Britain's fifth channel to reinvent itself in a changing television landscape. Using extensive corporate material, and revealing interviews, she details the strategy used by the channel to renegotiate its identity and position in relation to the remaining four terrestrial networks (BBC One, BBC Two, ITV, Channel 4). Her study, while specific, also offers a wider understanding of how *CSI* has been employed, in an industrial sense, to help remodel existing corporate identities and positions. In this, her chapter interconnects with Dermot Horan's on how *CSI* is used by RTE to position itself in terms of both Irish and overseas competition.

Moving on to questions of reception and audiences, the collection includes contributions from two people working in forensics. One, an experienced Australian pathologist, Shelley Robinson, and another, a British student studying forensic science, Daryl Vinall. Running these two pieces concurrently allows for a dialogue to emerge between an experienced forensic scientist and a rookie, about what they see in the show and its divergence from reality.

Matt Hills and Amy Luther explore the burgeoning world of *CSI* fan websites in order to determine the terms by which the shows are judged, evaluated and discussed as ongoing cultural phenomena. Their study shows the growing social hinterland surrounding the *CSI* franchise, in which the content delivered by the three strands is fiercely discussed, evaluated and personalised in an interactive form not feasible in conventional terrestrial, or even cable/satellite, television. Concluding this collection is David Bianculli and his witty and informed piece from 'across the pond', which seeks to position the *CSI* phenomenon, and *CSI: Miami* in particular, within its widest entertainment framework. He returns the collection, rightly, to its popular appeal; its strangely, almost perversely, popular appeal.

Each paper in their own way aims to consider why such a strictly formulaic, endlessly repeated, modular drama has come to command such a massive, global television audience. Together, these various contributions seek to understand both its fantastic popular appeal and its particular intellectual address to wider issues of identity and what it means, fundamentally, to continue to be human in our contemporary age. For all the enigmatic emotional framing of its main characters – indeed perhaps even because of this resistance – *CSI* reaffirms the fundamental conditions of existence. And not only the basic conditions but also, in the face of relentless death and destruction, the stoic, limited but determined respect for life. In a world in which what it means to be human is forever taken apart, dissected, examined, analysed and virtually reassembled, what other possible outcome can there be? The *CSI* teams' relentless examination of the human condition reaffirms what it means to be innocent rather than guilty, neither the 'vic' or the 'perp', but simply, gloriously, alive.

:1:

THE HOOK AND THE LOOK

CSI and the Aesthetics of the Television Crime Series
SUE TURNBULL

On 25 June 2004[1] the entry for the original *CSI* series set in Las Vegas on the Internet Movie Database offered the following 'user comment' from George Parker, Orange County, CA:

> CSI takes the viewer into the world of forensic criminal investigations set against the glitz and glitter of the Las Vegas strip. 'Mr Vanilla' (Petersen) leads the Crime Scene Investigation (CSI) unit comprised of a bunch of actors who look like a bunch of actors while playing it fast and loose with the forensic sciences. Tight, fast moving, and formulaic, CSI solves cases like an Energizer bunny on 'Speed' with no room for character development, emotional investments, back stories, buy-ins and drama. The result is a hugely popular fare of fast food for small screen freaks which will play best with less sophisticated and discerning TV viewers. More sophisticated audiences might want to check out 'Homicide: Life on the Streets', 'Prime Suspect', 'Cracker' and the like to satisfy their more jaded appetites (B-).

I have chosen to begin with Mr Parker's comments because they reveal how inevitably judgements of aesthetic value can slide via the mechanism of personal taste into unwarranted judgements about the imagined consumer. Because the hugely popular *CSI* is 'tight, fast moving and formulaic', and Mr Parker doesn't like it, then he is a sophisticated TV viewer and anyone who does like it is not. It's a fairly typical move in the language of popular television criticism where such hierarchies of value abound.

Mr Parker is, however, right to suggest that the style and the format of the show might be an important factor in its popularity and success, and I want to take his hint here to explore in more detail the aesthetics of the series. *CSI* may indeed be a very different television crime series from *Homicide: Life on the Streets*, *Prime Suspect* and *Cracker*, but how and why? What is it about the style, format and indeed content of *CSI* which makes it different, and so hugely successful? What's the hook and what's the look? As I write this in August 2006, Season Six of *CSI* is now airing in Australia and is still winning its timeslot as the highest-rating drama show for Channel Nine, a commercial free-to-air network which has otherwise struggled to hold its own against fierce competition from rival Channel Seven's other import winners, *Desperate Housewives*, *Prison Break* and *Lost*.[2]

In order to address issues of style and format, I therefore want to locate *CSI* within a highly selective history of the television crime series as a genre. In other words, I want to trace its bloodline from the 1950s to the present as a way of understanding just what kind of an Energizer bunny it might be. And, in so doing, I want to suggest that an historical approach to the televisual aesthetics of *CSI*, in terms of format and style, might lead to a rather different assessment of its quality as a crime series than that of Mr Parker quoted above.

For a variety of reasons, not least because it usually figures first in histories of the genre (except when these are British), I want to begin with *Dragnet*, created, written, produced, directed, narrated, and starring Jack Webb. *Dragnet* was apparently inspired by Webb's small role in a film noir entitled *He Walked by Night* (1948) directed by Alfred Werker, although Anthony Mann is regarded by many as the uncredited auteur of many scenes (Silver and Ward 1980: 121). The film begins with the titles over a street map of LA, followed by a screen of text which reads, 'This is a true story ... only the names have been changed to protect the innocent.' While various shots of Los Angeles appear, a documentary-style voice announces (just in case we haven't got it yet), 'This is Los Angeles' and goes on to tell us a range of statistics about the city including the fact that it is 'the largest police beat in the country and the toughest' and that 'The work of the police, like that of a woman, is never done'. Ten minutes into the film, the police captain, who is on the trail of a cop killer, announces,

'Let's go downtown and see what they picked up in the dragnet,' referring to a prior command that all likely suspects be pulled in for interrogation. The stylistic parallels of *CSI* with the opening of a typical *Dragnet* TV episode are thus immediately apparent, not to mention the origin of the title.

In the film *He Walked by Night*, Jack Webb plays a 'lab technician', or rather what might now be called a medical examiner, or even a crime scene investigator. We first see him dusting a car for fingerprints, then comparing spent bullets for striations, and finally performing an early form of photo-fit composition, projecting slides of facial parts onto a screen as a room full of witnesses construct a collective portrait of the suspect which will lead to his identification. It's a coincidence, but a nice one, that Webb appears in a *CSI* role in the film which not only inspired his subsequent radio and TV series, but which also helped establish the foundations for the television crime series as a genre, concerned with documenting the minutiae of police procedure and the role of science in detection.

Dragnet first aired on NBC radio in 1949, running for seven years to 1955 and with a television version broadcast from December 1951 until 1959. Regularly rating in the TV top ten, at the height of its success in the 1953–1954 season Webb's show came second only to *I Love Lucy*. Resurrected as a telemovie in 1967, a new series in colour was produced, directed and written by Webb which lasted a further three and a half seasons. Exhumed once again in 1989–1990 after Webb's death in 1982, the show failed to find an audience; probably, as one online commentator suggests, because the style of the television cop show had changed so dramatically in the interim: a set of changes I will try to delineate here.[3]

As a TV series, *Dragnet* therefore had three possible origins in three different media forms. The first and most obvious source is the highly stylised noir film of the 1940s, of which *He Walked by Night* is a less celebrated example. As Jason Mittell points out, the concept of 'film-noir' as a genre would hardly have been available to Webb at the time, the term only just coming into currency amongst French film theorists at the end of the 1940s (2005: 129). However, in its atmospheric lighting, especially in the final scenes set in the storm-water drains under Los Angeles through which the suspect frantically runs, the walls illuminated only by his torch, the film is highly effective in its use of noirish lighting, or rather darkness. Indeed, these scenes prefigure the stylistic use of concentrated sources of white light (especially the strategic use of torches) employed by the *CSI* series some fifty years later. The second and third origins involve a combination of the distinctive narrative voice of the hard-boiled detective, most usually identified with the crime fiction of Dashiell Hammett and Raymond Chandler, with that of the documentary commentary.

By the time he conceived and produced *Dragnet*, Webb had not only appeared in a film noir about the LAPD police, but had also played the part of a hard-boiled detective on radio in the series *Jeff Regan – Investigator* in 1948. The significance of the radio connection should not be underestimated given that *Dragnet* continued to run simultaneously on radio. One consequence of this doubling up meant that Webb regularly used radio actors in the TV series, employing them for their voices rather than their looks: a decision which had a considerable impact on the visual style of the show. The people looked 'real', not pretty, a look which underlined its documentary impulse.

In assessing the televisual aesthetics of *Dragnet*, its particular content and form, it is therefore hard to get past the existence of Jack Webb as a TV auteur long before the concept of auteurship had even been broached in film theory, never mind television studies. While film theorists in the 1960s nominated the director as auteur, thus seeking parity with literary studies in the academy, Newcombe and Alley suggested that television was in fact *The Producer's Medium* (1983). More recently, John T. Caldwell has thrown the bedraggled cat back among the pigeons by suggesting that it really doesn't matter whether we cite producers, directors, writers or performers as key personnel in television, as long as we pay attention to the ways in which producerly 'intention' is fabricated and wielded; both within individual programmes and amongst programmes in the flow (1995: 105). Spotting 'producerly intention' is easy in the case of *Dragnet* since, as David Marc suggests, Webb was even CEO of his own company, Mark VII Productions, which sold the show to NBC (Marc 1995: 135).

With twenty select episodes from the first eight seasons recently re-released on DVD, it's possible to revisit *Dragnet* to gain a snapshot of the kind of television it was.[4] For a start, it was the first TV series to be shot on tele-film, which permitted the repeated use of film footage of the city: a strategy by now very familiar in the television crime series to establish location and point of view. *CSI*'s reiterated swirling helicopter shots of the Las Vegas, Miami and New York skylines by day or night spring to mind. In its use of such footage, and location shooting, *Dragnet* was therefore in immediate contrast to the stage-bound 'live' detective shows offered by the other networks at the time, adopting a cinematic approach and frequently echoing the style of film noir in its artful lighting and placement of characters. Indeed, Webb is on record as having announced that his intention was always to create 'a half-hour of motion pictures, not a half-hour of TV films' (Mittell 2004: 143).

The episode entitled 'The Big Show', the eleventh in Season Two first broadcast on 22 January 1953, begins as usual with Walter Schumann's much quoted (and parodied) 'Dum de dum dum' Dragnet March (aka 'Danger Ahead'), as Badge 714 of the Los Angeles Police Department appears on screen and Webb announces in his mellifluous clipped tones the phrase adapted from *He Walked by Night*, 'Ladies and gentlemen, the story you are about to see is true; the names have been changed to protect the innocent.'

Webb's claim to documentary realism may have had some foundation given his close connection to the Los Angeles Police Department and its police chief, William Parker, who, as Mittell points out, not only set up a system to provide storylines, but also offered his own, vetted scripts and provided expert advice to 'satisfy Webb's yearnings for authenticity' (2004: 134). As Schaeffer (2006) suggests, *Dragnet* thus emphasised 'authentic police jargon, the technical aspects of law enforcement, and the drudgery of such work'. So close did Webb become to the LAPD, who not only admired the way he represented them to the public but also used episodes of the show as training films, that after his death in 1982 he was buried with the full honours befitting an LAPD detective, including a seventeen gun salute.[5]

As usual, the first shot in the episode entitled 'The Big Show'[6] is of the city, as the camera pans from left to right and Webb offers the voiceover statistics and terse observations which echo those of his inspiration, *He Walked by Night*:

> This is the city. Four million people. Something for everybody. Houses to live in [shot of an apartment complex]. Places to work [shot of a factory]. Places to relax [shot of men on a golf course]. Churches to pray in [shot of a church]. Most of them enjoy a life and they try to hold on to it. A few of them have lost their grip [shot of three cheerful derelicts under a bridge, laughing and talking, surrounded by empty liquor bottles]. In my job I get to know them all. I'm a cop.

This may be radio with pictures, but the pictures are intriguing since they quite clearly fix the commentary to specific places and moments: factories, golf courses and happy drunks. As Webb continues, a new image appears: that of a bus terminal which looks less like a location shot and more like a set on a sound stage:

> It was Monday August 12. We were working the Day Watch out of Juvenile Division. My partner is Frank Smith. My Boss is Captain Stein. My name is Joe Friday. We'd got a call that a seven-week-old baby had been abandoned in a bus terminal. We had to find him.

As we watch Friday and Smith (Herb Ellis) walk through the terminal, something interesting happens. The camera picks up on a large man with a bulbous nose as he enters a photographic booth. Our point of view of the terminal is now *through* the booth to where Friday and Smith approach a woman seated with her back to us. The man inserts his coin in the slot, adjusts his hair, smiles, and then pulls the curtain across, blocking our view.

What I particularly love about this moment is that it is, of course, completely untranslatable in radio terms. It is a visual aside which serves no narrative purpose at all: a moment of stylistic and even comic excess. It is also extremely artful in its framing, thus pointing to the possibility that early television (as many commentators have already pointed out)[7] was frequently made and shot by those whose previous experience was in film, and thus routinely achieved such cinematic moments in the pursuit of a distinctive televisual style.

The camera position then changes as we meet Marjorie Lewis (Vivienne Gregg), the woman holding the baby and she narrates her story about how it was left in her care on a bus by a young woman who has now disappeared. The scene is long, the delivery fast, apparently as the result of a production decision; in order to save to save rehearsal time, Webb required his actors to read their lines right off the teleprinter (Schaeffer 2006). Odd though this staccato style of delivery may be, it is remarkably effective, contributing a pace and rhythm to the series which adds to its semi-documentary feel. It also cues the camera to go in extremely close on the speaking face at moments of high tension – as in the climax of this episode when Marjorie Lewis confesses her deception, telling such a sad story of hopelessness and confusion that not only does Webb's hard-edged Friday visibly soften, but I was moved to tears as a viewer, thus revealing the dramatic function of style.[8] As usual, the episode then concludes with a pronouncement of the sentence meted out by law to the offender, except, in this case, the charge of abandoning a child is commuted; the law and justice are for once shown to be in step.

While this may be an unusual episode, it nevertheless proves that generalising about a TV series may hold inherent problems, since the object of study can be such an amorphous creature, changing direction, style and mood just when you think you've got a grip on it. Thus, even though Marc and Robert J. Thompson might dislike what they describe as Webb's paranoid law and order homilies, which in their opinion placed him somewhere on 'the right side of J.Edgar Hoover', there were clearly moments of compassion in the original series which suggested that the law might have a human face.

Setting aside Webb's supposedly conservative politics for the moment, what I want to take from this discussion of *Dragnet* are the following observations about format and style. *Dragnet* was shot on film and, despite its claims to documentary realism, was highly stylised in terms of both performance and look, frequently displaying cinematic self-consciousness in the set-up of elaborate and carefully lit shots. The series was fast paced and tightly structured around a half-hour format in which a single case was proposed and solved through the pursuit of evidence. (Like Gil Grissom in *CSI*, Joe Friday just wants the facts.) There is little on-going character development amongst the major characters, the emphasis being on policing rather than policemen.

This was all to change as the television crime series increasingly intruded on the emotional lives of the policemen and women over the ensuing years. One key series in this regard is another NBC show from the mid 1970s, *Police Story*. Created by a former policeman and crime writer, Joseph Wambaugh, *Police Story* was an anthology series which every week dealt with a different couple of policemen, and indeed policewomen, on the beat. Episodes focused largely on the relationships of the policemen with each other first and the job second: the TV series *Police Woman* starring Angie Dickinson was perhaps the most notable spin-off. It might be mentioned in passing that Michael Mann, producer of 1980s crime series *Miami Vice* and *Crime Story*, which will be discussed in more detail below, wrote for this series after his return from the UK. I mention *Police Story* here because it is quite frequently omitted in genealogies of the crime series genre, which point to *Hill Street Blues* as the moment when melodrama meets the crime series in an explosion of personal angst amongst the officers. However, while *Police Story* may have got to the melodrama first, it is *Hill Street Blues* which marks both a connection and a break with the past in terms of format and style during the 1980s.

As Marc points out, *Hill Street Blues* is clearly indebted to Webb's episodic police procedural formula as it structures every episode around a day in the life of the precinct. Except, of course, *Hill Street Blues* then departs from the formula by offering the viewer no resolution to the plot conflicts which are set up (1984: 95). Instead of a tightly written single plot structure leading to a neat denouement, what *Hill Street Blues* gave us instead was:

> a large ensemble cast of thirteen to fourteen central characters, overlapping dialogue, multiple narrative strands ... documentary-style camera work, a multi-ethnic cast and strong female characters, [as well as] a liberal attitude towards policing and social issues (Cooke 2001: 23).

In its use of overlapping dialogue and hand-held camera work, techniques which are vividly apparent in the roll-call scene which opened the pilot episode, like *Dragnet* before it, *Hill Street Blues* established a sonic and visual aesthetic which was quite unlike anything which had been seen on television before; textual innovations supporting Mittell's observation that, ever since *Dragnet*, police dramas have been in the forefront of stylistic innovation in television (Mittell 2004: 146).

Hill Street's stylistic innovations were, however, neither easy to archive nor welcomed. The show rated poorly in its first season, even though it went to scoop the Emmy pool in 1982 (Cooke 2001: 23). Writer/producer Steve Bochco and his co-creator Michael Kozoll apparently fought long and hard to get creative freedom from NBC to make the kind of crime series they wanted to make. Fred Silverman, President of NBC, had seen the rushes of the film *Fort Apache: The Bronx* (1981) and wanted a TV series to match. Bochco had seen a low-budget black-and-white verité documentary entitled *The Police Tapes* (1976) by Alan and Susan Raymond, about the daily routine of South Bronx cops, originally aired on public service television, and wanted to make a TV series closer to its style and mood; once again signalling the documentary impulse in the crime series as a genre. Bochco's vision triumphed, at least until 1985 when he was fired from the series (as result of his refusal to compromise over high production costs), whereupon he moved to Twentieth Century Fox to develop the legal series *LA Law*. As Marc and Thompson point out, the significance of Bochco's producerly contribution to *Hill Street Blues* is confirmed by the fact that the series apparently changed direction 'overnight' after his departure, losing its stylistic cutting edge (1995: 224).

As a result of *Hill Street Blues*' stylistic innovations, and the fact that

Bochco's name was prominently used to promote it, Caldwell identifies Bochco as one of television's showcase producers of the 1980s and 1990s, amongst whom he includes Michael Mann and David E. Kelley (the latter having first worked with Bochco on *LA Law*). Such producers Caldwell describes as network banner carriers, the citation of whose names gave the networks' seasonal offerings a more personal touch in the promotion of new shows, much in the way that Jerry Bruckheimer's name is currently used in relation to the promotion of *CSI*, in all its manifestations, as well as *Cold Case* and *The Amazing Race*. In summarising Bochco's contribution to television, Caldwell further credits him with developing a 'house look', which he defines as the 'wall-to-wall visual look that becomes a defining property of both each episode and of the ensemble of quality actors as well' (1995: 65-66). This 'house look' then becomes a signature both for the show and its showcase producer. It is interesting to note that the showcase producer whom Caldwell perceives as standing next in line to Bochco is Michael Mann, whose television crime series *Miami Vice* has often been accused of 'excessive stylishness' in a decade in which 'style quite frankly seemed to count for more than anything else' (Marc and Thompson 1995: 231).

In her comprehensive review of Mann's career, Anna Dzenis traces the development of Mann's visual aesthetic from his early days at the London International Film School in the 1960s, in the company of Alan Parker, the Scott brothers and Adrian Lyne, directors who all began their careers in the commercial, highly stylised pictorial fields of advertising (2002: 1). After returning to the US, where he worked as a producer, director and writer on a variety of projects during the 1980s, Mann embarked on his first cinematic feature, *Thief*, in 1981, which he also produced, directed and wrote. Significant amongst the list of other producers is the name of Jerry Bruckheimer who went on to produce Mann's next feature film, *Manhunter*, in 1986, based on Thomas Harris's crime thriller *Red Dragon* (1982). Here, a much younger and thinner William Peterson plays Will Graham, a policeman with an unfortunate gift for empathising with serial killers. Bruckheimer clearly appreciated Mann's cinematic style, and produced films directed by a number of the other directors with whom Mann studied in London, including Adrian Lyne on *Flashdance* (1983) and Tony Scott on *Black Hawk Down* (2001). If there's a producerly Bruckheimer look, it would therefore seem to lie in his choice of directors who will provide him with a particular visual style.

Dzenis describes *Thief* as 'a visually and sonically stylised work, with metaphoric images set in the wet night time streets of Chicago accompanied by the techno sounds of Tangerine Dream' (2006: 2) and notes that, as a consequence of *Thief*'s expressive stylisation, James Naremore positions it in a lineage of 'neo-noir' films. Naremore's positive assessment of the film invites reflection about at what point '*expressive* stylisation' on film becomes '*excessive* stylisation' on television and whether or not a double standard might apply: a point which has some relevance to aesthetic evaluations not only of *Miami Vice* but also *CSI*, which has been similarly accused of celebrating style over substance. This is a point to which I will return.

Miami Vice which, according to Caldwell, also established Mann's reputation as a showcase television producer, was the original idea of NBC executive Brandon Tartikoff, who had come up with the two-word concept 'MTV Cops' as a way of cashing in on the recent success of the newly established cable access television station geared towards the youth market. Tartikoff's concept found its way to the desk of writer-producer Anthony Yerkovich at MTM Enterprises, who wrote a script for a pilot which was sent to Michael Mann. Mann's first instinct was to make it into a film, but was apparently persuaded under duress to turn it into a TV series (Marc and Thompson 1995: 235). However, given what Mann did with the series, it is clear that he hardly abandoned his initial desire to make it as a film; he simply proceeded to shoot 'a movie a week' as he explains in a DVD feature accompanying the recently re-released first season.[9]

In terms of structure, each episode of *Miami Vice* involved at least one finite plot line whilst dealing, like *Hill Street Blues*, with the relationships of the ongoing characters. It was, therefore, not unusual for the emotional lives of the cops to impinge on, or even motivate, the weekly crime story. Sonny Crockett (Don Johnson) and Rico Tubbs (Philip Michael Thomas) played undercover cops living the affluent life of drug dealers, dressed by Versace, driving Ferraris and, in Crockett's case, living on a luxury yacht. One of my favourite and most emblematic episodes from the first season, entitled 'Evan' (1:21),[10] involves a blast from Crockett's past in the shape of a former Police Academy colleague, Evan Freed (William Russ), who is still blaming himself for the suicide of a gay colleague whom he taunted about his sexuality. Evan, himself now an undercover vice cop, is an alcoholic mess, eventually breaking down in Crockett's arms; an embrace witnessed by Tubbs when he walks into the interview room. Crockett and Evan spring apart, at which point one can't help wondering just what Evan's homophobia was all about anyway. Evan recovers himself, and goes off to do his duty, which results in him taking a bullet for Crockett.

As Crockett cradles the dying Evan in his arms, Tubbs places a hand on Crockett's shoulder as the final credits roll, forming a perfect male pietà. Far from being all about style, for me *Miami Vice* was more often about masculinity in crisis and was all the more interesting for that. The style, including the clothes, I would therefore argue, was indeed more usually *expressive* than *excessive*.

The use of colour, lighting and music in this episode is both dramatic and typical of the series as a whole. The station house is brightly lit in shades of white and lime green; the crime boss's house is a blaze of light and glass walls, a stellar example of modern Miami architecture. In stark visual contrast, the final scenes are conducted at the harbour in blue-black darkness, illuminated only by spotlights and torches, as Jan Hammer's atmospheric audio track sets the ominous mood. However, this episode also includes the use of two strategically placed popular music tracks by Peter Gabriel, establishing the innovation which has since been much emulated, especially by teen TV series and indeed the *CSI* franchise, for using already-released music tracks to enhance their sonic appeal.

As Marc and Thompson suggest, in the use of 'complex camera angles, state of the art editing, synaesthetic use of music with image and elaborate colour design', *Miami Vice* actively sought, and indeed achieved, a 'completely new video [and sonic] aesthetic for that old network standby, the cop show' (1995: 232). It also said a great deal about masculinity in the 1980s, but that's another essay. Of particular interest here is what Caldwell has described as Mann's 'house look' for *Miami Vice*, frequently involving the use of different visual styles and colour codes within a single episode to signal different narrative moments as described above (1995: 66). Mann's move thus prefigures the very precise colour coding frequently used between the Plot A and Plot B storylines in the original *CSI*, as well as the development of three distinct colour palettes to distinguish the locations of the subsequent franchises from the original Las Vegas (neon reds and electric blue), to Miami (coral, yellow and white) and New York (graphite, black and gold). It is in this way, as in *Miami Vice*, that the strategic use of colour becomes an intrinsic part of the visual landscape and narrative strategy within the *CSI* franchise.

While still engaged as a producer on *Miami Vice*, Mann was not only working as a director on the film of *Manhunter* but also producing another television crime series entitled *Crime Story*, featuring the Manichean struggle between mob boss Ray Luca (Anthony Dennison) and Detective Mike Torello (played by real-life former detective Dennis Farina). Set in stylish Chicago in the 1960s, Season Two relocated to Las Vegas where, as Marc and Thompson suggest:

> The stark film noir-ishness of Ness versus Nitti [characters in another television crime series, *The Untouchables*, 1959–1963] collides emphatically with the Sunbelt tones of *Miami Vice* to become the televisually gorgeous struggle of Torello and Luca amid the neon blues and flaming pinks of the famed desert oasis (1995: 238–239).

In other words, I would argue, Mann was setting the stage for *CSI*.

There have, of course, been many other television crime series in the intervening years. In 1990–1991 Bochco had a stab at producing his own MTV crime series, *Cop Rock*, which interspersed the police drama with musical numbers less in the style of a video clip and more in the style of a Broadway musical number, much in the way attempted by the 2004 British TV series *Blackpool*. Although a critical success, *Cop Rock* died mid season, afflicted by poor ratings (Marc and Thompson 1995: 229). Far more successful was *NYPD Blue* which, in its first season, took the hand-held and disorienting camera work of *Hill Street Blues* to new and dizzying heights. One almost needed a motion sickness pill to watch. Over the Atlantic, writers Lynda La Plante and Jimmy McGovern were providing British viewers with *Prime Suspect* and *Cracker*, crime series which, while they reveal an awareness of the kinds of stylistic innovations initiated by Bochco and Mann, nevertheless belong to a tradition of British crime, the rather different aesthetics of which I do not have time to explore here. It might also be noted in passing that these series were promoted in terms of their *writers* rather than their producers, perhaps signalling a rather different promotional climate in the UK.

Nor do I have time to develop an argument about a growing interest in forensics which would not only have to backtrack to such forensic TV series as *Quincy ME*, but would also need to consider the relationship between television and crime fiction, especially the work of Patricia Cornwell; the success of Cornwell's first novel, featuring medical examiner Kay Scarpetta in *Postmortem* in 1990, was but one indication of a compelling and growing interest in forensic science in the 1990s. While there has been much speculation about what such an interest might mean, *CSI* producer Jerry Bruckheimer himself suggested that this was fuelled by the very public debate about the accuracy of the forensic evidence presented at the trial of O.J. Simpson, which he regards as a key factor in the success of their show.[11]

Bruckheimer has recently been described by John Caldwell as a 'superproducer' whose easy transition between film and television production in the new millennium signals a shift in the old film versus TV hierarchies, with television finally being recognised by many in the American media industries as possibly more exciting and innovative than film. As Caldwell suggests:

> ... the Grazer/Bruckheimer series 24, *Arrested Development*,
> *CSI: Crime Scene Investigation* and *Cold Case* offer far more
> challenging exercises in cinematography, editing, dramatic
> structure and narrative form than the endless big-budget
> blockbuster and flat comic book features that are mindlessly
> cranked out by the major movie studios (2005: 91).

While Bruckheimer might stand accused of having produced a fair number of those endless big-budget blockbusters himself (*Pearl Harbor* (2001) springs immediately to mind although all was forgiven with *Pirates of the Caribbean* (2003)), it might be remembered that he was also the producer of Mann's *Thief* and *Manhunter*, and clearly had a strong idea about how *CSI* should look when he approached young British director Danny Cannon to direct the pilot. As Cannon tells it in an extended interview feature accompanying the Season One DVD:

> The look of the show came about from the first conversation I
> had with Jerry Bruckheimer where he said to me, 'I need that
> cinematic look in television. How do we do that?' (2004a)

The look which Cannon gave Bruckheimer was therefore partly an effect of series creator Anthony E. Zuiker's original script (with its inherent contrasts in locations including a hi-tech lab); the original Las Vegas setting (in which, as Cannon puts it, 'the contrast, the colour, the intensity is always there for us'); but was primarily a consequence of a desire to make the series look like a film (Cannon again: 'it appears as if we are making a feature film every week because we are'). Shot on Super 35mm film stock, and subjected to a high degree of post-production colour manipulation, the fact that the weekly feature thus produced so often echoes the work of Michael Mann may be both a conscious and an unconscious effect of working in the same genre, similar locations, and the striving for a neo-noir cinematographic effect whilst fighting the format limitations of television. That Cannon is aware of Mann's influence is apparent in his voiceover commentary to the *CSI: Miami* pilot when he announces that the look of a particular scene is 'like a tribute to Michael Mann'. Although a number of different directors have subsequently worked on the *CSI* franchise, I would argue that it is Cannon who is the creator of the *CSI*'s house look in all its expressive stylishness and that this is no accident, given producer Bruckheimer's cinematic vision for television based on the visual (and sonic) style of the directors, including Mann, with whom he had previously worked.

In terms of *CSI* then, the larger points I want to make about its format, style and visual aesthetic and how these relate to what has gone before are these. Firstly, in terms of format, with its return to an episodic narrative structure with a focus on documenting the work of the police, *CSI* in all its franchises constitutes a throwback to the early days of *Dragnet* in its bid for authenticity. Although there have been some attempts to develop characters and relationships in the fashion of *Hill Street Blues*, these have largely been subordinated to the crimes of the week which usually unfold as Plot A and Plot B which are often visually coded to look quite dissimilar. A very clear example of this strategy is apparent in the Season Three episode of the original *CSI* entitled 'Random Acts of Violence' (3:13), directed by Cannon, who suggests that while the serious and emotionally dark Plot A derives its stylistic influence and colour coding from the Steven Soderbergh film *Solaris* (2002), the much jokier Plot B uses more upbeat white, blue and flashes of red in order to narrate a locked-room mystery which Cannon considers an homage to the British comedy crime series, *Jonathan Creek*.[12]

Secondly, as in *Dragnet*, the often tedious nature of detection is compressed to fit the format demands of the genre. In both, the emphasis is primarily on police procedure with attention to getting the details right. While Webb consulted the LAPD, *CSI* employs the services of Elizabeth Devine, a former forensic examiner with the LA County Sheriff's office as a consultant on the series. Both series also offer closure, with the criminal usually being caught and publicly admonished. Justice is seen to be done, raising questions about whether *CSI*'s popularity, like *Dragnet*'s in its day, might be related to forms of political conservatism or the need for certainty in an era of uncertainty. In this regard, David Marc once described the TV crime show as a sitcom in which the Law is married to Chaos, 'In each episode Chaos steps out of line, but the Law whips her back into shape before the final commercial' (1984: 69). While such a description would hardly fit many of the crime series of the 1980s and 1990s such as *Hill Street Blues*, *Miami Vice*, or even *Cracker*, in which the Law often spectacularly failed to keep Chaos even remotely under control, in *CSI*, with the significant assistance of science, the Law would appear to be doing much better.

Thirdly, in terms of visual style, like *Dragnet*, *CSI* also aims for a cinematic look on television: a look which is not so much film noir (as in *Dragnet*) but neo-noir, achieved via the artful use of lighting and colour. *CSI* thus recalls and reiterates the work of director Michael Mann, in particular the stylistic expressiveness of both *Miami Vice* and *Crime Story*. Cannon's voiceover commentary to the Season Two episode, 'Alter Boys' (2:6), describes his effort to achieve a visual style which, I would argue, is pure Mann in both intention and effect:

> I'm always fighting the television format ... What we do
> in colour correction is constantly a vignette with blacks, a
> graduated filter that goes all the way around the lens and draws
> your eyes into the centre of it (2004b).

Not only does *CSI* echo Mann's visual style and use of colour but also his construction of a sonic landscape composed of a specially produced electronic score (in *CSI* by Richard Keane), and strategically placed current pop music tracks which are used to similar expressive ends.

Consider for example the Season Two episode 'Slaves of Las Vegas' (2:8) of the original *CSI* set in Las Vegas. After a body is found in a children's sand pit by a kissing couple, Grissom begins his examination of the corpse in the lab. This sequence takes two minutes and thirty-one seconds, although it is clearly intended to condense a much longer time frame, and was responsible for the series featuring its first partial nudity warning. The episode, written by Jerry Stahl (writer of the Bruckheimer-produced feature *Bad Boys II*) and directed by Peter Markle, also garnered an Emmy for 'most outstanding make-up for a series (non prosthetic)', indicating that *CSI* is occasionally recognised as quality TV, if only in terms of its technical proficiency.[13]

The sequence begins with Grissom in the autopsy lab slowly circling and photographing the body from every angle to the accompaniment of an eerie ambient music track entitled 'Svefn-G-Englar' by the Icelandic band, Sigur Rós. The filters are blue, Grissom's coat is bluish-white, the corpse is greyish-blue. The effect is dream-like. The body is turned over and Grissom examines the back, removing a small piece of metal from a bloody wound. He puts on infra-red glasses and switches on a hand-held blue fluorescent light, intensifying and darkening the blue in order to once again inspect the surface of the body, this time revealing a luminous speck of white on the calf. Finally he begins to wash the body, after thoughtfully testing the temperature of the water (dead bodies may not feel the temperature but living actors do), pausing to examine the marks on the wrist which he prepares to lift with a liquid latex imprint. Nothing is said; only a mournful human voice on the soundtrack is heard singing an indistinguishable lament. The sonic and the visual landscapes are perfectly attuned.

I would argue that it is in a scene like this that we can locate the primary fascination of CSI as it allows us to 'look' with Grissom at the body, witnessing every stage of his post mortem (albeit in a condensed time frame). As we follow his examination step by step, we are therefore invited to think along with Grissom, to spot the clues, to solve the case. In an era when the goal of audience participation is more usually assumed to occur via an interactive telephone or computer link-up, CSI beckons its viewers into the show by inviting them into the world of the Crime Scene Investigators to participate in the solving the crime by looking at the evidence.

As Danny Cannon suggests, while scenes about sifting evidence might be all 'talk' in other crime series, in CSI they are all about 'show': a claim confirmed by Karen Lury who argues that the function of CSI's visual style is not only to dramatise the action, but also to demonstrate the evidence (2005: 46–51). One of the ways in which CSI achieves this is through the use of CGI animated effects, including insert 'pops' which take us inside the human body to explore the forensic evidence from within. In this way, CSI becomes, in Caldwell's terms, supremely televisual, the screen becoming more like that of a computer which, with a click of a mouse, opens up its graphic interface to reveal proliferating fields of information.

Brad Tannenbaum of Stargate Films, the company which creates the CGI images used in the show, describes these inserts as 'the money shots', the term used in pornography for that climactic moment when proof of orgasm is achieved through the depiction of male ejaculation on screen.[14] I find the use of this term within the context of CSI powerfully suggestive in the light of Linda Williams' path-breaking history of pornography entitled *Hard Core: Power, Pleasure and the Frenzy of the Visible* (1990). It is my contention that, like pornography, CSI also participates in a 'frenzy of the visible' which, as Williams would argue, entails the pursuit of knowledge through visualisation. However, far from disapproving of this move (which seems to be the position taken by Lury, who is worried about the 'stylistically pornographic nature' of the images presented (2005: 56), like Barbara Stafford, I am keen to rescue such forms of visual communication and knowledge (about sex, about death) from the accusation that they are somehow less valuable ways of knowing than the linguistic or written (1996). Indeed, as Stafford points out, since the Enlightenment the problem of imaging what was 'out of sight' has become central to the fine arts and the natural sciences as they sought to reveal and reconstruct what was invisible to the naked eye (1991). CSI, I would argue, clearly participates in such an Enlightenment project in an era when, for most people, science is a discourse to which they have no access except through the popular medium of a television programme which not only tells but shows as well. Furthermore because, like sex, death has been rendered an 'obscenity' which is largely hidden from view, CSI becomes a place where we are allowed to inspect it on screen, as it reveals what is so often hidden from view and 'out of sight'.[15]

Other inserts might include the use of flashbacks, frequently shot in a contrasting filter, or at an off-kilter and disorienting angle and accompanied by distorted sound, in order to visually and aurally distinguish them from the present and to suggest the haziness of memory.[16] However, such flashbacks may also 'lie', in so far as the character telling the story, or the CSI reconstructing the event, tells it or imagines it wrongly. We may therefore see many versions of the same event before the truth of the flashback is confirmed by the logic of the forensic evidence. According to writer/creator Zuiker, in his voiceover commentary to the episode 'Lady Heather's Box' (3:15), this is 'the theme of the entire franchise, it's all about the evidence'. As confirmation of this claim, in the pilot episode of the original CSI, Grissom informs another character to 'concentrate on what cannot lie, the evidence'.

In an era of postmodern uncertainty when the possibility of locating even a simple 'truth' seems faint, such faith is patently nostalgic. Unlike the medical shows of the 1990s such as ER or Chicago Hope, which Jason Jacobs suggests articulate a pessimistic disenchantment with science, CSI reasserts an optimistic faith (2003). Science, it is implied, can interpret the evidence thus enabling the location of truth and the apportioning of blame. As Lury points out (in this volume), this is a post-Enlightenment and pre-modern version of science as a 'supremely rational discourse' untroubled by the 'doubts and confusions opened up by twentieth-century discoveries such as the theories of relativity and chaos'. To restate Marc's thesis with a twist, Science will banish Chaos and enable the reaffirmation of the Law. Except, of course, when the evidence is tampered with or the CSIs are inefficient, as in the Season Three opener where everyone except Grissom screws up. Such failures, of course, are not about the failure of science, but simply about the limitations of the human. For actor William Petersen, 'evidence thus becomes a whole character in and of itself' (Peterson 2002); a character, I would suggest, not unlike that of the quintessential lawman, Joe 'Just the facts ma'am' Friday', who never once doubted himself as an instrument of the Law.

However, while *Dragnet* offered its viewers the innovation of documentary authenticity couched in the stylistics of film noir, what *CSI* in all its franchises offers its viewers is the crime show as a neo-noir digital spectacle. In other words, the ongoing characters function like avatars in a game world whose point of view we are invited to share as they go about their business of forensic analysis. This world is thus made intelligible to us through the process of visualising knowledge. That the crimes can be solved simply by looking at the evidence as revealed through science is the compensatory fantasy on offer; a fantasy which is at the heart of the success of the show. That this fantasy can be realised in spectacular visual images within the formally pleasing aesthetic of a 44-minute television episode is the triumph of *CSI* as a work of televisual art. As a spectacle, *CSI* gives us 'the look', which not only fascinates, but which also promises knowledge, truth and certainty. That's the hook.[17]

:2:

NO NEED TO PATHOLOGISE...

Reprinted from *The Observer*,
Sunday 13 August 2006
ANDREW ANTHONY

According to the *Radio Times*, a publication which is seldom wrong, the world's most popular TV series is *CSI: Miami*. When you realise that the Colombian soap *Te Voy a Enseñar a Querer* (*I'm Going to Teach You to Love*) is fourth in the list of global favourites, and *Emmerdale* isn't even in the top ten, you get a measure of the show's achievement.

So what is the recipe of its extraordinary success? Putting the show under the kind of intensive forensic analysis to which it likes to subject dead people, I can reveal a list of simple but by no means cheap ingredients. The first, to quote the great Allsopp, is location, location, location. Or to be more specific, Miami, Miami, Miami.

The opening scene of Tuesday's show featured a blameless blue sky, a helicopter, a young woman with large fake breasts in a skimpy vest, a yacht, a marina, a bald cop with a gun and a black youth on the run. Before a word was spoken there was more action and glamour on view than in a year's worth of *The Vice*, *Waking the Dead* and *Silent Witness*, not to mention – in any circumstances – *Heartbeat*. Try filming the same scene in, say, Gateshead or Portsmouth and those fake breasts would have looked somehow gratuitous. In Miami they just looked part of the scenery, like the palm trees.

Playing opposite the sun-baked city of silicone is the second key ingredient, David Caruso. You would have to search deep in the Siberian wastelands to find a being who looks less comfortable in the quasi-tropical glare of Florida. He plays the criminal pathologist Horatio Caine, which is inspired casting because Caruso knows a lot about death, having died a lonely one himself after he left *NYPD Blue* to become a Hollywood superstar. *Kiss of Death* was the prescient title of Caruso's brief and unhappy spell as a leading man. Audiences found his scrawny ginger features strangely resistible when displayed on the 30 x 60ft dimensions of a cinema screen.

In truth, even on the small screen Caruso's appeal had been a little mystifying. Radio was the more natural medium for his looks. But on *NYPD Blue*, through the combination of a soft voice and hard stare, he managed to fill the position of the tough skinny cop that had been vacant in popular culture since Frank Sinatra's 1968 role in *The Detective*. Like Sinatra before his comeback in *From Here To Eternity* (1953), Caruso went from here to obscurity. If he has returned from the dead in *CSI: Miami*, he still wears the pallor of a corpse. That's with his sunglasses on. When he takes them off he looks more like he went out for a drink in NYC and woke up in Miami squinting, dry-mouthed, and plagued by horrifying flashbacks.

But the fragile Caruso need not worry. As this is a Jerry Bruckheimer production, he does not have to contend with anything so burdensome as acting. Each week he turns in the kind of minimalist performance that can't lose much in Latin American and Asian dubbing suites. Though compared with Emily Procter, who plays Horatio's assistant, Caruso is a one-man study in method mannerisms. Procter comes from the Botox school of acting in which facial gestures are strictly forbidden. Which leads us to the third essential ingredient: character efficiency. In *CSI: Miami* people make murder confessions more readily than most of us would admit to overpaying for a pair of shoes. An especially tough interrogation can last up to 10 or 15 seconds. Then Horatio only has to say 'DNA swab' and the sound of canary song fills the air.

Once ads are accounted for, there's little more than 40 minutes to solve a case, so this is no venue for character actors to show their stuff. What really matters is the methodical march of scientific crime detection.

In many ways *CSI: Miami*, like its Vegas-based stablemate, *CSI: Crime Scene Investigation*, is the anti-*NYPD Blue*. Whereas the New York show was full of commotion and ambiguity, *CSI* presents a vision of slick investigative procedure. Routinely referred to as 'vics' – and they're not talking nasal spray – the dead are no more than bodies of evidence. Ultimately *CSI*'s international success may come down to the fact that in place of postmodern doubt it offers post-mortem certainty. As Horatio whispered in his closing speech to a black youth he'd just saved from a lifetime of prison rape: 'Here's what I think. Here's what I know. That at the end of the day, the truth, Toby, the truth is all we have.' Noble words, but given the preceding plot, there are more things in heaven and earth, Horatio, than are dreamt of in your philosophy.

:II:

INTERROGATION
Narrative and Narration

:3:

ANATOMISING GILBERT GRISSOM

The Structure and Function of the Televisual Character
ROBERTA PEARSON

Famous movie star Tom Haviland (Chad Michael Murray) commits a gory murder in a Las Vegas hotel room. At the preliminary hearing, Philip Gerard (Raymond J. Barry), the high-profile forensic expert on his defence team, seeks to discredit the forensic evidence by discrediting those who have amassed it. Supervisor Gil Grissom is reluctant to gather evidence lest his increasing deafness cause him to falter on the witness stand and inadvertently undermine the prosecution's case. Gerard uses Catherine Willows' past as an exotic dancer and Warrick Brown's gambling problem to cast doubt on their professional abilities. Gerard implies that Sara Sidle's romantic attraction to Grissom may bias her testimony and objects to her paramedic boyfriend having moved evidence at the crime scene. And Nick Stokes has somehow managed to bungle the blood evidence. The collective personal failings of the Las Vegas Crime Scene Investigation graveyard shift may permit Haviland to escape justice. But Grissom's last minute discovery of conclusive evidence and convincing presentation thereof persuades the judge to put the case forward to trial.

Tying the outcome of a case directly to the characters' personal weaknesses, the third season episode of the original CSI, 'The Accused is Entitled' (3:2), represents the programme's compromise between an episodic, procedural format and the tightly serialised character arcs now common in so many American television dramas. The occasional, casual viewer would have inferred enough of the characters' backstories to follow the case of the week while the dedicated, competent viewer would have had her enjoyment enriched by detailed knowledge of the backstories. Showrunner Anthony E. Zuiker has recently commented on the episodic/serialised compromise:

> We simply did not want to handcuff the viewers to their television sets from week to week. We wanted to make great television, earn the viewers' trust and welcome them back 24 times a year. What works best for *CSI* and many procedurals today are 'stand-alone' episodes with serialised character arcs. This lessens the pressure on the viewers to tune in every single week, yet encourages loyal viewing by serialising character beats. We'd rather have you watch 20 or 24 episodes rather than miss two episodes and tune out forever (Carolina 2006).

In response to Zuiker's comment, television critic Rick Kushman reflected on the increasing cultural consensus around quality television. 'Serials let writers tell better stories. They offer the size and depth of a novel.' (2006) The tension between stand-alones and serials is that between art and commerce: complex and continuous character arcs win critical plaudits but risk losing viewers. The positioning of post-network television dramas on a continuum from the strictly episodic and loosely character-based (e.g. the original *Law & Order*) to the usually episodic and somewhat character-based (e.g. *Law & Order: Special Victims Unit* and *CSI*) to the tightly serialised and strongly character-based (e.g. *Battlestar Galactica*, *The Sopranos*) reflects this tension. *CSI*'s placement in the middle of this continuum makes it an ideal text for the investigation of televisual character. This investigation begins with an anatomisation of the problematic concept of the fictional character before moving on to address the character's function of introducing novelty and divergence to the programme format.

Narratologist Marie-Laure Ryan makes a bold claim concerning the relationship of the reader to the text. 'If readers are caught up in a story, they turn the pages without paying too much attention to the letter of the text... And if readers experience genuine emotions for the characters, they do not relate to these characters as literary creations nor as "semiotic constructs" but as human beings' (1994: 12). Readers might relate to characters as human beings, but even the most beloved of literary, cinematic or televisual creations ultimately exist only as words on a page or images on a screen. This confusion between semiotic constructs and real-seeming human beings is the paradox at the heart of the fictional character. Another narratologist, Shlomith Rimmon-Kenan, offers helpful guidance on setting a course between the Scylla of realism and the Charybdis of semiotics:

> Whereas in mimetic theories... characters are equated with people, in semiotic theories they dissolve into textuality... The two extreme positions can be thought of as relating to different aspects of narrative fiction. In the text characters are nodes in the verbal design; in the story they are – by definition – non (or pre-) verbal abstractions, constructs. Although these constructs are by no means human beings in the literal sense of the word, they are partly modelled on the reader's conception of people and in this they are person-like. Similarly, in the text, characters are inextricable from the rest of the design, whereas in the story they are extracted from their textuality (1983: 33).[1]

Television writers, working in the psychologically realist mode dominant in American television dramas, model their characters on their culture's conceptions of people, making them person-like. As a result, to quote Tzvetan Todorov, 'the fictional character becomes endowed with character: he acts in a certain way, *because* he is shy, weak, courageous, etc.' (1988: 413). In a psychologically realist text, psychological motivations appear to drive the action but, in practice, actions and psychological traits are two sides of the same character; traits motivate actions and actions connote traits. As H. Porter Abbott argues in *The Cambridge Introduction to Narrative*, 'Characters... have agency; they cause things to happen. Conversely, as these people drive the action, they necessarily reveal who they are in terms of their motives, their strength, weakness, trustworthiness, capacity to love, hate, cherish, adore, deplore and so on. By their actions do we know them' (2002: 124). In one of the few film studies texts that touches on the topic of character, David Bordwell acknowledges the intertwining of character and action. He defines a character as 'a bundle of qualities, or traits' (1985: 13–14), but continues:

> Their traits must be affirmed in speech and physical behaviour, the observable projections of personality... Even a simple physical reaction – a gesture, an expression, a widening of the eyes, constructs character psychology in accordance with other information... Hollywood cinema reinforces the individuality and consistency of each character by means of recurrent motifs.

> A character will be tagged with a detail of speech or behaviour
> that defines a major trait (1985: 15).

The first few episodes of a television series tag the central characters with the speech/behaviour that defines the major traits that will motivate them over the course of the season, and, if all goes well, several seasons. In an early first season episode, ('Pledging Mr. Johnson', 1:4), Gil Grissom rebukes Catherine Willows for becoming too caught up in a case. Catherine responds that most people do 'bring ourselves to our cases. We can't help it. I should be just like you. Alone in your hermetically sealed condo watching Discovery on the big screen and doing genius level crosswords. But no relationships, no chance any will slop over into a case.' Grissom corrects her. 'Technically it's a townhouse and the crosswords are advanced not genius. But you're right. I'm deficient in a lot of ways. But I never screw up one of my cases with personal stuff.' Catherine ripostes, 'Grissom, what personal stuff?' The behaviour Catherine mentions (watching documentaries, doing crossword puzzles, living alone, avoiding relationships) all relate to Grissom's major trait of emotional disengagement/repression as does his calm and objective response to her criticism. Similar interactions with others on the CSI team reinforce this trait. In 'Too Tough to Die' (1:16), Grissom counsels Sara Sidle against become too emotionally involved with the victims. Sara responds, 'I wish I was like you. I wish I didn't feel anything.' A major trait will occasionally be explicitly reinforced during the course of a series. In the third season episode 'Random Acts of Violence' (3:13), Grissom reprimands Warrick Brown, whose personal connection to a case has led him to behave inappropriately. Warrick's words echo Catherine's and Sara's. 'I can't be like you. I'm not a robot. I actually care about these people.'

Continuing to document instances of tagged speech/behaviour together with the televisual codes that convey that speech/behaviour would dissolve Gilbert Grissom into the textuality of which Shlomith Rimmon-Kenan speaks, not only rendering the character 'inextricable from the rest of the design' but making this chapter inordinately long and boring. Thankfully there is no need for such fanatical documentation; the televisual character's paradoxical personhood lies precisely in his abstraction from the rest of the design. Television characters are not like holograms. Each tiny fragment does not contain the sum of the whole, but rather becomes fully intelligible only when juxtaposed with all the other tiny fragments in all the other scenes in all the other episodes in which the character appears. Television characters are to some extent autonomous beings; autonomous, that is, of the televisual codes and individual scenes/episodes that construct them, existing as a whole only in the minds of the producers and the audience. It is here that the characters take on the quasi-human status so baffling to literary theorists, but so obvious to television producers and audiences. Anatomising the televisual character requires identifying the elements that constitute a character abstracted from the design of the text and existing in the story, that is, in the minds of producers and audiences, rather than conducting a close textual analysis of individual scenes/episodes/codes.

THE STRUCTURE OF THE TELEVISUAL CHARACTER

Bordwell suggests that traits, physical behaviour and speech constitute a character. I expand this to a taxonomy of six key elements: psychological traits/habitual behaviours; physical characteristics/appearance; speech patterns; interactions with other characters; environment; and biography. I have abstracted Grissom and the other characters from textuality by using online episode guides to identify what showrunner Zuiker refers to as character beats, which in practice meant watching fifty-plus episodes. Here's the taxonomy of elements that construct *CSI*'s central character, that quasi-human being, Gilbert Grissom.

PSYCHOLOGICAL TRAITS/HABITUAL BEHAVIOURS

As I have said above, Grissom's major trait is that of emotional disengagement/repression. In keeping with this, he is almost always calm and controlled, has difficulties with intimate relationships and avoids self-revelation. He is for the most part, however, a good leader, loyal to and protective of his subordinates, even if occasionally insensitive to their personal needs. His intolerance of incompetence at higher levels in combination with his political maladroitness causes problems for him and his team. He is an empiricist deeply committed to the scientific method, although sometimes takes this to bizarre, 'mad-scientist' extremes as when he asks new recruits to donate a pint of blood for his experiments or spends his nights off at the body farm. His dedication to his job is primarily motivated by intellectual curiosity and the desire to be smarter than the criminal, although he despises men who hit their wives, sexual abusers and drug dealers who deal death to kids. His particular area of expertise and passion is entomology and he keeps a pet tarantula and races cockroaches. His listening to classical music and opera together with his knowledge of literature marks him as a cultured intellectual.

Although his knowledge of popular culture is limited, he's a good poker player, a baseball fan and likes roller coasters.

That the above could well describe a 'real' person is by no means coincidental: the *CSI* producers, working within the psychologically realist model, have consciously conformed Grissom to the realist literary ideal of the 'rounded' character. The motivated connection between traits and behaviour together with the realist details, some of which (roller coasters, baseball) resemble the quirky contradictions of a 'real' person, are intended to render him lifelike. But the construction of this 'lifelike' character also depends upon referencing readily available cultural tropes (the emotionally repressed male; the dedicated professional; the 'mad scientist'; the intellectual) which make Grissom instantly legible to a wide range of viewers.

PHYSICAL TRAITS/APPEARANCE

Gil Grissom, like all television characters, is conflated with the actor who embodies him. Grissom must look and talk like William Petersen; the actor's facial configurations/expressions, body posture/gestures and vocal quality/mannerisms all contributing to character meaning. The actor's performance is a key constructor of character meaning; other aspects of the character's traits and appearance are constructed by various other production personnel. The scriptwriters give Grissom the hereditary otosclerosis which physically externalises his isolation and the costume designers dress him in the neutral colours appropriate to his emotional repression.

SPEECH PATTERNS

Scriptwriters use dialogue to distinguish one character from another and to point up key psychological traits. Grissom's somewhat more formal speech emphasises his emotional distance from the rest of the characters while his gnomic utterances and Zen-like aphorisms reinforce his air of mystery. In the first season episode 'Friends and Lovers' (1:5), Gil tells a story told to him by a Harvard professor who once sat next to him on a plane. For several days the professor went to the toilet to find a spider in the bowl; each day it had fought its way back from the powerful flush of the day before. Eventually taking pity on the spider, the professor took it out of the bowl but returned the next day to find it dead. Grissom concludes, 'We don't impose our will on a spider. We don't impose our will on the evidence.' The story is a longer variation on his central mantra, 'follow the evidence, evidence is truth'. The writers conform the character to the cultural trope of the intellectual by sprinkling literary/ historical quotes and allusions through his dialogue. For example, he calls a guy dealing drugs to kids 'Humbert' (somewhat inappropriately I'd say), quotes Sun Tzu ('If you wait by the river long enough the bodies of your enemies will float by') and explains the principle of Occam's razor (if you hear hoof beats, assume it's horses, not zebras).

INTERACTIONS WITH OTHER CHARACTERS

All fictional characters are partially defined by the other characters with whom they interact. Even Robinson Crusoe had Friday. The potentially long run of a television series, coupled with a stable ensemble cast of characters designed to complement each other, multiplies the opportunities for interactions which reveal different aspects of a character. A key determinant of character in workplace dramas, those with ensemble casts in professional settings, most famously the 'cop and doc' shows among which CSI is numbered, is position in the workplace hierarchy. The primacy of CSI's episodic, procedural format over serialised character arcs makes Grissom's job as supervisor of the graveyard shift the single most important definer of his character; should Gil cease to be supervisor he would also cease to serve his key narrative function of heading investigations. The character's key narrative arcs and most marked emotional responses arise from threats to his job. His deafness, a disability which prevents him performing competently, and his political ineptness, which causes his team to be disbanded, destabilise the character and, as I discuss below, potentially the series format.

Grissom's relationships to his subordinates are not limited to professional interactions, but encompass the personal as well. As do other heads of television workplace hierarchies (e.g. Jean-Luc Picard, Tony Soprano, Jed Bartlett), Grissom functions not only as boss but as paterfamilias, even though his other character traits don't particularly suit him to this role. In 'Burden of Proof' (2:15), an episode in which Grissom exhibits greater than usual insensitivity to his subordinates, Catherine admonishes him. 'You are the supervisor. You have responsibilities. And people are making a family around you whether you like it or not, whether you give permission or not. We don't have to go the Grand Tetons together. Just every now and then you've got to lift your head up out of the microscope.' Grissom's strongest emotional ties are to females: Catherine; the other female CSI, Sara Sidle; and romantic interest, the dominatrix Lady Heather. He can express the vulnerabilities and fears hidden from his male colleagues and the rest of the world to these women, his closest confidantes and those who seem to know him best. It is Catherine and Lady Heather who first detect his hearing loss and Catherine who comes to visit/comfort him in the hospital before his operation. Sometime before the end of the sixth season, Grissom consummates a romantic relationship with Sara.

ENVIRONMENT

A great deal of the action in workplace dramas perforce takes place in a workplace that constructs character; cops are defined by their seedy, shabby offices and White House staff by their expensively furnished ones. CSI staff spend a great deal of time in stark and clinical labs which signal their unbiased and scientific professionalism. But, as Karen Lury points out, Grissom's office differs from the rest of the workspace. 'There is a strong sense of ordered chaos: metallic shelves are filled with specimen jars; there is a fridge with mysterious liquids and yet more glass jars; photographs and posters featuring insects adorn the walls, as well as preserved moths in frames'. The office, says Lury, is 'clearly designed to suggest the repressed "mad scientist" aspect of Grissom' (2005: 47).[2] The decor indeed points up Grissom's mad-scientist aspect but the office's liminal position between the public lab and the private home also marks it as a privileged space for personal interactions and the revelation of Grissom's thoughts and emotions. In the third season episode 'The Execution of Catherine Willows' (3:6), the first season's serial killer reappears and once more eludes the CSIs. At the episode's end, Grissom has an end-of-shift drink in his office with Captain Brass and admits to being worried that the killer is smarter than he is. At the end of the same season's 'Play with Fire' (3:22), Grissom, finally determined to deal with his hearing loss, looks up his doctor's number on his rolodex. Sara stops by and says, in reference to the unresolved sexual tension between them, 'Let's have dinner. Let's see what happens.' Grissom confesses, 'I don't know what to do about this.'

As this use of Grissom's office illustrates, location inflects behaviour, with characters, just like 'real' human beings, performing different aspects of the self in different settings. Workplace dramas with tightly serialised character arcs often stage action involving family and romantic partners in domestic spaces; ER, for example, shows us Carter's mansion, Abby's house and Luca's flat. CSI, with its emphasis upon the episodic and the procedural, takes us to the characters' domestic spaces infrequently. But, when it does, Grissom's home deliberately contrasts with the 'ordered chaos' of his office; it's a spacious white-walled loft, the metal grey and black of the high-end kitchen appliances and stereo emphasising an austerity broken only by the colourful framed butterflies on the wall. This is not the lair of the mad scientist, but rather the inner sanctum of the intellectual, the decor of office and home keyed to different aspects of the character. In the first season's 'The Strip Strangler' (1:23), Grissom retreats to his home after the sheriff takes him off a high-profile case on which he has publicly clashed with the FBI. Catherine, temporarily in charge of the team, comes to see him. Grissom tells her, 'I'm not used to having people in my house,' underlining how unusual it is for action to be staged in his private space. Catherine replies, 'You just don't like it when you can't solve a case. Or command your troops.' As Catherine understands, the sheriff's threat to Grissom's professional status has motivated this unusual withdrawal into private space. Catherine and the rest of the CSI team set up temporary headquarters at Grissom's flat and, working under his direction, solve the case, permitting him to return to his more usual environment of lab and office. The scriptwriters' banishing of Grissom to a private space has signalled the temporary instability of a character defined primarily by his role in the workplace hierarchy.

BIOGRAPHY

A character's biography performs two functions; it augments the reality effect of the quasi-human being and it provides plot lines. Biographical details can flesh out established traits or introduce the contradictions characteristic of 'real' human beings. Grissom's having a Ph.D. contributes to the construction of the character as a consummate professional. His having almost blown the house up with his chemistry set as a six year old, and funding his first body farm with his poker winnings, enhance Grissom's mad-scientist aspect. His replacement and framing of his Roy Rogers certificate granting him part ownership of Trigger strike a convincingly incongruous note. These details deepen the character but have little narrative consequence; other details jump-start the novel and divergent plot lines so necessary to the long-running television show.

Some of these biography-based plots last only an episode while others encompass multiple episodes. A one-off example occurs in Season Two's 'Alter Boys' (2:6), which reveals that Grissom is a lapsed Catholic who believes in 'God, in science, in Sunday supper', but not in 'rules that tell me how I should live'. He nonetheless still shows respect for a priest and revises his opinion of murder suspect Ben Jennings (Corbin Allred)'s guilt based on the priest's estimation of Ben's character. But the episode's end closes off this character beat. Grissom visits the priest and apologises for having been unable to clear Ben, who is going to take the fall for his guilty brother. The priest says that, despite having renounced the Church, Grissom still suffers like a Catholic. Grissom responds, 'That guilt's not in me anymore.' Grissom's having inherited otosclerosis from his deaf mother initiates a character arc that starts at the end of Season Two, runs through all of Season Three and is resolved at the beginning of Season Four. An even lengthier character arc concerns the unresolved sexual tension between Grissom and Sara, which begins in the second season and is apparently consummated sometime before the end of the sixth. In the second season episode 'Burden of Proof' (2:15), we learn that Grissom may have a fear of romantic involvement stemming from a very bad relationship. Catherine talks to Gil about Sara's request for an extended leave, which, it is implied, stems from frustration at his lack of response. Grissom says, 'Sara gets very emotional,' to which Catherine responds 'Are you in denial? Wow, you got burned bad.' The detailing of Grissom's romantic past provides some motivation for the plot line to continue over the next several seasons.

Biography is the last element in my six-part taxonomy of the televisual character; scriptwriters and other production personnel skilfully weave these six elements together to create convincingly 'real' pseudo-human beings. But the shaping of character also depends on the deployment of readily available cultural tropes; this is where ideology most proximately influences character construction. As I said above, Grissom is made instantly legible to a wide range of viewers through the tropes of the dedicated professional, the' mad scientist', and the intellectual. Clearly such tropes have strong gender biases; in western culture 'mad scientists' are almost always male and dedicated professionals and intellectuals frequently so. A singularity of focus often thought to be typically male is common to each trope; psychological traits and associated behaviours have strong gender associations. Gil's central trait of emotional repression/distance and the isolating behaviour associated with it is often thought of as more typically male than female.

Gender is a key constructor and differentiator of character in ensemble workplace dramas; many academics have criticised *Star Trek: The Next Generation* or *The West Wing* for restricting female characters to conventionally female roles such as counsellors or communicators. Both the female CSIs participate as fully in the workplace as their male colleagues but, in keeping with the culture's construction of femininity, family plays a far more important role in the lives of Catherine Willows and Sara Sidle than it does in the lives of Gil Grissom, Warrick Brown or Nick Stokes. Catherine is a divorced single mother whose male relations (ex-husband, recently discovered biological father) become directly involved in CSI cases and whose daughter is a constant worry. Sara Sidle's extremely traumatic childhood causes her problems with both personal and professional relationships. The boundary between the female characters' public and private lives is blurred to a far greater extent than with the male characters. Race is also a key constructor and differentiator of character. The Warrick Brown character is coded within cultural tropes of black masculinity. Warrick's grandmother and male mentor having saved him from a life of crime draws upon common conceptions of a black community with strong matriarchs and absent fathers. Warrick's gambling problem, associated with criminality and corruption, recalls the black hustler of the street-corner craps game. The female characters and the black characters perform the same roles as the white male CSIs, but the blurring of the boundaries between their public and private lives often causes the personal to impact negatively upon the professional. Gil's and Nick's personal problems and motivations rarely interfere with their professional obligations. In Gil's case, however, his repression and isolation is itself constructed as a problem by contrasting it with the greater emotional engagement of the female characters. Foregrounding the imperfections of the white male primary character enhances the necessary polysemy of a television show aimed at millions of viewers and points to the ambiguities of ideological critique.[3]

THE FUNCTION OF THE TELEVISUAL CHARACTER

The character taxonomy works for characters in all moving-image forms – film, television and video games. However, the function of the six elements varies with respect to the narrative structure appropriate to each medium. Take, for example, biography. In video games, biographical details produce a reality effect but are largely narratively irrelevant; the hero of *Resident Evil* (1996) continues to kill zombies no matter what his backstory is. In films, biographical details produce a reality effect and provide motivations for involvement in the central plot line; Scotty Ferguson pursues Madeline in *Vertigo* (1958) because of his problem with heights and attendant psychological traumas. In television, biographical details produce a reality effect, provide motivations for involvement in the plot lines of single episodes and also for involvement in narrative arcs encompassing multiple episodes; Grissom's deafness, Catherine's complicated family life, Warrick's gambling. Seriality is American television drama's defining characteristic, distinguishing it from both films and video games. The requirement that television characters sustain a series distinguishes them from their counterparts in psychologically realist cinema. The core psychological traits and behaviours of film characters can alter as they experience the narrative trajectories that bring them to the denouement; indeed, such alteration is seen as the hallmark of 'good drama', as when the heroine of *Now Voyager* (1942) goes from awkward spinster to sexually confidant woman. The lack of an immediate denouement requires that the core psychological traits and behaviours of television characters remain stable; Gil's ceasing to be the mad scientist, consummate professional and committed empiricist would threaten the series' format by undermining the character's central narrative function. Gil must behave like Gil until cancellation or the departure of William Petersen. At the same time, CSI's loose degree of seralisation requires some element of personal development. Gil, Catherine and Warrick cannot quit the crime lab but Gil can face impending deafness, Catherine can establish a workable relationship with her biological father and Warrick can deal with his gambling problem.

Characters are suited to their particular fictional forms. Protagonists of one-off novels, plays or films may complete teleological trajectories to life-changing epiphanies. The central protagonists of television dramas must perforce exhibit relative stability in keeping with the repetitive nature of the series/serial format. But the familiarity and even boredom that can arise from this necessarily repetitive nature motivates television scriptwriters' constant search for novelty and divergence. The most extreme novelties and divergences are seen in the so-called 'stunt shows' aired at key moments in the broadcast year (season premieres, sweeps and season finales) and featuring unusual storylines or famous guest stars both in front of and behind the camera. CSI normally begins with a well-established pattern of shots: aerial shots of Las Vegas and/or its desert surrounds, either the crime or the discovery of the body, CSIs at the crime scene. Stunt episodes immediately signal their novelty by departing from this sequence. 'Kiss Kiss, Bye Bye' (6:13), starring Faye Dunaway as a famous former showgirl, begins with black and white footage of Las Vegas in the 1960s. 'Grave Danger' (5:22 & 23), directed by Quentin Tarantino, begins with Nick driving to a supposed crime scene from which a kidnapper will abduct him. The novelty and divergence of 'Grave Danger' lie not only in it being helmed by a famous film director but also in putting the Nick character into an unusual and life-threatening situation.

Stunting constitutes a flashy, attention-getting divergence from the basic series format. Less obviously, novelty can arise from the introduction or development of psychological traits and biographical details. 'The Accused Is Entitled' (3:2), in which the collective failings of the CSIs almost permit a famous murderer to escape justice, demonstrates that, while Gil, Catherine, Sara and Warrick may often be bad crime fighters, they are good characters whose key elements give rise to novel and divergent storylines. *CSI* has five character-based variations upon the basic procedural format: 1) personal problems outside the workplace; 2) personal problems outside the workplace brought to a case; 3) relatives/ friends directly involved in a case; 4) personal conflict/romance in the workplace between team members; and 5) the team's problems with outsiders.

1) Personal problems outside the workplace: One indictor of the primacy of the procedural format over character arcs in *CSI* is that personal problems are almost inevitably brought into working spaces, if not to the case itself. Elements of the characters' biographies can sometimes motivate scenes not directly related to the central plot lines, but taking place in labs or at crime scenes. For example, Warrick has a difficult phone conversation with new wife Tina Brown (Meta Golding) while sitting in a lab at a workplace ('I Like to Watch', 6:17). A few episodes later, in the penultimate episode of Season Six, Warrick, on crime-fighting business in a casino's panoptic control centre, spots Tina on the gambling floor with another man and mistakenly assumes her infidelity. Such scenes minimally advance a character's narrative arc, while at the same time augmenting the weekly procedural plot/plots to fill up the requisite forty-five minutes of screen time, a blessing for harassed scriptwriters working under the highly pressured conditions of American television production.

2) Personal problems impinging upon the workplace or a case: Sometimes the way in which cases resonate with characters' biographies and psychological traits causes the loss of personal objectivity. As mentioned above, this happens to Catherine Willows in 'Pledging Mr. Johnson' (1:4). Separated from her philandering spouse, she reveals to the husband of the victim that his dead wife was having an affair. Grissom blames Catherine when the husband kills the wife's lover. Sometimes personal problems directly affect professional performance. Catherine, with her complicated family life, is the character who struggles most to separate the private and the public. After the murder of her ex-husband in the third season, Catherine inadvertently contributes to a lab explosion in which Sara and Greg are injured ('Play with Fire', 3:22). She tells Grissom, 'I'm spending sixteen hours working, three pretending

to sleep and the other five lying to my daughter that everything is going to be alright.' Sometimes cases seem to directly parallel the character's personal circumstances. Catherine's daughter (Madison McReynolds), exhibiting increasing behavioural problems as a result of her father's death, gets picked up by the cops for hitchhiking in the fifth season episode, 'Harvest' (5:3). The mother of a dead and abducted girl lashes out at Catherine, comparing their parenting. 'What kind of a mother are you? You work nights. You probably don't even know where she is half the time.'

3) Relatives/friends directly involved in a case: All television programmes augment character biographies with relatives and friends who serve the function of introducing divergent plot lines. Catherine has the most extended cast of relations, friends and acquaintances who become directly involved in cases. In 'Who Are You?' (1:6), Eddie Willows (Timothy Carhart), her ex-husband, is a suspect in a murder case until Catherine finds the evidence that exonerates him. In 'Lady Heather's Box' (3:15), Eddie is murdered, leaving Lindsey trapped in a sinking car from which Catherine heroically rescues her. In 'Felonious Monk' (2:17), Catherine reopens the case of her murdered best friend only to discover that her mentor, detective Jimmy Tedero (Bruce McGill), fixed the evidence. But it is Catherine's biological father, Las Vegas bigwig and casino owner Sam Braun (Scott Wilson), who provides the most continuous source of plot lines. In several episodes, starting in the third season, Sam becomes a central figure, or even a suspect in CSI cases. In the third season finale, 'Inside the Box' (3:23), it transpires that a professional heist of a bank vault was staged by Sam to retrieve evidence connecting him to the murder of a Las Vegas showgirl. In the fourth season premiere episode, 'Assume Nothing' (4:1), the bank robbery case against Sam is dropped because Catherine had tampered with the evidence by having Greg run a DNA test to establish Sam's paternity. Sam appears again at the end of the fourth season in 'No More Bets' (4:22), this time suspected of beating and perhaps even killing a card shark. In the Faye Dunaway stunt episode, Sam, who knew the victim and was absent from the room at the time of her murder, is once again a suspect. Catherine, at Sam's insistence, meets him in his flashy limo. She tells him, 'This is the second time that I thought you might be a killer.' By my count, it's the third time; Sam's novelty and divergence potential may be wearing thin.

4) Interpersonal personal conflict/romance in the workplace: A common psychological trait among the CSIs is ambition; all are dedicated

to their jobs and desire professional advancement. At times the friendly rivalry transmutes to outright interpersonal conflict, becoming a minor, and sometimes a major, element of episode plot lines. In the fourth season episode, 'After the Show' (4:8), a suspected killer of a showgirl is attracted to Catherine and will talk only to her. Nick and Sara resent this, knowing that such a high-profile case will help their bids for promotion. Gil, Catherine, Sara and Nick discuss who will lead the investigation.

Nick: This is a career case, Grissom. You know Sara and I both put in for promotion. If we work this we're on the departmental radar.

Catherine: I've got the most high-profile cases under my belt. I think the sheriff would rest easier knowing that I was handling it.

Gil: It's a big department. There's a lot of room at the top.

Nick: We wouldn't ask for it if we couldn't do it.

(Gil remains silent)

Sara: Fine.

(Nick and Sara leave)

Catherine: You going to have my back?

Gil: I always have your back.

As does 'The Accused is Entitled' (3:2), 'After the Show' diverges from the standard procedural plot lines by devoting greater time to the characters. In this case, however, the characters' psychological traits and biographies contribute to, rather than detract from, their crime-solving efforts, with Catherine's background as an exotic dancer particularly helpful. She says to Sara, 'I saw that look in Howard's [the suspect's] eye. I used to make my living off that look. He wanted me. We needed him. I decided to exploit that situation.' When Catherine does eventually break the case, Gil asks her, 'How are you with Nick and Sara?' She responds, 'We're good. They're pros.' Another shared trait, dedicated professionalism, ensures that equilibrium is restored and the team readied for the next week's episode.

Workplace romance can undermine professional relationships, not only for the couple concerned but for the entire team. But it also provides yet another source of novelty and divergence and the filling of screen time; hence the prevalence of UST (unresolved sexual tension) plot lines in workplace dramas and other television programmes. While some fans have detected a vaguely flirtatious relationship between Catherine and Warrick, CSI's primary UST plot involves Gil and Sara. As I've said above, a biographical detail partially motivates Gil's reluctance to commit; he's had a bad relationship in the past. But Sara's traumatic childhood causes her to be attracted to Gil. In 'Nesting Dolls' (5:13) she tells him, 'I choose men who are emotionally unavailable', gesturing towards him as she makes her admission. Judging from an emotionally intimate scene between Gil and Sara set in a bedroom in the sixth season finale, the couple do get together at some point. Executive producer Carol Mendelsohn confirms that the two are in a relationship and that it's 'not so new' (Ryan 2006). According to Mendelsohn, the romance with Sara is part of Grissom's character evolution. 'I think Grissom has changed over the six seasons of CSI', says Mendelsohn. This is in keeping with the element of personal development required by CSI's loose degree of serialisation; characters can evolve within certain limits without threatening the procedural format. The consummation of UST, however, can potentially undermine a series format with too great a degree of novelty and divergence; c.f. *Northern Exposure, Star Trek: Deep Space Nine* and *Frasier*. Mendelsohn is aware of this pitfall. 'We are not a soap opera. We are not a serial. We will always be a show about science, mystery, clues, and twists and turns. And this is a twist and turn. But it's not going to be the Grissom-Sara show from now on' (ibid).

5) The team's problems with higher authority: Characters in all workplace dramas clash with higher authorities; mavericks are a much better source of drama than conformists. Of the CSI team, Gil's and Sara's psychological traits make them the most predisposed to conflict with, or to ignore, their often inadequate superiors. As I've said above, Sara's traumatic childhood frequently impinges upon her workplace performance and causes her, as she says, to have 'a problem with authority' ('Nesting Dolls'). In Seasons Four and Five, Sara's character beats include a drinking problem, a drink-driving incident, an enforced vacation and counselling. Her difficulties culminate in 'Nesting Dolls', a case that involves the murder of mail-order brides. Catherine, her supervisor on the case, says to her, 'Every time we get a case with any kind of domestic violence or abuse you go off the deep end. What is your problem?' As this episode finally reveals, her problem is that her abused mother stabbed her abusive father to death, after which Sara was put into a succession of foster homes. In 'Nesting Dolls' Sara finally goes too far, having a public

argument with Catherine, who refuses to support her request for a search warrant of the male suspect's home. Deputy lab director Conrad Ecklie (Marc Vann), one of those incompetents whom scriptwriters delight in putting in charge, wants Grissom to fire her. Grissom refuses, saying 'She's a great criminalist and I need her.' She's also a good character and the scriptwriters need her.

As we have seen above, Grissom has his own problems with authority; for example, in 'The Strip Strangler' (1:23) he was awarded an unwanted two-week vacation for failing to support the sheriff's and the FBI's choice of murder suspect. The political naivety that causes his temporary suspension eventually leads to his team's disbanding in the fifth season. In 'Mea Culpa' (5:9), Sheriff Ecklie uses the reopening of an old case as an excuse to mount an investigation into Gil's management of his team, particularly his handling of his subordinates' personal problems. Captain Brass warns Grissom, 'This isn't just about the one case. He's looking into your whole team and your ability to lead them. When it comes to politics he whips your ass. So watch your back. It's going to get ugly.' It does indeed get ugly; despite Grissom's being exonerated of overlooking crucial evidence, Ecklie achieves his goal. At the episode's climax he says to Grissom, 'I question the effectiveness of your team and your ability to lead it. I'm breaking you guys up. Catherine Willows will be promoted to swing shift supervisor. Warrwick and Nick go with Catherine. Greg, Sofia, Sara and Grissom will work nights.' Short of character death, the breaking-up of the workplace team is the ultimate divergence from the series' format. In fact, so novel and divergent is the break-up, that the scriptwriters immediately resort to various devices to reassemble the standard team; for example, in 'Nesting Dolls', Gil lends Sara to Catherine and then works on the case during his free time.

Grissom's lack of political nous leads directly to a divergence from the series format so extreme that it must immediately be undone; by the end of the season the team is officially reunited. Customarily, scriptwriters use previously established or newly introduced psychological traits and biographical details to institute less extreme forms of novelty, enough to maintain viewers' interest but not enough to destabilise the series format. Over the course of a long-running series, the routine augmenting of traits and biographies for novelty purposes can lead to highly elaborated characters. But a highly elaborated character is not the same as a well-developed character; just as characters are suited to their particular fictional forms, so must our critical language be. For literary and dramatic critics, development has often meant that the protagonist grows, achieves a higher degree of self-awareness and makes life-transforming decisions. But the repetitive nature of the television series dictates a relative state of stability for its characters, whose failure to perform key narrative functions and to interact with other characters in pre-established fashion could seriously undermine a series' premise. Gil Grissom can't have a life-changing epiphany and become a priest or a vagabond, but the character can be augmented with any number of biographical details, from the narratively trivial (card signed by Roy Rogers) to the narratively significant (deaf mother). In television, it's more accurate to talk about character accumulation and depth than it is to talk about character development. The long-running American television drama can create highly elaborated characters of greater accumulation and depth than any contemporary medium. A medium-specific critical language of this kind is crucial to any project hoping to develop standards of evaluation for popular culture, but that's another essay.

:4:

SO MANY DIFFERENT WAYS TO TELL IT

Multi-Platform Storytelling in *CSI*

MICHAEL ALLEN

> Let's face it: we have entered an era of media convergence that
> makes the flow of content across multiple media channels
> almost inevitable... Everything about the structure of the
> modern entertainment industry was designed with this
> single idea in mind – the construction and enhancement of
> entertainment franchises (Jenkins 2003).

Although George Lucas has been widely credited with ushering in the
modern era of film tie-in merchandising with the massive range of toys,
book, T-shirts and other paraphernalia created in support of the release
of *Star Wars* in 1977, movie tie-in merchandising has been a factor of the
industry since its inception. In contemporary Hollywood, however, it is
inconceivable that a wide range of multiple-media products would not
now accompany the release of a major movie, designed to maximise its
earning potential. More charitably, perhaps, it can be seen that developing
film worlds (characters, locations, narratives) in other media – novels,
Internet websites, etc. – can also be a creative move, designed to open up
and expand the possibilities set up in the original work.

Television is similar in this respect, perceiving a fanbase keen on
taking their interest in a particular show further than catered for by the
programme itself. Certainly, Joss Whedon, creator of *Buffy the Vampire
Slayer*, has used other media – comics in his case – to extend the world of
his fictional creation, in addition to the merchandising available for fans

to purchase. *CSI* is no better (or worse, depending on your viewpoint) in this matter, allowing its fans to purchase everything from coffee mugs and windcheaters with 'CSI' emblazoned on the back, to miniature forensics kits for those wanting to be the lab geek rather than the cool field agent. For the world's most popular television franchise (at least, that is *CSI: Miami*'s current boast, as of November 2006), maximising such ancillary earning power is an opportunity too good to miss.

What I would like to focus on in this chapter is how certain specific products in this range of *CSI* merchandising interconnect with the particular format of the original television series. This format is highly repetitive and formulaic in its structure; notoriously reticent in offering any substantial character insight or development; and stylistically both restrained in its main part but periodically excessive – the now-famous 'CSI-shot' – in describing the gruesome violences which are the cause of the 'C' (crime) in each episode. This chapter, as a result, will explore a particular strand of the franchise's merchandising product: the narrative-based tie-ins of novel(isation), graphic novel, and video game. It is my intention to show that, together, they create an expanded *CSI* 'narrative world' which cannot be accommodated within the familiar structure, generic constraints, and visual style of the television shows themselves. In so doing, they explicitly work *with* the constraints imposed on the television shows to provide a range of different reading and viewing pleasures. In beginning this exploration, however, it is wise to keep in mind Jesper Juul's observation that, 'While it is clear that stories can be passed between a novel and a movie and back, it is also clear that not everything passes equally well. For example, novels are strong in creating inner voices and thoughts, while movies are better at conveying movement' (2005: 48).

CHARACTER DEVELOPMENT

CSI has been frequently noted, and criticised, for denying its viewers/fans any substantial insight into the main characters. In some respects this is simply the conventional technique of narrative retardation that is a natural element of any serial narrative: holding back information, delaying revelation, keeps viewers hooked, waiting expectantly to be told more. Roberta Pearson, in this volume, explores the rationales behind the constraints placed upon character development in *CSI* due to its serial format. Specifically in terms of *CSI* and the crime genre it loosely inhabits, it is also because the focus of each episode is the private lives and motivations of the victims and culprits who suffer and commit each week's crime. In this respect, spending precious screen time (barely 43 minutes without advert breaks) coming to know more about the CSI teams' personal lives would detract from knowing all we need to know about those involved in the crimes. And yet ... Gil Grissom, Horatio Caine, Mac Taylor, Sara Sidle, Catherine Willows, Nick Stokes: each week we set aside time to be with them; it's natural that we want to know more about their lives and feelings beyond their obvious consummate professional skills and knowledge.

Because the television episodes furnish little in the way of character detail and 'backstory', and the graphic novels and video games, due to their specific media forms, do not have character development at the forefront of their *raison d'être*, this task is left to the series of novels written to accompany the three strands of the television franchise. Importantly, these novels offer completely new stories rather than novelisations of existing television episodes. Therefore, they are not trying to 'flesh out' the detail presented in pre-existing narratives but, rather, offer additional visits to the CSI-world and its characters. In doing so they offer 'proof', in a different medium (as do, in other ways, the graphic novels and games), that the characters continue to operate, to live and to feel, outside the events and time presented in the television episodes.

More importantly, the length and format of the novels offer the possibility of more detailed character development than do the television episodes. They employ the standard techniques of prose fiction – an omniscient narrator who describes and explains events and is able, through internal monologue, to 'get inside the head' of any character to describe how s/he is thinking and feeling; extended dialogue interchanges between characters that would seem overly extended in the more action-based emphasis of a television crime show – to potentially create more psychologically detailed protagonists than those seen on television. It is here, perhaps, where our natural curiosity regarding the CSI teams' private lives and thoughts might be answered and satisfied.

Personal details in the novels interconnect with the hints offered in the series. At the end of the pilot episode of *CSI: NY*, for example, Mac, sitting by the side of the episode's final victim as she lies in hospital, sadly recollects the death of his wife in 9/11 and how she remains with him in the trace of her breath, still in a beach ball he cannot bear to throw out ('Blink', 1:0). As Janet McCabe argues in this volume, this scene, and Mac's subsequent journey to Ground Zero, are profound moments which reference a national as much as a personal trauma. But having offered us this early insight into Mac's psyche, the series, characteristically, closes this access down, and we are only able to both hypothesise further emotional depth, and read Mac's subsequent actions and moods through this momentary revelation.

In the *CSI: NY* novel, *Dead of Winter*, however, Mac's grief is explored at length throughout the course of the narrative. Very early in the story, for example, Mac and his wife are described struggling through deep snow to buy groceries at a local supermarket:

> When Mac slipped on a hill and sank, rear end, into the snow on the way back home, Claire had laughed. Groceries were strewn around him making their own indentations in the snow lit by the hazy streetlights. Mac hadn't been able to laugh. He looked up with an exaggerated frown, but the frown became a smile. Claire was ankle deep in snow, her ears red, her blue watch cap pulled down her forehead, her red-knit, gloved hands clutching shopping bags. She was laughing. He could see it all now, dark street, white snow, streetlamp glowing, her laughing (Kaminsky 2005: 15).

Later, in a Proustian moment of gustatory remembering, the realisation that he has, yet again, bought a chicken salad to eat causes him to think of her again:

> Mac's wife, he remembered, had liked chicken salad, which was probably why he had been eating it. The taste, the smell, reminded him of her. It was something like pinching a taste bud to remind him, though he took no pleasure in it. Tonight he semi-planned to pick up a couple of kosher hot dogs and a large Diet Coke. The date was coming soon, a few days. As it grew closer, Mac Taylor felt it deeper and deeper inside him (ibid.: 89).

The date in question is his wedding anniversary, and the novel's epilogue will see Mac, joined by his team, at his wife's grave as he lays a bouquet of roses down to commemorate the occasion.

Later in the novel, discussion of the opera causes him to remember that 'His wife had loved opera. And Mac had gotten used to the artificial, inane stories, the overacting, and the semi-pomp of dressing up. He had especially liked watching Claire dress for a big night out. She always smiled in appreciation' (ibid.: 118). Later still, standing before a famous oil painting he is able to identify the work, to the surprise of his colleague, Stella Bonasera, because:

> 'My wife had some prints of his work,' said Mac. 'One of the highlights of our trip to Europe was to see Millet's *Angelius* in the Musee d'Orsay.'
>
> Stella nodded. It was more information about Mac's dead wife than he had ever given up before.
>
> Mac's smile was broader now.
>
> 'She saw beauty in that painting,' he said. 'And you see a woman with a medical condition' (ibid.: 245).

The important point here lies in Stella's final realisation of having received 'more information about Mac's wife than he had ever given up before'. Certainly more than in the television series. She, with Mac, like us with all of the *CSI* characters as we watch each week, learns virtually nothing about his inner emotional life and memories even though, in the early episodes of *CSI: NY*, Stella is obviously concerned about him and his inability to sleep. At least we as viewers, unlike Stella, are privy to Mac's revelation about his wife's breath in the beach ball.

But, through the omniscient narrator controlling our privileged position as readers of the novels, we are told far more; detail that would hamper the smooth forward narrative flow of the time-pressured television episode and compromise both the professional agenda of the crime investigation and the professional distance maintained between the teams of CSI investigators. In another media form, however, the valuable information is there for the grateful taking. And taking it allows us to understand those characters a little better. It is a double-level of knowledge that enables us to derive a double pleasure: of not knowing from the programme itself, thereby letting the detailed investigation of the crime provide our entertainment, and, if we read the novel, of knowing *in spite* of the programme's emotional reticence, so that the characters' actions and reactions are framed in a broader psychological context.

Other aspects of character development are enabled by the length of novels as opposed to the brevity of TV episodes, such as protracted banter between characters which indicate a greater bonding and affection for one another than generally comes across in the television series. At times, intriguingly, this character interrelating takes on a more significant dimension, to act as a bridge connecting together currently incomplete character and action arcs from the series. The main example of this, certainly the most potentially entertaining for *CSI* fans, is the simmering sexual attraction between Grissom and Sara. This is insinuated from the moment they first meet in the series, in the episode 'Cool Change' (1:2) of the Las Vegas strand, when Sara makes her first appearance with Grissom. With his back to her, and in response to her quip that it is understandable that a victim might have jumped to his death, considering who he was married to, Grissom replies: 'I don't even have to turn around. Sara Sidle.' Having posited the possibility for a central departmental romance, however, the producers retreated by putting the mutual attraction into the background (until the end of Season Six), periodically flirting with it by allowing a sexual frisson to exist between the two characters.

The novel *Cold Burn*, however, continues the storyline. Grissom and Sara are snowed in at a New England hotel where they are attending a pathology conference and a murder there has commanded their attention. Although booked into separate rooms, she soon comes to call on him at his. His simple comment that she looks rested makes her think (using internal monologue):

> 'Wow – that was one of the nicest things he'd ever said to her.' Encouraged, she tried, 'You wanna go for a walk?'...
>
> ... 'I don't do snow,' he said. He was still in the black slacks and black three-button shirt. Gesturing with the bug book, he said, 'It's cozy, reading by the fire. You should try it.'
>
> That sounded almost romantic... (Collins 2003: 37–8).

Later, Sara tells him that he smells good and asks what cologne he's wearing. 'His eyes tightened as he processed the question. Then he said, "Thanks... it's aftershave," and pulled the door shut' (ibid.: 93–4); the closing of the door possibly representing the closing down of his emotions. Finally, on the last pages of the novel, with Grissom and Sara back at the CSI lab, Catherine teases Sara about the snow having ruined the conference:

> Sara paused at the door. 'Last day – Sunday? That was nice and

cozy, though. We spent the day reading by the fire.'

She slipped out, leaving behind two co-workers who were looking at each other with wide eyes and open mouths.

'No,' Catherine said.

'No way,' Nick said.

In the hallway, Sara was smiling to herself. Nick and Cath didn't know that she and Grissom had separate fireplaces in their separate rooms.

And they didn't need to know.

Let them wonder (ibid.: 302–303).

Obviously, none of the above examples are evidence of consummation of the relationship between Grissom and Sara. For that we must wait for the Season Six television finale, 'Way To Go' (6:24), the very last scene of which shows Grissom and Sara in dressing gowns in the same bedroom. Whether this scene actually means they have slept together and are now a couple, or that there is another plausible reason they had to share a room (on a case, caught in a storm, motel only had one room available...) remains to be seen. Season Seven will answer these questions.

This ambiguity notwithstanding, the repeated inclusion of new scenes in the novels describing the flirtatious, sexually charged interplay between Grissom and Sara maintains the reality of that attraction, confirming that it continues when the characters are off our screens, between television episodes. Again, the existence of this relationship in another medium acts as a second source of reliable information, as it were, confirming the truth of the flirtation.

In the graphic novels, such moments of personal revelation are, not surprisingly, handled primarily in a visual way. The individual panels become synecdoches for complex actions, a single image representing an often much longer action or event. In this way, they become representative of an intense restriction of possible detail, throwing even greater emphasis on the focus of the narrative – the crime – and even less on any possible character depth. There is very little access to any personal dimension in relation to the characters. But this radical restriction, caused by the formal properties of the medium, makes it all the more powerful when access is momentarily offered. At one point in *Bad Rap*, a *CSI: Crime Scene Investigation* graphic novel (Collins et al 2004), for example, a small panel shows Grissom and Catherine discussing newly found evidence when Sara approaches in the background. The subsequent panel shows Sara alone, filling Grissom in on latest developments, while a third has her continuing to talk to him, Grissom positioned along the left frame edge and Sara now dominating the foreground in the middle of the panel, Catherine nowhere to be seen. Graphically, we read this as Sara usurping the position of the other female, Catherine, and asserting her access to Grissom. The next panel shows Grissom retreating to the background as Sara tells him, 'I'd like to print our witnesses tonight: that security guard, the tourist, Al Rockwell, even Doug Clennon. Okay with that?' to which Grissom replies, 'I love it.'

But then in the next panel, in a startling reversal of perspective, we move behind Grissom so that he is now in the foreground of the frame, with Sara behind him. She asks him whether he knows of Al Rockwell, the old rock 'n' roll star who is one of the main actors, and suspects, in the story. In reply, Grissom recites verbatim the poignant set of lyrics from one of the singer's ballads: '"A teenage boy's a lonely soul, alone right from the start, and when the girl he loves is gone, he has a broken heart"... Yeah. I've heard of him.' His last words appear in a caption bubble in the final panel, which shows Sara staring intently out of frame back at Grissom, surprised by his melancholic admission (Collins et al 2004: 45).

The final two panels stand out as a moment of stasis in the relentlessly forward-flowing crime narrative; a relentlessness emphasised by the staccato nature of the comic book, whose format of several dynamically drawn panels per page privilege action over psychological depth. Although minimal in terms of character revelation, certainly in comparison to the novels and even to the television series, within the graphic novel's primary agenda of describing action and events, this moment of poignancy from Grissom carries a significant punch. In a few lines of dialogue and a progression of drawn panels, Grissom's idealism and possible youthful emotional heartbreak are offered up to us as one more fragment of his inner emotional complexity.

The arrangement of these panels, therefore, detail the force of feelings between Sara and Grissom, even when the dialogue is ostensibly concerned with discussing details of the case. As such, it is not much different from the choice of camera framings in scenes showing the two characters together in the television episodes, or the choice of details described in prose in the novels. But the pure graphic quality of the panels – single, condensed images summing up complex situations and emotions – strips the unspoken text of hidden desire to its bare essentials, offering the simple power of unresolved feeling.

Similarly, the television series' emotional reticence maps onto the general bias towards action rather than emotion in the video game:

> Video games generally focus on manipulating and moving objects, and less commonly address the more complex interactions between humans such as friendships, love and deceit... the game form lends itself more easily to some things than to others – it is hard to create a game about emotions because emotions are hard to implement in rules (Juul 2005: 20).

A circuit of repression is thereby set up, predicated on media form and expectation, which allows the denial of emotion and personal revelation in the televisual world of *CSI* to be confirmed and indeed intensified in its computer-game counterpart. The video game is wholly business oriented: just gather the evidence, process it using the virtual technology at your disposal, interview and determine the guilt of the suspect, but do not expect to have any access to the private lives of the CSI team. The game isn't programmed that way.

One further aspect of the logic of video gaming might be appropriate to consider here. This is the inherently repetitious nature of video game playing. A relatively simple range of rules are learned and a set range of operations performed to manipulate the characters and events on screen towards the resolution of the overarching game narrative.

> While nothing prevents a game from combining all imaginable kinds of challenges, there is a convention that the challenges presented throughout a game have a similarity that allows the player to face them by refining the same basic repertoire (Juul 2005: 115-6).

In this repetition of operations and similarity of challenges, video games in general, and *CSI* video games very much in particular, echo the formulaic structure and narrative progression of any *CSI* episode. In this way, one of the features of the television series, that has been regarded negatively by its critics, not only makes the programme ideal for conversion to video-game format, but also, perhaps, explains its popularity for at least a certain section of its potential audience; a sector that welcomes the familiarity of procedural repetition.

VISUAL STYLE

All three *CSI* strands display a pronounced, and markedly distinct, visual style. This is figured both in terms of their overall colour scheme – Las Vegas' neon glare, Miami's oranges and whites, New York's muted greys and blues – and in the explosive shift from these to the bloody, graphic and visceral camera movements showing bullets and knife blades cutting through human flesh in extreme close-up, which have become the trademark *CSI* look. The latter act as virtual reconstructions of the truth of the crime itself, or visualisations of hypotheses by a CSI member or pathologist of what might have occurred, based on the evidence so far.

The novels rather clumsily figure these 'alternative realities' in both prose description and in simple differences in font – plain text for the main narrative, italic for the imagined scenes. In this sense, the novels admit their relative inability to mimic and replicate the full terms of their original source reference: the television series. For this, the consumer must look elsewhere.

The graphic novels (the clue is in their format name) fare better than the novels in their ability to represent the contrasting visual styles of normal narrative and hyper-stylised 'internal damage' and/or imagined 'hypothetical solution' sequences:

> The editorial staff came up with the brilliant notion of using two artists, one (Gabriel Rodriguez) for the realistically portrayed investigatory work with the familiar TV faces; another (Ashley Wood) for expressionistically-depicted flashbacks and re-enactments... The approach parallels the striking visual style of the show – something that can only be suggested in a prose novel. Despite their differences, film and comics are, after all, both visual mediums (Collins et al 2004: 1).

Curiously, however, the detail in the two types of image is reversed in the graphic novel relative to the television series. Instead of the imagined sequences being far more spectacularly detailed than the main narrative sequences, it is the latter which are fully realised, while the mental images are sketchy and vaguely detailed. While obviously a pragmatic choice – to avoid the majority of drawn panels looking poorly sketched and amateurish and therefore not worth the cover price – the raw, crudely drawn images also visually reflect both the edgy violence and the often hazy and imperfect memories they represent.

The video-game versions of CSI restore the contrast between the visual representation of a flashback event presented in a hyper-slick form and the normal image quality of the rest of the narrative. There is, however, a significant difference in the rationale for the shift from the 'normal' image to the hyper-image. In the video games, the former has a clumsy, wooden quality. Technical limitations force the characters to become physically immobile, with only their lips moving crudely in time to the words supposedly being spoken by them. The game requires the player to interact with these rather cartoonish representations of the CSI personnel and the other characters acting as the various suspects, in an attempt to solve the crime narrative that is the purpose of the game.

When a stage of this hidden narrative is solved by evidence being gathered and processed, and an event or suspect identified, the graphic quality is transformed. The player's achievement in solving a part of the puzzle triggers the playing, in real time and with no ability to stop it, of a sequence of high-quality images that re-enact the event. Whereas such a sequence in the series is a spectacular confirmation of the knowledge and professionalism of the CSI teams, in the video game it is confirmation of the skill of the player, not only as a rookie CSI, but as an increasingly adept game player. It is as if the sequence rewards the player, not only by showing them that they are correct in the solution they have come up with, but by allowing them to watch an image sequence which explicitly echoes the kind that would be used in the television series itself. The player thereby, in some fashion, becomes the producer of their own televisual aesthetic; the result of determination and persistence to locate and uncover the evidence and the truth.

What is also interesting is that video-game protocols generally resist using such flashback and 'hypothesised' sequences, which are called 'cut scenes' in the gaming world:

> A somewhat controversial way of creating game fiction, a cut-scene is a non-interactive sequence of a game that typically provides backstory or informs the player of the task to be undertaken. Cut-scenes are often considered problematic because they prevent the player from doing anything and are in a sense a non-game element in a game. Still, they play an important role in projecting fiction in modern video games ...

... Cut-scenes are not a parallel time or an extra level, but a different way of projecting the fictional time. They do not by themselves modify the game state – this is why they can usually be skipped and why the user cannot do anything during a cut-scene. While play time is projected to fictional time in interactive sequences, cut-scenes disconnect play time from fictional time (Juul 2005: 135, 145, 147).

In the *CSI* games, however, what is seen as transgressive and harmful to the smooth playing of a video game becomes a marker of game-playing success. The shift in aesthetic registers and the jarring of the narrative flow signify the successful solving of a part of the crime puzzle. This temporal continuity and occasional fragmentation rebounds back to further consideration of the particular form of the television series and the processes by which the viewer engages with it.

THE VIEWER'S ACTIVITY

The narratives of the *CSI* television series have an interesting temporal framework – in that they largely remain in the present. The crime which typically opens each episode is seen as it takes place, and causes the CSI team to arrive on the scene, process the area for evidence, meet with suspects and related characters and eventually solve the 'whodunnit'. But dramatically interrupting this forward march of forensic analysis are visually heightened sequences which show either graphic close-ups of the injuries suffered by the victim – bullets and knives cutting through flesh, bouncing off ribcages, etc. – or imagined and hypothetical 'reconstructions' of what might have happened during the crime itself, based on the evidence gathered thus far at the point in the episode when the hypothesis is posited. At such moments, we move into a different temporal framework. In the case of the close-ups of injuries this time frame is a certain, if grossly magnified, past; the certainty of the event is confirmed in the professional authority of the describer, usually the resident pathologist. In the case of the reconstructions, the time frame is simply a 'maybe': this event *might* have happened in the past but it is uncertain both if and when it did.

It is the latter that I want to concentrate on now, in terms of the differences offered in this respect by the television series and the video games. David Bordwell, in his *Narration and the Fiction Film* (1985), discusses the difference, and relationship, between fabula (story) and syuzhet (discourse, plot); the first being the fictional events as they happened in time, the second as they are recounted by the storyteller, a version which involves non-linearity, omission, repetition, falsehoods; in short, manipulation of the order and detail of the basic story. Importantly for the present study, Bordwell spends some time analysing the particular operation of fabula/syuzhet relations in the crime/detective genre, within which the *CSI* narrative most comfortably resides:

> The fundamental narrational characteristic of the detective tale is that the syuzhet withholds crucial events occurring in the 'crime' portion of the fabula. The syuzhet may conceal the motive, or the planning, or the commission of the crime (an act which includes the identity of the criminal), or aspects of all of these. The syuzhet may commence with the discovery of the crime, or it may start before the crime is committed and find other ways to conceal the crucial events. In either case, the syuzhet is principally structured by the progress of the detective's investigation... The viewer creates a set of exclusive hypotheses – a closed set of suspects, a gradually defined range of outcomes. The genre creates suspense with respect to the twists and turns of the investigation and plays upon curiosity about the missing causal material.
>
> Since the investigation is the basis of the syuzhet, there is obviously a more or less constant revelation of prior fabula information... But the most pertinent missing causes will emerge only gradually, often near the end of the syuzhet. In other words, exposition about the investigation itself tends to be concentrated in preliminary portions of the syuzhet, while information about the motive, agent, and circumstances of the crime will be distributed and finally summed up clearly in later portions. Thus, no gap will be permanent (1985: 64).

The *CSI* narrative fits this schema very well. A crime has been committed through a series of events: the fabula. The duty of the CSI team is to piece together this fabula through the gathering of evidence which will confirm its linear sequence. The various dead ends of investigation, false testimonies by suspects and conflicting evidence are the efforts of the syuzhet to prevent this, or at least delay its inevitability. The fabula is then eventually presented, usually by Grissom, Horatio or Mac, in a summary scene which concludes each episode.

The pleasure for the viewer, the game that is effectively played between them and the programme, lies in trying to guess ahead in order to piece together the fabula before the CSI team does. In so doing, the key term is 'guess ahead'. For Bordwell, the film (and television) viewer is not simply a passive receiver of the information from the text, being told everything without questioning anything. Instead, s/he is an active hypothesiser, processing information as it is given up by the text and formulating theories and guesses as to its significance, importance or irrelevance, and how it might be used to anticipate what will happen next:

> To make sense of a narrative film... the viewer must do more than perceive movement, construe images and sounds as presenting a three-dimensional world, and understand oral or written language. The viewer must take as a central cognitive goal the construction of a more or less intelligible story ...
>
> ... people perform operations on a story. When information is missing, perceivers infer it or make guesses about it. When events are arranged out of temporal order, perceivers try to put those events in sequence. And people seek causal connections among events, both in anticipation and retrospect (Bordwell 1985: 33–34).

While Bordwell is describing the viewer's activity during the watching of a film or television drama, some of the terms he uses could equally well refer to the activities of the CSI team in 'cracking' the mystery of a particular crime. The analysing of movement, images, sounds, oral and written language – the 'performing [of] operations on a story' – are tasks the CSI teams routinely conduct during any of their weekly investigations. And while it is hard to imagine either Grissom, Horatio or Mac entertaining the notion of guessing or inferring anything (something they repeatedly warn their teams away from indulging in), that is effectively, in the hypothetical reconstructions that regularly pepper the CSI narratives, what the investigating teams do when they attempt to piece together an incomplete crime story based on the evidence gathered thus far. 'What if so-and-so did this?' 'What if this happened before that and led to the other?' Often they are right, and the partial sequence they have imagined proves to be as it actually happened. More often, however, they are wrong, and the reconstruction turns out to be a fantasy based on guesswork (educated though it may be) and supposition.

Partly this has to do with a combination of what Meir Sternberg (1978) calls the *curiosity hypothesis*, a strategy by which intentionally withheld story information prompts the viewer to make various kinds of hypotheses about present events, and a *suspense hypothesis*, in which anticipation is set up about future events. In *CSI*, as in most works in the detective/investigation genre, the latter produces knowledge that leads to the filling in and answering of the former.

The process of finding fragments of evidence, on which educated (or not, in this case) guesswork is then based, forms the central dynamic in the playing of any of the *CSI* video games. As a rookie CSI, the player is initially led by the hand by one of the regular *CSI* characters (Calleigh Duquesne in Miami, Catherine Willows in Las Vegas – interesting how it is the women who act as guides and helpers). Each piece of evidence allows the player to guess or hypothesise about its significance and meaning, and to then visit seemingly connected or implicated characters within the game's narrative. The step-by-step nature of the game – find a piece of evidence, visit a character, ask them pre-scripted questions, act upon the results (positive or negative) – intensifies the sense of hypothesising that is conducted at every step. And built into the game is the possibility of several wrong moves – attempting to question an irrelevant character, for example, or return to a now empty crime scene in the belief that another clue still lurks there – before the right one is eventually reached (or, in the case of this writer, a video-game virgin, blindly stumbled upon). In such a way, the video-game experience offers, in drawn out *in extremis* fashion, the processes with which the viewer engages during the viewing of an episode of any of the *CSI* strands.

CONCLUSION

The full terms of the *CSI* narrative therefore lies in the viewer/player's ability to operate in a range of different media forms: television, novels, graphic novels, video games. Each of these ask different skills of the person: the ability to read and process relentlessly forward-moving televisual images and sounds; to read and reread prose text from the pages of a novel; to interpret the dynamic operating between still images and word on the pages of a graphic novel; to interact with the video-game world by proactively making decisions that allow the searching of on-screen details for clues and the 'interviewing' of a range of possible suspects, in order to piece together the story of the crime. These various multimedia activities in many ways echo the range of activities and skills required of the CSI teams themselves, as they chemically test materials and stains, read complex chemical formulae from computer screens, study bullet striations under microscopes and interpret the actions and emotions of suspects and other characters.

Ultimately, the success of the *CSI* series lies not *in spite* of their relentless formulaic and structural repetition, but *because* of it. Certainly, one important aspect of the series' popularity lies in the emotional security inherent in the generic certainty of this repetition: that week in, week out, crime will be defeated by the methodical activities of the CSI team. But over and above this comfort-zone effect, the *CSI* narratives are popular because, in their procedures of continual hypothesis based on the gathering of evidence, facts and figures, they so completely mimic the activities of their viewers as they watch the shows. *CSI* represents audio-visual, fictional narrative viewing/reading at its purest, with few tangential distractions to throw us off the case or from our fundamental viewing task. In conducting its weekly on-screen investigation, it invites its viewer to conduct their own investigation: of the text itself, of its semiotic codes and of their own self-reflexive viewing pleasure.

The expandability of the world of *CSI* moves in various directions. Immediately, within the television franchise itself – Las Vegas, Miami and New York so far; others, possibly, to follow – with each strand maintaining the basic and endlessly repeatable structure of crime, investigation and resolution. A second direction moves the television series into the transmedia environment – novels, graphic novels, video games – in order both to maximise the commercial potential of the programme (hit the fans hard while the franchise is hot), and to explore how the essential elements of the series – the processes of scientific analysis, narrative structure, etc. – can be made to function artistically in new and different media environments. The pleasure of this second movement comes from seeing these familiar elements of the series played out in these other less familiar media landscapes. The final move then reverses the direction of the transmedia dynamic, feeding back the possibilities opened up by these different narrative media forms to invest aspects of the series – character depth, backstory, developing relationships – with detail and depth not feasible of being included within the programmes themselves. It is an economic and artistic match made, if not in heaven, then certainly in the globally aware contemporary American television industry. And it is one which has helped make *CSI* phenomenally successful not only as a television show, but also as a range of other narrative products that feed its burgeoning fanbase. That is the marker of its success.

:5:
CSI AT THE BFI ...

KIM AKASS

The buzz began some weeks before the actual *CSI* event. The National Film Theatre's (NFT) annual Crime Scene festival of crime fiction in literature, film and television, organised by the British Film Institute (BFI), from 30 June – 3 July 2005, was to feature a special *CSI* weekend complete with a preview screening of the Season Five finale of *CSI: Crime Scene Investigation* – 'Grave Danger' (5:25), written and directed by Quentin Tarantino. This was to be followed by a *Guardian* interview with the man himself as well as executive producer and writer Carol Mendelsohn. The following day was billed as a panel discussion featuring Danny Cannon, director and executive producer, Max Allan Collins, author of the *CSI* novelisations, Mendelsohn, and possibly Tarantino, chaired by Adrian Wootton, Director of Crime Scene Weekend. Quite a line-up and totally impossible to get a ticket for the Friday night screening – believe me, I tried. And here's an irony. After years of attending screenings at the NFT, I could not get a ticket for a preview of a *television programme*. It may be that *CSI: Miami* has recently been named the world's most watched television show (2006), but does this adequately explain the fact that there was not a ticket to be had for love nor money on a balmy night on the South Bank in July 2005?

... OR, NO QT AT THE NFT
As it happens, Tarantino cancelled at the last minute due to pressure of work and my very lucky friend (who did manage to get a ticket) was absolutely correct in her assumption that if I just came along I would get a seat. Of course I would. How many people would turn up for the screening

of something that would be on television in the next few months? Quite a number as it happens; and even though I could have got in and shared the moment, the auditorium was packed. With good reason as, without a doubt, even *sans* Tarantino, it was quite an experience (or so I have been reliably informed) and as filmic as anything previously screened at the NFT. But the question still remains – director notwithstanding – what is it about *CSI* that prompted the NFT to feature the programme so prominently? This chapter will focus on the programming of a weekend event featuring a television series that a colleague once called 'the trashiest of all trash TV' (he shall remain anonymous in order to protect his professional reputation).

Before talking about the event itself, I have to return to the end of May 2005 when the buzz began. What was more exciting: the fact that Tarantino had directed a couple of episodes or that the NFT was featuring *CSI* over a whole two days? Both facts give the series kudos and provide a modicum of street cred for a fan that had always been forced to keep her dirty little secret to herself. It was not only my erstwhile colleague quoted above that had despaired of my taste in television. The fact that I wrote (and still write) about the medium at all was a source of much amusement, amazement and disparagement to many friends and colleagues. As anyone who works in British academe will tell you, there is a hierarchy of respectability among subjects, with humanities way down the scale. Film studies has only gained any kind of propriety since the 1970s; media studies is something that students allegedly only sign up for because it is an 'easy' option; and television studies lurks beyond even that particular pale. So, the thought of somebody at the NFT having the chutzpah to programme a weekend dedicated to *CSI* felt like two fingers stuck up at those who had not spent evenings curled up on the sofa sharing time with Gil Grissom, Sara Sidle, Catherine Willows, Warrick Brown, Nick Stokes and, more recently, Horatio Caine, Mac Taylor et al. As a (much more astute) colleague remarked to me on hearing about the event, the buzz generated by it and the rush to get tickets: 'You must be onto something if the NFT are showing *CSI*.' Yes, indeed I must.

To be sure, this is not the first time Quentin Tarantino has been involved in a groundbreaking TV show, giving the medium a whiff of credibility. Way back in 1995, shortly after the success of *Pulp Fiction*, he made his foray into television to guest direct an episode of *ER*, 'Motherhood' (1:23), which was aired in May of that year. Some ten years later his return to TV to both write and direct the *CSI* episode caused an even bigger stir. According to Adrian Wootton, it was quite a coup for the NFT to get permission (from both Alliance Atlantis and the UK broadcaster Five) to screen 'Grave Danger' before it was broadcast on British TV, but the presence of Tarantino would legitimise the decision for the NFT as well as bring in an audience that might not necessarily watch the series. 'I was always interested in doing a focus on CSI and... the Tarantino episode made the whole thing a much stronger proposition' (interview, October 2006). But it was not the sole reason that many attended. According to Wootton, 'overwhelmingly the attendances were from people who were huge fans of the show' (interview, September 2006). This was evidenced by the turnout for the Saturday afternoon event (which I *was* able to get an advance ticket for). The auditorium was certainly not as full as it surely would have been had Tarantino been on the panel, but those that did attend were obviously diehard CSI fans. And no, we weren't just sad freaks and geeks with little else to do on a Saturday afternoon (after all, we could have been watching Live 8 instead), but an assorted bunch, both fans and scholars, with a genuine fascination for the phenomenon that is CSI.

THIS MUCH I KNOW...

Why CSI? Why indeed? Especially when *Law & Order* could have been of equal interest in a crime fiction event. The series is longer running and has its own franchise to boot: *Law & Order: Special Victims Unit* and *Law & Order: Criminal Intent*. Wootton explains his choice thus:

> Well first of all I loved [CSI], and it was precisely its newness
> and the freshness of format we wanted to explore. Also and
> rather obviously *Law & Order* is a great show (which I am
> also a big admirer of and I have pretty much seen all of that
> too in its three different franchises) but it has never had the
> public appeal in the UK of CSI and, even in the US, I don't
> think that, despite its longevity, it has ever captured the public
> imagination in quite the same way (September 2006).

What strikes me immediately is how Wootton outs himself as a fan. But more interestingly he seems to justify his own fandom in the context of the show's enormous appeal in the UK and the US. Such unease epitomises for me the ongoing debate amongst TV scholars: what is the place of taste within television studies?

It is an issue that has long preoccupied contributors to the online journal, *Flow*. Launched three years ago (October 2004) with a mission statement aiming to bridge the gap between 'academics and an informed public', and 'to generate a new type of conversation' (similar to the one taking place at the NFT), *Flow* reflects on the taste debate. Brian L. Ott cites Susan Sontag's 'erotics of art' (2001: 14) and urges television scholars 'to develop modes of criticism rooted in pleasure'. Fast-forward two years and John Corner asks, 'How openly subjective should it [criticism] be, stressing a personal relationship ("response") between critic and work or, conversely, what level of objectivity can it attain, what "scientific" support can it draw upon?' (September 2006). In the same issue, Jason Mittell argues that this is part of a larger problem that must be addressed in order to re-evaluate how television in general, and television studies in particular, are viewed. Suggesting that 'Television has been too easily dismissed as disposable and not even worthy of evaluation', he contends that the debate should focus on '*what* should be valued rather than *whether* we should value' (ibid.). Adding that this will result in 'both the medium and our field [gaining] importance and legitimacy' (ibid.).

For me, the idea of '*what* should be valued' and the question of 'importance and legitimacy' are central to what the *CSI* weekend was all about. *CSI* was incorporated into the crime fiction event not only because it is perceived as changing the face of the one-hour procedural drama (for example, its technological innovations in television aesthetics), but more importantly because an institution that takes media seriously has absorbed it into its institutional mission and given permission to speak about it. Less important for me was not what was said (even though I now know what the deal is with Horatio's sunglasses; that *CSI: Miami* is all about being seen while *CSI: Crime Scene Investigation* is all about being hidden and some valuable insights from Danny Cannon about the *CSI* look) it was the fact that it was said at all.

If, as in Mittell's view, it is time to incorporate our opinions into our scholarly and pedagogical practices, then it is important that we should 'not hide [our] tastes and value judgements away in the closet, bringing them into public only when off-duty' (ibid.).

Many thanks to Adrian Wootton.

:III:

TRACE

Aesthetics, Style and Form

:6:

BODY MATTERS

Realism, Spectacle and the Corpse in *CSI*

DEBORAH JERMYN

Writing about Lynda La Plante's crime drama series *Prime Suspect* a decade after it was first broadcast in the UK, I argued in an article published in 2003 that the series had actively 'pushed back genre boundaries' in TV crime drama (Jermyn 2003). This had been achieved in part, of course, through its complex portrayal of a female detective working in a man's world. But beyond this, I suggested, through its frank, unflinching look at the dead, tortured and decaying bodies of its murder victims, *Prime Suspect* had '[rearticulated] forensic realism in television crime'. Increasingly, I argued, La Plante's oeuvre invoked 'special effects', 'graphic detail' and 'close focus' in ways which had forever shifted audience expectations, and television's evocation, of realism and the representation of the body in the genre (2003: 60). After *Prime Suspect*, the 'boundaries' which had once governed how much crime drama could show us of the corpse, and how it looked, would never be the same again.

If any TV text seems indebted to this shift and pertinent to this discussion now, illustrating the degree to which television has become increasingly enchanted by the dramatic possibilities of forensic detail, it is *CSI: Crime Scene Investigation*. That a programme built around the gruesome clues, secrets and promises embedded within, and articulated across, the image of the corpse could become the most successful television series in the world would have been unimaginable until relatively recently. The terms I invoked in reference to *Prime Suspect* – 'special effects', 'graphic detail' and 'close focus' – have remained conspicuously germane to the contemporary crime TV landscape, but particularly so in relation to *CSI*. The series' success cannot be extricated from its spectacular deployment of CGI and special effects, which focus very often on reconstructing a privileged point of view in which the 'real' fate of the victims and the forensic truth of their deaths is reconstructed and revealed. Fostering a potent kind of intimacy between the television audience and the body, *CSI* capitalises on the small screen space and the intimate nature of the medium by actually taking the viewer into the body's 'inner space'. The programme's signature evocation of penetrative 'wound-cam' technology in some ways mimics and borrows from the realist connotations of footage drawn from the endoscopic cameras used in surgery to explore the body, images which have become a staple of medical documentary programmes. But, at the same time, these sequences and their deployment of CGI – labelled the 'CSI-shot'[1] by the programme's producers – are clearly about *spectacle* and capture more of the physical drama of the body's interior than any real medical probe ever could. Through the 'CSI-shot' – penetrating skin, arteries and organs to take the audience on a spectacular visual ride through the corporeal – the boundaries not merely of the genre, or of television, but of the body itself, have been dissolved.

In this way, the representation of the body and corpse within *CSI*'s forensic discourses is crucial to its heightened evocation of evidential 'truth claims', a motif which has become increasingly commonplace in contemporary television (cf. *Silent Witness* and *Waking the Dead* in the UK, the titles of which both invoke the notion of communicating with the corpse in order to reach the truth). Interestingly, so apparently convincing is the programme's depiction of the capabilities of forensics that it has been credited as having impacted on 'real life' perceptions of crime and forensics and the outcome of real court cases, as witnessed by the emergence of the so-called 'CSI effect'. In a cover story taken from *USA Today* in 2004, according to legal analysts in the US, 'the CSI effect' points to how the massive popularity of *CSI* and comparable generic programmes such as *Law & Order* is 'affecting action in courthouses across the United States by... raising jurors' expectations of what prosecutors should produce at trial... Jurors who are regular viewers expect testable evidence to be present at all crime scenes', thus making it harder to secure convictions in the very many cases where such evidence doesn't exist (Willing 2004: 1–2). Certainly, one of the distinctive generic shifts the programme has brought to TV crime drama is its relative disinterest in the criminal mind and Gil Grissom's recurrent aphorism is that it is a CSI's job to read the evidence, not look for motive. For example, when Warrick Brown tells Grissom in the pilot episode that he doesn't know what to make of a suspicious 'self-defence' case that culminated in a man shooting his wife's friend, Grissom tells him, 'Forget about the husband, forget about the assumptions, forget about your promotion. These things will only confuse you. *Concentrate on what cannot lie – the evidence*' (my emphasis). In the same opening episode, from hair follicles to fingerprints, from toenail cuttings to the size of a bullet wound, the body is quickly established as a key channel through which evidence, and thus the truth, can be reached.

In this chapter I want to explore this construction of the body as purveyor of facts and evidence while arguing that, crucially, CSI's depiction of the corpse simultaneously *detracts* from the programme's sense of realism. While Karen Lury has noted that the bleached-out colour schemes of the programme (particularly evident in Season One) produce a 'grainy documentary effect' which speaks of 'a desire to create a mood of seriousness or lend a sense of edginess' (Lury 2005: 37), this desire and aesthetic coexist alongside a much more extravagant investment in elaborate spectacle. The flashy, bravura camera movement which takes us inside the body, the apparently limitless capabilities of technology in bringing order to evidence, the play with temporality through stylised flashbacks which take us back to the moment of physical impact, can all be seen in many ways as anti-realist. The glossy signature of its Hollywood blockbuster producer Jerry Bruckheimer is writ large in CSI's use of effects and CGI. Hence, despite the programme having what Martha Gever has called a 'basic commitment to well-supported, objective, deductive reasoning' (2005: 449), aesthetically, and to some degree narratively, CSI can be seen as echoing the generic worlds of action, fantasy and sci-fi cinema, rather than the gritty milieu of some of its TV crime drama predecessors. How does the programme tread this problematic, contradictory line; and what are the implications of its investment in the corpse as a conduit of truth?

Through textual analysis and discussion of other key cultural precedents to the show, this chapter examines how CSI treads a line between these apparently conflicting impulses. I explore how it balances a tension between spectacular, anti-realist excess on the one hand and (an apparent) investment in authenticity and forensic evidence on the other; evident, for example, in the role of Elizabeth Devine, a former LA County Sheriff's Department criminalist, employed as a writer and technical consultant on the programme (Lury 2005: 45). I want to contend that, ultimately, the representation of the corpse contributes to a conservative ideological impulse at work in the programme, which promotes a belief in an absolutist, definitive approach to 'solving' criminal behaviour. As commentators concerned about the repercussions of the 'CSI effect' have noted, the CSI franchise fosters 'the mistaken notion that criminal science is fast, infallible and always gets its man' (Willing 2004: 2); and this presumption has worrying implications for its promotion of a reactionary and punitive justice system.

CRIES AND WHISPERS: HOW TO 'TALK TO A DEAD BODY'

Pathologist Eugene A. Arnold has said of his profession that:

> The deceased, mute though they may be, have valuable things to tell us. The translator for these messages is the pathologist and the interpretation requires an attitude of objectivity, a systematic approach and the knowledge and experience to decipher the information presented (2004: 3–4).

This notion of the corpse as mute but 'speaking' witness, and pathologist/scientist as 'translator' or 'decipherer', is a position very much borne out by CSI. The body in CSI is made to 'speak' in a manner where the stories it tells and the clues it yields initiate a process of systematic rational enquiry. For example, when Sara Sidle is incensed by a wife batterer who is suspected of shooting his wife ('Sex, Lies and Larvae', 1:10), Grissom must both rein in her rage (and, it is implied, her highly personal empathy) and revisit and extend the forensic trail to ensure that any prosecution can be shown to be based entirely on evidence and not prejudice or 'instinct'. Sara's instinct is subsequently proven to be entirely correct, but the arrest is brought about, rightfully, through revisiting the victim's body; blue stains discovered around the gunshot wound to her head are traced back to the husband's ammo and thus prove his guilt. In contrast, perhaps, to Arnold's invoking of 'interpretation' above, the programme adheres to the myth of scientific certainty, deflecting attention away from a more complex or discursive engagement with crime. Indeed, in 'Cool Change' (1:2), Grissom perplexes a young detective guarding a scene-of-crime when he opts not to speak to the girlfriend of the victim, a man who has been found dead after falling from his suite at the top of their hotel. Instead, he invokes a 'conversation' with the dead man, and their exchange proceeds in the following way:

Grissom:	[Looking at the dead body] Right now I want to talk to him.
Detective:	How do you talk to a dead body?
Grissom:	I let him talk to me actually. In fact he just spoke. [Leans over the body and picks up the victim's shattered glasses] Didn't you hear him? He just told me that he didn't commit suicide.
Detective:	You lost me.
Grissom:	This guy fell to his death wearing prescription eyeglasses. Jumpers take their glasses off.[2]

The body continues to 'speak' to Grissom by offering up suspicious traces of black glass embedded in his arms (found to be defence wounds), as well as a distinct, diamond-shaped wound to his head which reveals he was dead before he fell. When the trail of evidence confirms the man's girlfriend killed him, Nick Stokes is disconcerted by her nonchalance and asks her, isn't she bothered that she took a man's life? Having proffered her wrists for handcuffs without resistance, she merely shrugs 'no' – thereby evading any discussion of motive, justice or remorse – is taken into custody and the case rendered 'closed'.

As such, CSI's use of the corpse contributes to the way the programme largely removes its murderous stories from their cultural contexts, placing an emphasis on merely resolving them through evidence – rather than seeking to understand them through more meditative explorations of motive, history and social environment, for example. The vicarious speed, drama and adrenalin offered up by the 'CSI-shot' facilitates a position of childlike wonder and excitement in regard to new technologies and the experience of high-cost, high-octane forensic television which, at one level, threatens to shatter the illusion of a realist world. Despite this, however, the representation of the body is ultimately co-opted into a largely ideologically conservative regime where, like criminality, the corpse can be read, classified and finally 'solved'.

'WE'RE GOING TO SEE THINGS NO-ONE HAS EVER SEEN BEFORE... NOT JUST SOMETHING UNDER A MICROSCOPE.'
Cora Petersen in *Fantastic Voyage* (Richard Fleischer, 1966)

The captivating power of the corpse and the autopsy scene are not in any sense 'new', of course, and *CSI* merely attenuates the history of western cultural fascination regarding the mysteries of dissection and the 'inner space' of the dead body. Most presciently, Jonathan Sawday has examined how the Renaissance, that period of European history celebrated more than any other for its revival of the arts, science and learning, was marked by a 'culture of dissection'. In his words, this was an age when 'a new image of the human interior, together with a new means of studying that interior, [left] its mark on all forms of cultural endeavour' (1995: viii). This culture of dissection existed across the social and educational spectrum but, to our contemporary minds at least, its most infamous manifestation arguably came in the form of public anatomy demonstrations. Famous physicians would command large fee-paying audiences made up of the learned and curious, who gathered in order to watch a human dissection take place. Sawday describes how, 'The Renaissance anatomical theatre combined elements from a number of different sources, drawing together various different kinds of public space in order to produce an event which was visually spectacular' (1995: 64). Architecturally, these theatres encompassed influences from 'the judicial court, the dramatic stage, and, most strikingly, the basilica-style church or temple' (ibid.); a description which particularly brings to mind the extravagant gothic-style *mise en scène* of *CSI: New York*'s initial autopsy space. More recently, we can see a revival of this kind of public display and the *performance* of the work of the autopsy in Gunther von Hagens' work. In the mid 1990s, von Hagens, a German anatomist who invented 'plastination' to conserve human body parts, developed the highly controversial 'Body Worlds' international touring exhibition, which consisted of dissected human cadavers arranged in various poses. In 2002 he courted controversy again for performing the first public autopsy to be shown on TV, broadcast on the UK's Channel 4. All of these ventures, like the Renaissance's public anatomies, tread an uncomfortable line between promoting themselves as educational ventures on the one hand and as theatrical displays on the other; and speak of our endless fascination with the interior of the human body, which the 'CSI-shot' similarly entertains.

Sawday also alludes briefly to another fascinating cultural precedent to *CSI*; fast-forwarding four hundred years, Richard Fleischer's sci-fi cinema classic *Fantastic Voyage* (1966) similarly contains striking parallels to *CSI*. At first glance, this text may perhaps seem a world removed from the grim criminal milieu of *CSI*. The film details the adventures of a team of medics and agents, miniaturised to microscopic size in order to be injected into the body of an Eastern bloc scientist who has information for the

US government. Following a botched assassination attempt by 'the other side' he is in a life-threatening coma; the team must travel through his arteries to treat the site of his brain injury from within his body in order to save him. Clearly, this is an utterly fanciful storyline, one played out amongst images of the bloodstream that transform it into a psychedelic mirage of luminescent bubbles. And yet *Fantastic Voyage* can be evoked here as a prescient and intriguing precedent to *CSI*, one to which the programme-makers themselves have acknowledged a debt (Lury 2005: 53). It too encapsulates a fascination with the authenticity of the 'inner space' of the body, clearly seeking to position itself as educational and grounded in 'real' science in one respect, while simultaneously relishing the unbridled spectacle of an imagined, physical world beyond the range of the human eye.

The film's investment in 'the real' is foregrounded from the opening credits, when a sombre inter-title appears declaring its truth claims: 'The makers of this film are indebted to the many doctors, technicians and research scientists, whose knowledge and insight helped guide this production', it announces. Throughout the film, its evident pleasure in the dramatic special effects[3] called on to envisage this 'inner space' is couched within discourses which simultaneously attempt to situate the film within a rather more erudite and philosophical context, as suggested by this opening inter-title. We can trace this same tension across the sixteenth-century public anatomy theatres evoked above, and Gunther von Hagens' work, right through to *CSI*; all share a sense that the text seeks to justify its morbid fascination through exploring it within an 'educational' framework. In *Fantastic Voyage* this discourse is particularly voiced through the character of Dr Duval (Arthur Kennedy) who, like Grissom, is constituted as a maverick figure from the labs acting as sage mentor to a young assistant, Cora (Raquel Welch). As in *CSI* (cf. Warrick's seemingly superfluous lengthy aside in the pilot episode clarifying what follicle 'pulp' is and how it proves that hair has been forcibly pulled out), *Fantastic Voyage* occasionally labours over its educational digressions. For example, when Grant (Stephen Boyd) comments that he thought blood 'was nothing but red', Dr Duval patiently explains for the benefit of the uninitiated character/viewer, just as Grissom and his team frequently do: 'Only to the naked eye. Those corpuscles carrying oxygen give the stream its colour. The rest of the plasma is very much like seawater. An ocean of life...'

Duval regularly shares, articulates and cues the audience's awe-struck response and sense of privileged access to the inner workings of the body.

Like the 'CSI-shot', then, the journey into and around the body in *Fantastic Voyage* leaves behind the more traditional, abstract medicalised view of it as 'just something under a microscope'. Rather, both texts promote themselves as moving beyond this dull and antiquated spectatorial position. Instead, through research which is presented by the film and programme-makers as properly grounded in authentic scientific progress and inquiry,[4] they each seek to create a unique and privileged vision of the workings of inner space; a vision which is enacted in such spectacular fashion that it can not but coexist in continual and uneasy tension with the texts' 'truth claims'.

Indeed, *Fantastic Voyage* proved subsequently to be the inspiration for *Innerspace* (1987), a comedy-sci-fi hybrid which recounts the adventures of Tuck Pendleton (Dennis Quaid) being miniaturised only to be mistakenly injected into hypochondriac Jack Putter (Martin Short). Both films represent the journey into the body and the quest to master miniaturisation as being a part of the American 'pioneer spirit', and *Innerspace* similarly contains moments of awe-struck wonder as the protagonists realise the enormous significance of what Pendleton is seeing. As Putter ponders at one point in the film, 'It's weird. You're seeing parts of my body that I will never get to see... faraway places with strange sounding names.' Here, just as in *CSI*, the inner space of the body in part represents still-uncharted territory to be conquered and made known by (US) science. In *Fantastic Voyage* and *Innerspace* this is arguably part of a cold-war/post-space race confirmation of US superiority. But in *CSI* it constitutes part of the programme's broader, conservative premise that science can furnish all the answers and evidence and can be harnessed by the CSIs to condemn the guilty. In the process, it eradicates acknowledgement of human fallibility in the application of science and the limitations of science itself.

ALL ABOARD 'A TURBULENT HIGH SPEED CHASE THROUGH THE HUMAN BODY'
(Wright Wiley 2006: 168)

But these pauses in the drama, where the characters of *Fantastic Voyage* and *Innerspace* stop to wonder at what they are seeing, are also part of the essential pleasure of the films, offering a reflective moment for the audience, via the on-screen protagonist, to enjoy the fantasy and spectacle of the films' premise and special effects. Such awe-struck moments among characters are said to have flourished in contemporary effects or blockbuster cinema in relation to the use of CGI, creating 'an increased self-awareness of the wonders of this new technology, which has increasingly been built into the texts themselves' (Abbott 2006: 93). While *CSI* may not include reaction shots to its 'CSI-shots', since these are especially privileged moments which only the audience, and not the characters, can see, these sequences nevertheless share this sense of wonder in the properties of technology. Time, which has often already been 'undone' in that the 'CSI-shot' is frequently utilised in flashbacks, seems suspended. There are echoes here of Tom Gunning's theory of the 'cinema of attractions' (1990), where early cinema audiences took pleasure in the display of the technology of the film apparatus itself. Similarly, there is an invitation in these moments to relinquish thoughts of logic or narrative and to give oneself up to the 'visual and aural rush' (Lury 2005: 53) proffered by the 'CSI-shot' and its deployment of CGI, to gaze on and be amazed by the image itself.

To reflect a little further on this notion of 'the rush' offered by these texts' journey into inner space, it is interesting to note that the basic premise at stake in both films has also seemingly inspired a theme-park ride; the Body Wars flight simulation 'thrill ride through the human body' (Sehlinger 2003: 515) at Epcot in Walt Disney World, Florida.

> The story is that you're a passenger in a miniature capsule
> injected into a human body to pick up a scientist who has
> been inspecting a splinter in the patient's finger. The scientist,
> however, is sucked into the circulatory system and you must
> rush throughout the body to rescue her (ibid.).

What is interesting here is how this physical, 'thrill ride' sensation of a journey through the body is borne out by the audience's experience, not merely of the more overtly preposterous and dramatic *Fantastic Voyage* and *Innerspace*, but by the 'CSI-shot'. As Sehlinger's guidebook description of Body Wars continues, 'The simulator creates a visually graphic experience as it seems to hurtle at fantastic speeds through human organs' (ibid.); an account which seems to entirely capture the way the CGI technology of the 'CSI-shot' is used to take the audience on a visceral 'trip' which moves at bullet speed through the body. Of course, the 'graphic' nature of the 'CSI-shot', accompanied by vivid sound effects, can sometimes make the viewer wince, and the shift between high-speed 'snap zoom' (Lury 2005: 45) and slo-mo photography in these sequences is comparable in some ways to the uneven movement of a flight simulator, producing a kinetic effect. Similarly, guidebooks warn against the capacity of Body Wars to make the participant ill, counselling, for example, that this 'intense' and 'turbulent' ride has 'queasy-making moments due to the subject matter as well as the eerie accuracy of the motion-simulation' (Wright Wiley 2006: 168).

The sensory nature of the 'CSI-shot', its frequently gruesome content, its discombobulating impact, also make it something akin to what Carol Clover (1987) and Linda Williams (1991) have described in the existence of 'body genres'. These are film genres marked by 'grossness', such as horror, porn and melodrama, which represent the 'excesses' of the body and which desire, in part, to produce a physical response in the viewer (fear, sexual arousal, tears – in these genres thus mirroring the on-screen action). CSI, too, has a similar fascination with exploring and exposing a 'gross' corporeality, revealing the liquids, the mucus, the organs that constitute our bodies. To paraphrase Wright Wiley (above), this is done with a kind of 'queasy-making', loving attention to detail which seems to similarly seek a physical response from the spectator. While the sexual connotations of the penetrative action of the 'CSI-shot' seem quite self-evident, it is interesting to note that Lury refers to the programme more broadly as 'stylistically pornographic'. Certainly, CSI's drive to show the unseeable, to render the interior visible, seems to mirror the revelatory drive and gaze of pornography. Lury suggests further that 'there would seem to be an obvious connection between the infamous "money shot" in pornographic film (the moment of ejaculation) with the "CSI-shot"' (Lury 2005: 56), an analogy also made by Gever (2005: 457). This parallel between CSI and sensational 'body genres' underlines again how the representation of the body in CSI does not call on it merely to speak as a witness and is not only bound up in the programme's truth claims and 'realism'. Rather, simultaneously, throughout its 'gross' display of the body's interior, the audience is invited to 'buckle up' and take a ride through the breathtaking spectacle of the body, its inner space, its visceral pleasures.

From the cadavers publicly displayed and dissected in the anatomy theatres of the Renaissance, then, to the theme-park rides of the new millennium, our cultural fascination with the corpse and the infinite intricacies of inner space show no sign of abating. On the contrary, they have gained a renewed visibility through the success of CSI. Sawday links this fascination to the impossibility of ever knowing our own inner space: '[It] is perhaps this very impossibility of gazing within our own bodies which makes the sight of other bodies so compelling. Denied the direct experience of ourselves, we can only explore others in the hope (or fear) that this other might also be us' (1995: 8). Like numerous other cultural forerunners, CSI explores this simultaneous hope/fear through simultaneously embracing both the 'realism' and the spectacle of the body. What is intriguing about CSI, however, is its concomitant implication that forensic science can produce unquestionable certainty, that this can be used to convict and condemn the guilty criminal without a shadow of a doubt and that this process can justifiably occur without more liberal reflection concerning context or motive. As such, for all his quirky habits and maverick ways, Grissom's science and the work of his acolytes amounts to a very narrow and conservative vision of how our world and its criminal underbelly can best be understood.

:7:

EVIDENCE OF THINGS UNSEEN

The Pornographic Aesthetic and the Search for Truth in *CSI*

ELKE WEISSMANN
AND KAREN BOYLE

In *Interpreting Television*, Karen Lury argues that the *CSI* franchise (hereafter referred to as *CSI*) is 'stylistically pornographic' (2005: 56). Like film horror (Clover 1992; Pinedo 1997), *CSI* has been defined in these terms largely because of its graphic depiction of the body and failure to respect its boundaries. The other parallel most commonly drawn between horror and pornography is, of course, the direct engagement with the body of the viewer through the elicitation of physical responses: fear, disgust, arousal (Dyer 1985). This argument sits less comfortably with *CSI* for, while the show's signature shots may indeed elicit a physical response, the embedding of these shots within the context of forensic-science drama seems to provide the viewer with an alibi: this is not gore for gore's sake, but gore that demonstrates and ultimately helps to bring narrative resolution.

The implications of equating (porno)graphic bodily intrusion with the search for 'truth' in *CSI*, a franchise centrally concerned with the role of science in the (re)solution of crime, are central to this chapter. We will focus, specifically, on what has become known as the 'CSI-shot': the sequence that apparently recreates, through the use of prosthetics, models and computer-generated images, the impact of criminal (and, less often, accidental) violence on the body of the victim. Although much of the existing writing on *CSI* has either presented the franchise as a unified whole or focused on the original series in isolation, the use of 'CSI-shots' varies considerably across the three series and these variations point to ideological differences in their conceptualisations of science and truth arising, in large part, from their differing gender dynamics. This chapter outlines these differences and begins to consider their implications but, firstly, considers what the franchise's distinctive visual style owes to pornography.

PORNOGRAPHY AND TRUTH

At the centre of much of the contemporary academic debate about pornography is the question of pornography's relationship to the 'real'. Hardcore pornography's distinguishing feature, at least in its audio-visual forms, is 'real' sex. While contemporary mainstream and soft-core sex scenes rely on the suggestion of intercourse and climax, hardcore shows. What, and how, hardcore shows has varied over time, but in the contemporary context the signatures of hardcore would include close-ups of aroused genitals and other body parts, penetration shots and the so-called 'money shot' of male ejaculation. There is no optical point-of-view structure in these shots: we see what the bodies *do*, not what the performers *see*, the bodies posed according to the principle of maximum visibility (Williams 1990: 48). Achieving this visibility requires artifice – the selection of sexual positions that show the most of bodies and organs; the over-lighting of easily obscured genitals; the emphasis on external ejaculation (ibid.: 49) – but the visible is offered as a guarantee of authenticity: this is what real people having real sex look like (and, not unrelatedly, what they *sound* like).

Of course, it is never that simple.

Pornography is also representation. For Linda Williams, hardcore's 'frenzy of the visible' has a pre-history dating back to Eadweard Muybridge's photographic studies of motion which recorded the mechanics of the body, its movement and functions (1990: 38-9). Yet, whilst Muybridge's early human studies had the status of scientific, objective evidence, the socio-cultural context of their production is clearly detectable in the differences between the photographs of men and women, differences which point to the greater sexuality already culturally encoded in the woman's body. The photographic studies, in turn, establish conventions for the cinematic representation of the gendered body which their status as 'science' naturalises. The invention of (cinematic) photography is, therefore, more than simply a technology for recording: it *produces* certain kinds of knowledge about the body and naturalises the hierarchical relationships of power between different bodies.

Similarly, Williams argues, 'although the cinematic hard core will present itself as the unfaked, unstaged mechanics of sexual action, the representation of this movement is shaped... by techniques of confession that are applied first and foremost to female bodies' (1990: 48). However, the female body poses a problem for pornography because the *visual* proof of female sexual arousal and climax remains elusive. She continues:

> Hard core desires assurance that it is witnessing not the voluntary performance of feminine pleasure, but its involuntary confession. The woman's ability to fake the orgasm that the man can never fake (at least according to certain standards of evidence) seems to be at the root of all the genre's attempts to solicit what it can never be sure of: the out-of-control confession of pleasure, a hard-core 'frenzy of the visible' (1990: 50).

There are three points we want to emphasise here. Firstly, note that the pornographic body is a body of evidence (of arousal and pleasure) and that, despite the inherent difficulties, there is an attempt to render that evidence visible. Secondly, our language here is deliberately objectifying, as the pornographic body is, curiously, *disembodied*, by which we mean that it is disconnected from the affective experience of the performers and their characters. This is implicit in the statement that hardcore desires assurance of the *involuntary* or *out-of-control* confession of pleasure, a confession that may – as Williams goes on to note – be most effective when elicited in situations of force (rape). In other words, the (apparent) responses of the body are deemed more authentic than the affective or intellectual responses of the subject. Thirdly, pornography, in soliciting or, more accurately, constructing that 'confession', provides the (implicitly male) viewer with pleasure and the reassurance of mastery. That pleasure is registered physically on the body and that physical response in turn authenticates the 'eroticism' of the involuntary confession of the female body for the male spectator.

SCIENCE, TRUTH AND THE PORNOGRAPHIC AESTHETIC

Like pornography, *CSI* is obsessed with making the evidence of the body visible, only here the context is the investigation of crime rather than pleasure. As its title indicates, the *CSI* franchise is concerned with the *scene* of crime; a scene that is, almost without exception, ultimately narrowed to the body of the victim. Of course, that body is usually discovered in the opening scenes of the programme in a specific location, a location then designated as a 'crime scene' by the distinctive yellow and black tape. Nevertheless, whilst the scene yields important evidence that can be photographed and analysed in the lab, it is the body, removed to the clinical space of the autopsy suite, that is *CSI*'s primary scene. The implications of using the body *of the victim* to 'confess' the truth of the crime will be returned to later. For now we want to point to the contradictory aspects of these bodily confessions that bring us ever closer to and, indeed, within the body of the victim without ever adding to our knowledge either of the body (as a person) or of the crime.

Like pornography's signature shots, these sequences are divorced from the fictional narrative, set apart as offering a unique and privileged access to the 'truth' of the crime. The viewer of *CSI* does not, of course, mistake the bullets and blood of the 'CSI-shot' for real bullets or blood. However, these shots, which Martha Gever (2005: 457) refers to as the 'money shots' of the programme, arguably rely, like their pornographic namesakes, on our belief (that they present a general scientific truth) rather than on the suspension of disbelief demanded by the fictional text. This is achieved through two main formal devices. First, the sequence is generally narrated by the scientist (medical examiner or criminalist) in the guise of an explanation to a colleague that has much in common with a scientific lecture. The discussion of evidence over and through the body of the victim provides the alibi for the viewer's voyeurism. That is, the scientists explain, in the language of their profession, the specific effects and impacts of an act of traumatic violence on the body. Crime is, therefore, read as a series of symptoms and the 'CSI-shot' is presented as scientific fact divorced from the specifics of the fictional narrative. Even if the investigators do not identify a suspect (an admittedly rare occurrence in *CSI*), the 'CSI-shot' stands as an authentic recreation and display of a specific bodily injury or internal bodily feature.

Second, the sequence, like the longer reconstruction of the crime in which it is sometimes embedded (especially in *Miami*), is visually set apart. The sequence is usually preceded by a quick dissolve into white which gives the impression of a camera flash, separating the diegetic world from the movement into and through the victimised body. The apparent penetration of the body is actually achieved by use of precise continuity cuts and dissolves, from the body of an actor into CGI and plastic models, which are rendered invisible due to the speed of the sequence and the movement of the camera. The 'CSI-shot' breaches the fictional mode of the text by presenting something that *cannot* be seen, that is not (and could not be) anchored to any character's optical point of view and that is temporally removed from the narrative. The most explicit examples of this are sequences that, although apparently taking us *into* the body, present not the messy interior but an isolated organ or bone against a black background. Therefore, although the 'CSI-shots' are quite obviously 'fake', they are granted a demonstrative power within the text providing a visual model of the scientist's spoken explanation. Their scientific 'authenticity' is underlined both in the extra-textual claims repeatedly made about their credibility by those involved with the programme and, as Lury (2005: 48) notes, by the increasing use of similarly animated visual sequences in public science displays and scientific documentaries.

There is an implicit assumption, then, that by seeing more, by going deeper and closer, the viewer of *CSI* is placed in a position of greater knowledge: a 'reality effect' that Joe Black (2002) also observes in film culture. In *CSI*, the very excessiveness that maximum visibility provides could be argued to be destabilising. The body is shown to be disgusting, abject, beyond the control of the viewer though, of course, not beyond the control of the scientist who dissects, cleans, weighs, measures and tests the body in its constituent parts with a wide array of increasingly spectacular technology. For the viewer, though, this is a body without boundaries. It is a body that leaks, erupts, dissolves, rots, stinks. It is a dead body that is reanimated by the camera's movement or by the blood and pus that rushes towards the camera lens, catching us off guard. It is a dead body that is made to 'speak' by the investigators, both thematically, as the scientists use the body to tell the story of the crime, and aurally in the squelching, slurping, gushing sounds made when it is opened, penetrated, dissected. As Lury also suggests, one effect of the excessiveness of *CSI*'s signature shots is to make this a kinetic experience. In other words, like pornography, these sequences arguably move the body of the spectator whilst, as we will go on to show, adding little to our intellectual understanding of the crime.

If orgasm authenticates the 'eroticism' of the involuntary confession of the female body for the male spectator in pornography, is it too far of a stretch to argue that the physical response that *CSI* elicits authenticates the confessions of the victim's body, confessions that are only accessible through, and meaningful within, a scientific discourse? In other words, our very tendency to look away, or to see only gore, reaffirms the power of the scientist who looks and who sees and understands evidence. Perhaps this is the 'CSI effect' that commentators in the US have claimed has led jurors in real criminal trials to place undue faith in scientific evidence, a phenomenon that franchise creator Anthony E. Zuiker has reportedly welcomed as evidence of viewers' increasing knowledge-base: 'People know science now. They watch CSI' (Gonzales 2005).

The ideological implications of this are not, however, limited to the faith placed in science. It will be noted, for example, that we have not once referred to the perpetrator of crime in our discussion of CSI thus far. This is not accidental, and in the discussion that follows we will investigate to what extent the emphasis on the body of the victim de-emphasises the perpetrator's violent agency. Certainly, this would be nothing new: feminist critics have long critiqued media representations of male violence for failing to hold men accountable for their conscious and purposeful actions (Boyle 2005). Whilst the proportion of female perpetrators in CSI remains disproportionate to criminal statistics, the majority of perpetrators of violence in the franchise are still male (Weissmann 2006).

However, it is important to note one significant way in which CSI differs from both pornography's and horror's fascination with the *female* body: in CSI the victims are predominately male, a fact that many critiques of the show have conveniently ignored (e.g. Tait 2006). A quantitative analysis by Elke Weissmann (2006) finds that across the first four seasons of CSI: *Crime Scene Investigation*, the first two seasons of CSI: *Miami* and the first season of CSI: *NY*, 57.5 per cent of all victims are male. Moreover, again unlike in horror, it is *not* the case that that female body is necessarily the object of more lingering and graphic investigation and bodily intrusion: 60 per cent of the 'CSI-shots' focus on the male body.

Clearly, then, the pornographic aesthetic in CSI does not demand a female corpse. However, gendered structures of looking are arguably retained to a certain extent, at least in the original series. In *Crime Scene Investigation*, both of the regular medical examiners are male and, despite the fact that two of the central characters in the CSI team are female, 57.6 per cent of the bodies investigated in the show's first four seasons were examined by all-male teams. This picture is, however, rather different in *Miami* where the central medical examiner is female. In order to begin to examine the implications of these differences we will now explore each of the series in turn.

CRIME SCENE INVESTIGATION

Crime Scene Investigation, the original series, centres on the celebration of science as an investigative tool. Science is here displayed as the only means to objectively find out what really happened and to establish guilt.

Within this context, the victim's body is part of the evidence and the victim is rarely established as a human being in their own right. This is stressed again and again: in 'Gentle, Gentle' (1:19), for example, Gil Grissom points out to the parents of a baby victim that 'as difficult as this sounds, Zackary [the baby] is evidence'.

This emphasis on the body as evidence is visually highlighted by a distancing of the camera from aspects of the body, such as the face, that mark its individuality. Rather, the body appears only 'as a collection of injuries and evidence' (Jermyn 2003: 56) to be read by the investigators. When we are shown the victim's face it is often in a mediated form: on a television screen in the autopsy suite or in a reconstruction scene narrated by the investigators. Further, when victim and investigator appear in the same frame it is usually in medium- or long-shot, with the investigator looking down on the prone body. In other words, *Crime Scene Investigation* visually underlines the scientists' objective distance and the victim's object-status.

The 'CSI-shot' – which is visually spectacular and usually divorced from any clear ocular point-of-view structure – also contributes to the objectification of the victim in the name of science. This is established with the very first use of the 'CSI-shot' in 'Pilot' (1:1). The sequence begins with a close-up of Gil's hands placed over those of a female investigator as he imitates the shooting of the body currently on the slab. There is then a cut to a medium shot of the clean, unwounded chest of the victim. The camera rapidly moves towards and then, by inserting a few frames of black, into the chest where it hits an undistinguishable organ and briefly comes to rest. It then rapidly zooms back out of the body to a medium shot of the chest (which now shows a bullet wound) before cutting to a close-up of the female investigator looking at the wound. Thus, the victimised body comes into view as an itemised wound, a wound constructed as evidence and rendered meaningful only by Grissom's commentary and re-enactment. Indeed, the body itself looks 'fake,' according to the female investigator, and the face remains at the margins of the frame.

In this first use of the 'CSI-shot' there is simply a cut from the fiction of the text to the scientific display of the 'CSI-shot'. However, from 'Anonymous' (1:8) onwards, it is a quick dissolve to white that marks the beginning and end of the 'CSI-shot' and separates it out from the fiction of the investigation. This clearly resembles the flash of a camera, an apparatus often used to assist the investigation in CSI and which is given an unproblematic status within the franchise as an objective recorder of evidence. This is consistent with the franchise's investment in technology and the visual more generally. It is notable, for example, that even sound evidence is generally translated, via technology, into a series of increasingly spectacular images (as, indeed, in 'Anonymous'). Evidence, then, is that which can be rendered visible, apparently for the purposes of scientific analysis.

However, CSI's investment in the visual as evidence is contradictory and nowhere is this more apparent than in the 'CSI-shot' itself, where the visual information is typically excessive, adding little to our knowledge or intellectual understanding of the crime. In the sequence from 'Pilot', for example, it is only the shape of the wound that is important to the resolution of the crime. The move into and through the body may be narratively superfluous but it allows for a kinetic engagement on the part of the viewer as we are taken on a virtual roller-coaster ride, enhanced by sound effects that amplify the gruesome messiness of the wounded body (Lury 2005: 32). As a consequence, the body does not only appear as the object of the medical gaze; it is also invested with the iconography and, more importantly, the acoustics of the slasher film. This shares with pornography an emphasis on carnality, as Isabel Christina Pinedo points out:

> It is this very carnality that relegates hard core and gore to the status of disreputable genres. As Richard Dyer points out about porn…, both are disreputable genres because they engage the viewer's body, elicit physical responses such as fear and disgust, and arousal in indeterminate combinations, and thereby privilege the degraded half of the mind-body split (1997: 61).

Similarly, the 'CSI-shot', because of its speed and its emphasis on gore, is able to engage the viewer's body. However, while porn and the slasher film privilege the bodily reaction, *Crime Scene Investigation*, with its medical discourse, also engages the mind, creating a complex series of effects where our cerebral knowledge about the body is complemented by our bodily experience of this knowledge. In effect, this enhances the 'CSI-shot''s ability to present the real, as it suggests that the spectator can feel it and, in a positivist world, it is exactly this ability that makes the experience real.

It is important to note that it is the body of the *victim* that is made to confess the truth, a twist on conventional crime drama which typically relies on the perpetrator's confession. This truth is foremost a physical truth given up involuntarily by the dead body brought back to life by the animation of photography. In this way, the truth of the 'CSI-shot' in *Crime Scene Investigation* is most closely related to the truth that hardcore attempts to elicit from the female body. But the bodies in *CSI* are predominantly those of men and it is male bodies who are most often bored into by the camera in the ways described above, suggesting that it is actually the male corpse that is *Crime Scene Investigation's* primary fascination (Weissmann 2006). However, this fascination pushes against the conventions of the medical gaze which, as Mary Jacobus et al. (1990: 6) point out, has traditionally gendered its object feminine while the subject of the gaze has been constructed as masculine. This creates a distinct tension that *Crime Scene Investigation* negotiates through different means.

A juxtaposition of shots in the autopsy scene in '$35K O.B.O.' (1:18) provides a good example which illustrates both the problematic fascination with the male body and the means to negotiate this problem. Here, two victims, husband and wife, are examined. The visual examination of the wife begins with a close-up of her face, before panning down to the fatal wound on her neck. In contrast, the first shot of the husband is a close-up of defensive wounds on his *hand*: that is, we focus on the wound and not on the face of the victim. This separation of wounded body and face appears as something that is specific to the representation of male bodies. Whilst wound (death) and face (subjectivity, life) cannot be reconciled in representing the male body, the female body poses no such problem: conventionally beautiful apart from the fatal wound, the female victim is placed within a long tradition where a woman's death is, as Elisabeth Bronfen highlights, 'the most poetical topic' (1992: 62).

The female body in '$35K O.B.O.' remains *intact*: the pan down onto the neck wound is the only image of the female body in this scene. In contrast, the male body is investigated in detail: there are several close-ups of the multiple stab wounds on this body and two 'CSI-shots' 'penetrate' the orifices of the wound tracks. That the abject, wounded body – ruptured, leaking, boundary-less – has traditionally been gendered feminine (Kristeva 1982: 71) perhaps offers a further clue as to why this body is *only* a body, a collection of wounds divorced from any markers of (masculine) individuality. Male subjectivity is, however, retained within *Crime Scene Investigation* by the privileging of the male criminalists and their rational, scientific knowledge within the autopsy suite (Weissmann 2006).

The fascination with the body as evidence results in a significant shift away from the perpetrator who is at the centre of the investigation in conventional crime drama. Conventional crime drama relies primarily on talk to establish what happened (Todorov 1977; Walton and Jones

1999). The investigators interview first family and friends of the victims to find out who the latter were last with; i.e. who had the opportunity to kill them. Opportunity alone, however, is not enough to establish guilt which, as John Sumser points out (1996: 82), must be complemented with capability and motive (who would be capable of, and had motive for, killing the victim). Indeed, motive is often one of the first aspects that the investigators chase in conventional crime drama in order to line up their suspects. Moreover, conventional crime drama relies on a confession of the perpetrator to gain (re)solution, implying that the perpetrator has the power to speak about the crime and, therefore, also the victim. In other words, the perpetrators' agency continues into the confession.

In *CSI*, however, guilt is established by analysing the evidence, finding out what happened to the victim and understanding trace evidence (*CSI*'s whole philosophy is based on Locard's Theory: every contact between two people leaves trace evidence on both). Motive, therefore, is not necessary to identify the perpetrators or to establish guilt. If a motive is established, it is typically a coda to the investigation, positioned *after* the crime has been solved as an affirmation of the accuracy of the criminalists' investigation rather than as a resolution in itself. The relative unimportance of these scenes is underlined by the lack of suspense (after all, we are regularly reminded by the criminalists that the evidence never lies), combined with the lack of visual interest (the elaborate camera movement, gadgetry and visual effects that otherwise dominate the show are typically absent). In *Crime Scene Investigation*, then, power and agency lies with the investigators. Whilst the investigators repeatedly claim to give 'voice' to the victim, this extends only as far as the evidence allows: that is, we are given very little additional information to humanise the victim and give them an existence beyond the 'confessions' of their body at the crime scene and in the autopsy suite.

CSI: MIAMI AND *CSI: NY*

Although there has been a tendency in critical writing to treat the three series within the franchise as essentially similar, *Miami* and *NY* differ from the model set up in the previous section in significant respects.

Miami directs all its empathy and care to the victims of crime. This is partially facilitated by the casting of a black woman as its medical examiner. Indeed, Dr. Alexx Woods is shown to have a very empathetic approach to pathology. Where the medical examiners – and, with them, the investigators – in *Crime Scene Investigation* look at the body and its symptoms as evidence, Alexx sees the human being first. She usually begins her examinations by addressing the victims with pet names, stroking their hair and looking at their faces. Furthermore, Alexx often crouches over the victims and the composition of the shot emphasises her physical proximity. For example, in marked contrast to *Crime Scene Investigation*, a close-up shot of Alexx's face at a crime scene or in an autopsy sequence will frequently position the wounded body within the same frame. Alexx, therefore, does what Sue Thornham (2003: 79) suggests female investigators have to do, namely, she interrupts and speaks through her own body and its proximity to the victims.

This closeness to the victim, however, constitutes a problem for the 'CSI-shot' which, in order to speak the truth of the body, relies on the medical distance from the actual body of the fiction. Unsurprisingly then, *Miami* presents a 'CSI-shot' which is fundamentally different from *Crime Scene Investigation*'s. *Miami* uses the 'CSI-shot' far less regularly in relation to bodies but instead provides similar sequences in relation to technology, particularly computers and guns. Indeed, in *Miami*, these technological variations on the 'CSI-shot' are more frequent than body-shots (Weissmann 2006). In 'Big Brother' (2:8), this sequence begins with a close-up of Calleigh Duquesne as she looks out from the scene of the crime into an adjacent building. The camera then follows her look, flies towards and into the other building to a wireless internet dish which it examines for a moment from the outside. It then cuts inside and speeds along the cables into a computer to a close-up of a chip where it again comes to rest before panning to the side to reveal Tim Speedle in a medium shot, working on the computer. The sequence is accompanied by several rush and beep sounds, emphasising the technological environment. In its effects, this 'technology CSI-shot' is not unlike its counterpart showing the penetrating of a body: the viewer is again taken on a roller-coaster ride. However, it does not include the more sinister aspects of rupturing the boundaries of a mutilated body, allowing this sequence to function as a spectacular but ultimately safe ride through a cold, inanimate thing.

There is also a general emphasis on the face of the victim. Where *Crime Scene Investigation* divorces the images of the mutilated body from markers of male identity, *Miami* highlights these markers. Often, the autopsy theatre is filled with screens which show the victim's face and disrupt the unhindered look at the mechanics of the investigation. In 'Complications' (2:11), for example, the scene begins with a low-angle long shot of the autopsy theatre, showing the observation room in the background. The slab is at the centre of the frame, horizontally cutting it into halves. The top half of the frame is dominated by three screens – one large and two smaller – showing the male victim's face in close-up. The victim's face itself is clearly visible in profile on the slab, behind which Alexx and Horatio Caine stand. The screens here do not present the individual only as representation; rather, they contribute to the *disruption* of the medical gaze, refocusing the attention onto the individual victim. Moreover, as the scene progresses, the camera returns to close-ups and extreme close-ups of the victim's actual face.

Miami tends to present the 'CSI-shot' as part of a reconstruction. In 'Entrance Wound' (1:12), for example, the close-up of a male victim on Alexx's slab dissolves into white and into a close-up of the perpetrator (at this point, simply represented as an unidentified hand) holding a gun which is shot in slow-motion. The camera follows the path of a bullet as it flies towards the man, who opens his mouth in a scream, making way for the camera to follow the bullet into his mouth where it hits the tongue. A dissolve into white, and into an extreme close-up of the man's mouth as Alexx extracts the bullet, follows. The sequence, therefore, does not present the victim as inanimate and already dead but as a living being reacting to his environment.

Notably, the 'CSI-shot' in *Miami* is most often connected to the *living* body and its story. Whilst the 'CSI-shot' is still marked as a moment of truth in the ways already described, it is placed at one remove from the (female) scientist, whose concern is thus established as telling individual stories in which her science plays a central part, rather than establishing a general, scientific principle. *Miami*, therefore, presents a subjective and narrativised truth in which the individual victim is at the centre, thus submitting science to the narrative of an individual's life. This, we want to argue, is facilitated (if not necessitated) by the feminising of the scientific gaze. Alexx's power is, in some ways, less scientifically authoritative than her colleagues in *Crime Scene Investigation*: it is not simply that she 'gives voice' to the victim, but rather that she enables him to speak 'for himself'.

NY differs from both other series in its reluctance to actually include 'CSI-shots' that suggest the camera penetrates the body. In 'Outside Man' (1:6), for example, the whole sequence is reduced to one shot: the extreme close-up of the tip of a drill drilling into the leg, shot from the inside. The gore is still there but the *movement* in and through the body that characterises *Crime Scene Investigation* and *Miami* is missing. As a consequence, the 'CSI-shots' lose their affectiveness that is central to their ability to move the viewer's body, leading to a less kinetic investment in the science. Science is here presented as something that adds truth to the narrative but not as something that we ourselves need to understand with our minds and bodies. This suggests that NY moves back to a primarily cerebral engagement with crime which aligns it with more conventional crime drama. Indeed, of the three series, NY, especially in its first season, clearly has most in common with the conventions and iconography of a more realist tradition of American crime drama such as *Hill Street Blues*, *Homicide: Life on the Street* and the *Law & Order* franchise. As one of us argues more extensively elsewhere (Weissmann 2006), this imbues NY with a tone of nostalgia and mourning that cannot be divorced from its setting in post-9/11 New York: a context that the show explicitly acknowledges in Mac Taylor's own backstory. By showing less of the bloody messiness of crime, NY is able to assign guilt in a more moralistic and less objectively scientific way. The victims are even more sketchily drawn than in *Crime Scene Investigation* – significantly, survivors and witnesses play a far more central role (Weissmann 2006) – and the shift away from bodily interiors means that there is less tension in the relationship (thematic and visual) of the investigator to the corpse. Indeed, it is the investigator, and his ability to interact with living others, that is the narrative focus.

CONCLUSION

The 'pornographic' qualities that have been widely attributed to *CSI* in academic and popular responses relate not only to the penetrating camera and its graphic exposure of bodily injury and decay, but also, as we have argued in this essay, to the equation of maximum visibility with 'truth'. This poses problems for the franchise which, unlike most television crime narratives, deals primarily with male victims of violence rather than the usually assumed female ones. In *Crime Scene Investigation*, the tension between bodily intrusion and male subjectivity is resolved by the negation of the subjectivity of the victim and the emphasis on science and on male scientists in particular. Whilst both *Miami* and NY continue to place their faith in science – and retain the distinctive 'CSI-shot' which is by now the franchise's defining characteristic – this is tempered by the feminising of science and the focus on the victim's life in *Miami* and by NY's reestablishing of the investigator as the narrative focus. In both cases, science, despite its spectacular representation, serves, rather than provides, the narrative as in *Crime Scene Investigation*. Whilst the implications of these differences cannot be fully teased out in a chapter of this length, investigating *CSI* through the lens provided by pornography brings the show's complex and contradictory gender dynamics, and its fascination with the graphic as the guarantor of truth, more clearly into focus.

:8:

WHO ARE THEY?

Style codes
of the *CSI* investigators
ANNA KÖNIG

It's a cold light that shines in Nevada and, in the early days, the Las Vegas CSI forensic team reflected the harshness of their city: their faces were drained of colour. In stark contrast to the eyeball-popping hyper-real brightness of Vegas, the investigators were initially as grey and anonymous as the bodies they swabbed and probed. There was nothing overtly glamorous about them. Indeed, from the outset, their lack of cool was presented as a scientific thesis just asking to be challenged. The scriptwriters left nothing to chance: in the very first episode the team was introduced with a schoolyard put-down of 'here comes the nerd squad'. Yet, like the corpses they deal with, clues to the identities of these hard-boiled professionals can be found in their clothes, their hair, even the lines on their faces. Science will not tolerate generalisations, though: cold, hard evidence is required. So what can be learnt from the appearance of these professionals for whom objectivity is a way of life?

In many respects, Gil Grissom is an unlikely leading man. Certainly, in the early days of *CSI*, the oddball elements of his persona hinted of eccentricity and a life spent outside the loop of convention. Clean-shaven and sporting the denim shirts and practical outdoor jackets of an all-American everyman, the complexity of Grissom was revealed only in terse words. Oblique references to poetry, philosophy and the minutiae of eclectic miscellany said much more about him than his workaday appearance. When asked what sort of college student he was, Grissom replies, 'I was a ghost.' Outward appearances seem to be of limited interest or value to Gil Grissom.

Similarly endowed with alliteration, Sara Sidle's name alludes to vulnerability, or perhaps even self-destruction. Aside from her name, Sidle seems to harbour other secrets, for her path and Grissom's, we are told, have crossed previously. At the start of the series, her look is that of a pretty tomboy as she is tall, almost gangly, and wears clothes that play down rather than emphasise her femininity. In the early episodes, her lack of make-up contributes to an image of a precocious teenager. Unlike the composed mask of her older and seemingly more experienced colleague, Catherine Willows, Sidle's face wears an almost permanent frown of intense concentration. Unusually, for an American actor, she has a gap between her front teeth that has not been visited by orthodontic work. This small gap in its own small way helps define her as an individual, an unconventional beauty.

Undoubtedly the hippest of the Las Vegas investigators, Warrick Brown exudes a laid-back style that his colleagues can only hope to aspire to. Early on, his relative youth is exemplified by his casual dress – combat trousers, fitted T-shirts, denim jackets – which contrasts edgily with Nick Stokes' more traditional, preppy style of dress. A glimpse of a tattoo is another nod to his youth, some of which, we are told, was spent gambling and generally getting into minor-league trouble – fairly standard fare for African-American television characters. In a later episode, however, Brown talks the aspiring investigator, Greg Sanders, through the rituals of dressing for work. Preparedness, it seems, is the key, so any impression of casualness is merely an illusion. This is a man with self-awareness – he knows who he is and he shows it through his appearance.

In Miami, meanwhile, crime smoulders under a very different light. Bright southern sunshine saturates each frame, refracting colours that are reminiscent of a Mario Testino photo shoot. Against a backdrop of turquoise swimming pools and pink art deco buildings, dirty crimes are committed, discovered and solved. Yet the Miami investigation team generally leaves the hot, bright outfits to the models, drug dealers and miscellaneous party people that cross their path as victims, perpetrators and innocent bystanders. Against a backdrop of kaleidoscopic visual intensity, the investigators are relatively subdued.

In such a landscape, where brilliant sunlight sparkles off the ocean, sunglasses become obligatory. Indeed, for Horatio Caine they are the fulcrum around which his personality pivots. A man of few words, he makes his Las Vegas counterpart, Grissom, appear positively garrulous. As he is typically found wearing rather anonymous suits, the lines on his face and his shades are the only visual clues to his identity. And this is a face that appears to have been out in the Miami sun for an eternity, so etched are the lines; and lines on the face always speak of wisdom and experience. This late in the day, sunglasses will do little to prevent further wear on the delicate skin around the eyes. Instead, they are used as a prop, which he puts on or removes for effect or emphasis.

His colleague Calleigh Duquesne is a different creature altogether, though. She has the pale skin and golden hair of a classic southern belle: her ancestry is also evidenced in a slight drawl. This is not someone who has bought into the fake-tan glam of Miami. As a rule, her hair sits perfectly around her shoulders, curiously, never getting in the way of print-taking or close examinations of forensic material. Underneath severe black suits she wears tight vests or halter-neck tops, occasionally revealed when the Florida heat gets too much. Her role as a ballistics expert means that she is frequently found testing weapons, leading to scenes that are vaguely reminiscent of that niche form of soft porn that features 'girls with guns': the camera lingers as she steadies herself, takes aim and fires. This is a body that becomes progressively more toned with the passing of every episode, every season.

Like their Las Vegas counterparts, the backroom boys and science nerds in Miami are pointedly deficient in fashion savvy. With each new season, the investigators hone their personal style, albeit in imperceptible increments, yet the geeks are trapped in a purgatory of badly styled hair, unfashionable glasses and disproportionately flamboyant shirts that serve only to highlight their lowly status in the investigation food chain.

Latecomers to the *CSI* franchise, the New York team face the challenge of representing a city that has an almost mythical status within film and television. Yet the New York portrayed in *CSI: NY* is no friendly, smiling Big Apple – it is a dark, hostile, post-9/11 place that relentlessly denies the viewer the comforts of cheery familiarity. And, accordingly, this air of gravitas is reflected in the team and their dark-hued, hard-edged clothes.

The perpetually clenched jaw of Detective Mac Taylor tells a story in itself. It is an expression that speaks of unimaginable loss – his wife died in the attacks on the Twin Towers – and although the rest of the team have their share of hard-luck stories, undoubtedly it is Taylor's that resonates most powerfully, binding him inextricably to his city. As with his counterparts Grissom and Caine, it is his face rather than his clothing that holds the key to his identity.

His colleague Stella Bonasera, meanwhile, represents a New York that has a powerful historical screen presence – the immigrant's city. Half-Greek, half-Italian, her personal history mirrors that of the city itself and her European origins are not only evident, but take centre stage. While her Las Vegas colleagues sport the looks, and indeed the locks, of smooth Waspy restraint, Bonasera wears an abundance of luxuriant curls like a mantle of ethnic difference. She may be an orphan, but the city is her mother and father.

But if we return to the original crime scene we see that things have changed over time. Perhaps in response to stakes raised by the Miami team, and in their own, rather more gritty way, the New York team, the Las Vegas investigators have, collectively, sharpened their image. Grissom still cuts a rather lumpen, slope-shouldered figure in his thigh-length workman's jackets, and yet even he has evolved. Gone are the black-rimmed glasses, and facial hair has appeared (as everyone knows, a beard can hide a multitude of chins). Sidle, meanwhile, is looking rather more grown-up and groomed than the eager ingénue who appeared at the start of the series, perhaps in preparation for the developing relationship with Grissom which, famously, marked the end of Season Six.

Yet the ultimate glamour is always reserved for the corpses: the big-time casino winner whose luck turned; the party girl whose fun was cut short; the promising college student who got caught up in something bad. Whether in Las Vegas, Miami or New York, it is always the victims whose bodies and clothing tell the most detailed stories. The investigators remain, by comparison, sartorially objective.

:9:
CSI
AND SOUND

KAREN LURY

In much of the academic writing on *CSI* there has been a great deal of interest in the visual aspects of the programme. The series' sensational use of colour, the integration of CGI and other special effects, as well as the development of signature framings – such as the so-called '*CSI*-shot' – have understandably been the focus of much critical attention (Lury 2005, Gever 2005, Tait 2006; Weissmann and Boyle in this volume). As a complement to this work, in this chapter I want to look away from the qualities of the image in *CSI* and focus instead on sound. What follows is an introductory but relatively wide-ranging description of the soundscape of *CSI: Las Vegas* and a more focused investigation into the narrative thread of Grissom's 'deafness' (which served as a recurring backstory for the character in Seasons Two and Three). By doing so, I hope to reveal the relationship between the overt scientific, mechanical and technological aspects of *CSI: Las Vegas* and a more covert fascination with the erotic and 'otherworldly' aspects such as spiritualism and religion.

Finally, I will argue that the meaning of 'deafness' for Grissom can be linked to the programme's obsession to promote (its particular practice of) science *as* religion. The science practised in the programme is, I would suggest, post-Enlightenment but pre-modern, in that it is a supremely rational discourse that is presented without the doubts and confusions opened up by twentieth-century scientific discoveries such as the theories of relativity and chaos. These are theories which insist that the process of interpretation and the position of the scientific observer must and do have an impact on their findings. This is in contrast to *CSI* where the investigators' role as scientists, and the way in which they interpret or process their evidence, is rarely questioned (even if their personal lives prove problematic). Ultimately, however, there are certain points at which the characters are forced to confront the limitations of their particular practice of science and, clearly, Grissom's deafness is one example of this. In this chapter my particular concern is to demonstrate that whilst his deafness is a mechanical problem for Grissom as a 'scientific observer', it is also (covertly) presented as a spiritual or *religious* crisis.

SOUNDS IN *CSI*

I will begin with a brief description of the key aspects of the series' 'soundscape', focusing on specifically:

1. 'Musical sounds': the composed score by John M. Keane and other musical sounds such as the 'sound wipes' at the conclusion of key scenes and, briefly, the 'source' music or non-diegetic popular music frequently played over montage sequences in the programme.
2. 'Sound effects': concrete sounds which give volume, depth and material substance to the objects and bodies we see on screen, and the 'ambient' sounds which tend not to have a visible location on screen but which aurally 'thicken' our perception of the environment.
3. 'Vocal sounds': the qualities and reproduction of the different voices in the programme concentrating primarily on the speech of the characters.

SCORE

Firstly, I want to draw attention to the score written by John M. Keane. Keane composes about 25–30 minutes of score for each programme and his 'brief' is to both create atmosphere and provide aural 'cues' for the audience. It is clear that the score for *CSI: Las Vegas* is heavily indebted to the work of the composer Howard Shore. Of Shore's compositions it is perhaps most obviously his score for the 1995 David Fincher film *Se7en* that is recalled in Keane's own music, but similar traits and practices can also be traced back to Shore's compositions for earlier films such as *Silence of the Lambs* (1991) and *Single White Female* (1992). A key distinction, however, is that working for film allows Shore the opportunity to work with a full orchestra, whereas working within the budget and time constraints of television obliges Keane to compose his music with a range of synthesisers and samplers. However, in following on from and developing Shore's work, Keane's scoring is distinctive in several ways:

1. There is a clear attempt to bleed the non-musical soundscape of the series (computer beeps, the sounds of footfalls and/or blood drops) into the musical score.

2. The music is produced through synthesisers, sampled loops and grooves and is characterised by looming ominous bass sounds with a 'sprinkling' of higher-pitched instruments (beeps, strings, piano sounds) over the top. In interviews, Keane has also suggested that he is frequently determined to introduce elements of an 'organic' performance into this 'techno bed' and will, in some instances, perform a piano element himself. He then adds this 'human touch' into his palette of digitally produced and archived sounds (Keane, 2004).

3. The arrangement of sounds is dominated by ostinato (repeating patterns), which encourage a sense of intensity and pace to the narrative. By echoing a frequent device in baroque classical music, the use of ostinato is appropriate to *CSI* as it serves to establish an apparently complex feel to the sonic environment of the programme.

4. It is also characterised by unfinished and tentatively repeated melodies and rhythms layered into the mix. As Richard Dyer has observed in relation to the music in *Se7en*, this arrangement can make the listener feel as if the music is constantly going to reach resolution or is going to 'get somewhere' yet it never actually does. As Dyer states, this is a 'tonal progression that endlessly promises melody and completion but never really delivers it, drawing one endlessly onwards through the darkness' (1999: 54).

The structure of the music, and Keane's practice of composing, also allow for an 'unpicking' of the music so that it is always possible to suspend and isolate a particular sound from the mix. Not coincidentally, this suspension often occurs just as the vital clue is identified by the investigators from the apparently confused environment of the crime scene.

Keane has suggested that:

The ambience on top of the music feels like the otherworldly part of the show. Cues aren't complete without the indefinable element or texture inside of the music, I guess most times it adds a darkness or unsettling feel to the show. A lot of the times the ambience needs to be in a different key or very dissonant to be effective. So much of the show is about compiling evidence. It's a great way to highlight all the different pieces of evidence and point to clues, sometimes subliminally and other times blatantly (2004).

Overall, therefore, the score has three related functions. Firstly, it creates atmosphere. Secondly, it might be said to 'echo' the scientific practice central to the programme's narrative – initially its layering, the use of ostinato and its technological feel relate closely to the complexity of the 'crime scene' environment and the puzzle to be solved. However, as the investigators begin to solve the puzzle, the suspension of sounds or short musical phrases relate closely to the 'unpicking' of the evidence portrayed by the investigators. Lastly, despite the predominantly technological feel to the score (its relation to ambient music and the use of synthesisers), there is often implicitly a human or organic touch integrated into the mix. It is this last aspect to which I wish to return in my conclusions.

SOURCE MUSIC OR NON-DIEGETIC MUSIC

Aside from the use of the Who track as a theme tune (a musical link for all three programmes – 'Who Are You?' for CSI: Las Vegas, 'Won't Get Fooled Again' for CSI: Miami, 'Baba O'Riley' for CSI: NY), the characteristic musical genres used in CSI: Las Vegas would seem to be dictated by the tastes and knowledge of the series' chief director, Danny Cannon, and the sound supervisor for the series, Jason Alexander, who are both British. Their choice of music reflect this; much of it is British in origin and the predominant genres employed are either 'indie' (New Order, Radiohead) or techno/ambient (DJ Shadow, Portishead, Euphoria). Other source music which is more 'gothic' or 'Nu metal' in character (such as Nine Inch Nails and Marilyn Manson) is more obviously related to the dark and occasionally blatantly 'gothic' content of the programme (Manson, for example, features heavily in an episode from the fourth season, 'Suckers' (4:13), which features a plot about 'real life' vampires). The way in which this more avant-garde 'gothic' music is used to label places is also made evident in an earlier episode from the third season, 'Lady Heather's Box' (3:15), where it is used to colour the diverse sexual activities that take place in Lady Heather's (Melinda Clarke) sadomasochistic brothel.

The use of techno or 'ambient' music is closely related to Keane's score, as these genres are also commonly characterised by a bleed between environmental and musical sounds and in their use of sampling. They also frequently involve repetition and manifest a complex feel. As in Keane's music, ambient and techno music could also be said to play with the idea of the 'ghost' in the machine, as human sounds such as voices are often integrated into, or 'floated over', the techno mix.

Superficially, therefore, the music in the series might be understood as clever or cool, thus contributing what could be called an 'aural gleam' and credibility to the appearance of the investigators and their work. Interestingly, however, the music is rarely directly associated with the apparent musical tastes of the major characters. For example, one of the quirky in-jokes of the Quentin Tarantino-directed double episode 'Grave Danger' (5:24 and 25) is that the music we first hear in the opening episode is *country* music and this is completely out of character with the series' familiar soundscape. The likely in-joke is that it emerges that this country track is actually non-source (diegetic) music being played by one of the characters in their car – and unsurprisingly it is revealed to be Nick Stokes, the jock and 'good ol' country boy' from Texas who is singing along. The only other character we commonly see playing or listening to music is Grissom who, defined by his refinement and intellectual prowess, listens, of course, to classical music and who also initially had his own wistful, Bach-inspired theme.[1]

In general, however, the choice and application of source music works, as Alexander claims, with a 'keen sense of companionship' between both score and the source. Furthermore, as I have suggested, another intriguing connection between the source music and score is the relationship or dynamic tension between fragile, 'organic' ghosts and the 'tech' machine. Alexander claims:

> We take a very organic approach to music, we solve crimes through science. That involves technical machines, the processing of DNA and very basic chemical processes. So it's not always high tech. Sometimes we take a low-fi approach to the music and a high-tech approach to the scene (or vice versa). If everything flowed the same way it would probably be too acute. That's why we love the word organic – it feels just right for us (Johnson 2003).

SOUND EFFECTS

The most explicit concrete sounds in *CSI* accompany the trademark 'CSI-shots'; the snap-zoom sequences where we follow bullets, knives or even infected blood into the body of the victims in a visceral re-enactment of the crime. These squelches, rips and gulps are shocking in that they animate the special effects of the image (made up of zoom camera shots, CGI and model animation) and they act most effectively as a kind of aural assault, but in their 'liquid' quality they also have an acutely intimate and even an 'oral' feel. This 'oral' quality of the sound encourages a sensual and erotic dimension, yet because these interludes are often associated with violence this is frequently disturbing. This visceral quality suggests that in these sequences there is a way in which the sounds remain believable since they are tangible (and thus appear 'truthful' at the level of sensation) even when the images they apparently support are fantastic or unbelievable (or as commonly occurs in the earlier 'reconstruction scenes' mistaken in their description of the event). What I'm suggesting is that although the sounds as well as the images used in the snap-zoom shots and the reconstruction scenes are 'fake' (these are not real sounds or real image-sequences) the sounds 'feel' real and thus serve to legitimate the truth claims of the image.

The other 'oral gulp' used in the programme is the sound wipe – a buzz of electronic noise that sweeps us in to the series title sequence or from one scene to another. This sound cue most obviously mimics the visual 'cartoon' wipe seen in *Star Wars* films and colludes with the comic-strip narrative and cartoon palette of the colours used in the series. At the same time, it also underscores (or points out) the quips, pieces of evidence and plot points provided by the CSI team. The 'wipe' between scenes is further emphasised by the way in which juxtaposed sequences will often have very different levels of sound (from loud club to quiet interrogation) producing a 'sound cliff' which jolts the viewer-as-listener to pay attention.[2] Thus the sound world, like the image world in *CSI*, is exaggerated, over the top – cartoon-like.

AMBIENT SOUND

The strong but limited colour palette of the visual image in *CSI* is echoed by the recurring series of ambient sound effects. Interior sounds used include: footsteps, phones ringing, technological beeps, whirrs, clicks, flashes and the buzz from cameras and computers and other forensic machines, some vocal hubbub, and a curious 'wall of air' (air conditioning?) often heard in the autopsy room. Inside, therefore, aural indicators covertly remind the audience that there is a continual and perhaps awkward 'rub' between organic bodies and technological machines. Exterior sounds used include: dogs barking, owls hooting, insects chirping or buzzing, camera flashes, sirens and police radios. For a series supposedly set in the city of Las Vegas it is surprising how nature often dominates the exterior soundscape although this perhaps only serves to exaggerate the interruption of the sounds of law and surveillance. Once more, therefore, it could be said that even at the level of ambient sound, there is a fairly explicit juxtaposition in the series between 'organic' sounds (which relate to nature and the body) and man-made or technological sounds (referring to machines, cameras, computers or cars).

VOCAL SOUNDS

The sound of the human voice in the dialogue in *CSI* is absolutely privileged in relation to the other sounds in the programme. Thus the voices of the CSI team and associated detectives are nearly always dry and close-miked. 'Realistic' sound perspective – which would reproduce the sound levels based on how far away the characters apparently are from the camera – is rarely adhered to. Instead, as Mick Fowler, the sound mixer on the show explains, the voices and the dialogue in the programme are recorded 'as if I'm standing right beside the actors. It doesn't matter whether the actors themselves are standing in close-up or 100 feet away in an establishing shot. The audience must feel like they're eavesdropping in on the conversation' (2003). Fowler suggests that the primary consideration here is that 'there are lots of clues provided in the audio'. In addition, I would suggest, voices are likely to be privileged because the interrogation and confession scenes, based, of course, on the sound of voices talking to one another, are integral to the crime-solving narrative of the programme.

In terms of performance, the fact that the actors' voices are recorded via the use of radio mikes taped to parts of their anatomy allows them (except when dramatically necessary) to effectively whisper their dialogue. This means that the majority of the conversations in *CSI* are performed in a low-pitched, breathy and intimate manner – the register of secrets and caresses. However, in certain situations, the sounds of different voices are made less intimate and are more distorted. For example, if an interrogation scene is first presented as if we were viewing the action via the two-way mirror and thus outside of the interrogation room, the sound will often – initially – sound tinny to place the audience 'outside' the room in accordance with our apparent point of view. Equally, the sound heard in the morgue/autopsy room is nearly always reproduced with a definite reverberation, encouraging the perception of the characters interacting in a cold, large space such as a church or meat locker. Additionally, in flashback/reconstruction scenes, voices are often made fuzzy and distorted to fit with the shaky and blurred quality of the image. In general, however, the audio position of the viewer – as Fowler makes clear – is as if they were an *eavesdropper*, thus echoing and supporting the voyeurism encouraged by the image. However, as I have also indicated, the audience's auditory closeness to the characters accentuates the amplified intimacy and the erotic potential of the voice. Stephen Connor, in his recent book *Dumbstruck*, suggests that 'The microphone makes audible and expressive a whole range of organic vocal sounds which are edited out in ordinary listening; the liquidity of the saliva, the hissings and tiny shudders of the breath, the clicking of the tongue and teeth, and popping of the lips. Such a voice promised the odours, textures, and warmth of another body' (2000: 38).

What Connor reminds us is that the voices we hear via a microphone are therefore distinct from those we hear in our 'everyday' listening; they are more obviously intimate and 'full-of-body', suggesting a mouth that clicks, hisses and a tongue which licks. The proximity of the voice in *CSI* is important since to hear someone who is speaking to you quietly you need to get close to them physically. But, as the series points out, you may also have to do this if you are, as Grissom does over the second and third seasons, slowly going deaf. As Lady Heather teases Grissom in Season Three, 'Do you like my lips... or are you going deaf?' ('Lady Heather's Box', 3:15).

CONCLUSIONS

The notion of the 'organic' body or the 'ghost' in the machine recurs in the different dimensions of the soundscape of *CSI*. In particular there is a sense in which the musical score sets up a kind of aural search for this missing ghost, reproducing the technically oriented search for clues enacted by the CSI team. Of course, audio puzzles (the disentangling of sound-as-evidence) do occur in the programme, although they appear far less frequently than the investigations of visual evidence undertaken by the team.[3] When such audio searches do take place, sound-based pieces of evidence are generally 'unpicked' via a digital sampling device, effectively reproducing (in reverse) the creative process of the series' composer John M. Keane who, as I've described, builds the score by using and layering different musical samples. Initially, therefore, there's a rather neat association between the scientific, diagnostic 'instruments' used by the CSI team and musical instruments used by the series' composer.

Hearing and sound, therefore, like the visual aspects of the programme, are presented as something that can be comprehended and organised via a rational, deductive or diagnostic process. Perhaps ironically given this rigorous science-based dynamic, the programme inevitably awards the CSI team superhuman (or supernatural) abilities: they can hear the dead 'talk'. This obviously ties in with an increasingly common 'spiritualist' discourse in contemporary television and thus aligns the programme with several other recent American and British series which also feature characters who can hear the dead speak, such as *Six Feet Under*, *Tru Calling* and *Afterlife*. For *CSI*, however, this 'supernatural' ability is made legitimate in relation to the scientific gloss of the series as it can be seen to be in accord with an enlightenment project identified by Jonathan Sterne. Sterne traces the use of sound-based medical instruments (primarily the stethoscope) which, he suggests, directed the understanding of bodies and disease away from the messy and unreliable vocal and sonorous confusion of the patient's own witness. These new instruments (stethoscopes and then other 'sound' based instruments such as CAT scans and ultrasound) allowed the enlightened medical practitioner to employ a more rational, learned process of 'educated listening', where the body's sounds could be categorised and interpreted to give a more exact understanding as to the patient's illness (or, as in *CSI*, the nature and cause of their death). Jonathan Sterne suggests that this separation and categorisation of sound (or 'mediate auscultation') 'was an artefact of a new approach to the work of sensation, in which listening too moved away from the ideals of an intersubjective exchange between doctor and patient into the quiet, rhythmic, sonorous clarity of reason and rationality' (2003: 136).

Satisfyingly, this would seem to provide another neat fit between the explicit aims of the narrative and the use of sound. However, in my further conclusions I want to suggest that this scientific or rational discourse cannot entirely repress the messiness of humanity or the otherworldly presences apparently inhabiting the unseen spiritual realm. In the final part of this chapter I want to explore the way in which hearing and sound are commonly related both to the erotic and the spiritual and how these associations are also played out in the programme. To provide a framework for this, I will adapt a model of 'hearing' presented in David Michael Levin's book, *The Listening Self* (1989), in which he presents four 'stages' of listening, arranged chronologically but which he indicates do not necessarily supplant one another. These are:

Primordial listening: This refers to the antenatal period and during infancy, where the human subject is awash with sound and, whether in the womb or at the mother's breast, sound and touch are closely associated. In this 'mode' of hearing there is little sense of figure-ground (that is a sense in which any one sound can be distinguished from background noise) and there is little categorisation of the sounds that are heard.

Everyday listening: This mode refers to the way in which the child and young adult has learned to connect sound to material events they can both see and/or feel, and in which they have some sense of figure and ground, i.e. they can identify which sounds are significant in relation to themselves. This may mean that they are able to identify specific sounds as threatening or welcoming.

Skilful listening: This mode is understood as a learned ability to distinguish between sounds, and involves an acute or culturally developed understanding of figure and ground, and is commonly expressed in musical and in educated listening – as in medicine, for example. Skilful listening is increasingly achieved via machines – such as stereo/quadraphonic speakers, microphones and digital sampling equipment.

Hearkening: This is a possibly unrealised stage which moves the subject as listener beyond skilful listening so that the 'ego' which has previously defined the significance of sounds only in relation to the self is 'disentangled' from the world of sound. This kind of listening is distinguished by a 'tuning' in to the world. Klein suggests that it requires submission and is often related to the sacred. It is in this mode in which we are able to listen in to a spiritual realm and where we might hear the voices of God, of angels or more simply the dead. In its deliberate refusal of the usual conventions of 'figure and ground', this kind of listening is a return to the primordial stage (although, in the primordial stage, the blurring between figure and ground is not a conscious choice to submit). Thus, like 'primordial listening', hearkening is passive and 'ecstatic'. It is also potentially erotic as it is characterised both by powerful emotions and a necessary submission, and is thus associated with a loss of control. As Leigh Eric Schmidt suggests, these sacred and erotic aspects of listening are not necessarily at odds with one another. 'It takes, indeed, a very short excursion into the auditory to know how closely listening is knotted with feeling, desire, responsiveness and touch, with the stirring and soothing of passions – whether joy, love, grief, courage, or heavenly yearning' (2002: 34).

HOW DOES THIS RELATE TO *CSI*?

The importance of sound and 'skilful listening' is made evident in numerous episodes of the series, but perhaps it is in relation to Grissom that the question of sound and hearing as a spiritual and erotic problem is made most explicit. I thus want to think about how sound – and its erotic and spiritual dimensions – relate to Grissom's character. And Grissom is important because he is clearly the moral centre of the programme. Interestingly, he is generally presented as if he is inhuman – a machine surrounded by machines. As such, he is tireless (he often works back-to-back shifts, rarely sleeps); he is characterised by a lack of emotional affect; and he demonstrates an extraordinary encyclopaedic and esoteric knowledge. Indeed, even his knowledge of the natural (organic) world – in particular, his obsession with insects – is primarily used to 'rationalise' the natural world as he most frequently employs this knowledge to construct a 'clock' or timeline for the decomposition of certain corpses.

When we first learn of Grissom's relation to the deaf community – revealed via his ability to sign (in the first season's episode featuring a deaf school, 'Sounds of Silence' [1.20]) – we do not know that *he* will go deaf, but two key facts are established. Firstly, that it is his mother who has a genetic 'fault' and went deaf at the age of eight. Secondly, in his final conversation in this episode he signs, unexpectedly, some personal history. Since the exposition of a personal history for any of the characters is deliberately underplayed in the series, it is entirely appropriate that this revelation is actually hidden – seen but not heard – both from the majority of the television audience (at least in its original transmission) and initially from the CSI team.

In this conversation (which is translated in a DVD 'extra'), Grissom explains that he asked his mother what it sounded like to be deaf. Apparently, he signs, she suggested that he should stick his head underwater. There are two possible interpretations in relation to this response – firstly, it could be seen as a jokey rejoinder to a naïve question. Alternatively, the response, and more specifically Grissom's personal memory of what deafness 'sounds like', provides an association for him which would link deafness to a relationship between his mother and to water (and thus potentially to the womb). Thus deafness for Grissom is potentially associated both with femininity and with the antenatal 'bath of sound' and thereby, potentially, with the lack of control experienced in the primordial stage of listening. This implied association between deafness and the sound of water is amplified by the way in which this episode ends with the sound of a water fountain pictured in the foreground of the shot being pushed up in the sound mix so that it eventually dominates the final seconds of the soundtrack.

If Grissom relates his deafness to submission and femininity, it is perhaps less surprising that at one of the key points in the third season, in relation to the crisis of his increasing deafness, Grissom ultimately 'submits' to the sexualised mother figure of Lady Heather (she is a dominatrix). It is also not surprising that the moment he decides to undergo an operation in which he is able to retrieve his hearing (at the end of the third season), it is also the point at which he formally rejects the romantic and sexual advances of his colleague Sara. Initially, therefore, Grissom's deafness and his 'listening crisis' are associated in the series with the erotic, the feminine and submissiveness. Yet, I would suggest, deafness is also associated with a spiritually inclined or quasi-*religious* submission to a willed (or in Grissom's case an enforced) silence, to a submission where one must 'listen without ego' and 'hearken'. Arguably, if Grissom goes deaf, it is not just that he will be a machine that is broken (and will fail as a scientist-observer) but that it serves to remind him of the humanity and the spirituality more commonly associated with the 'voices of the dead'. In his state of enforced deafness, Grissom must acknowledge the limits of a 'skilful listening' without humanity and without God. Grissom's deafness thus suggests that he must, at some point, acknowledge the nature and power of the emotions, the spirituality and the 'messiness' of both himself and of other people. For in real life these are the aspects that cannot be contained or interpreted by the controlled environment of the laboratory or by scientific rigour. I'm suggesting, therefore, that Grissom's problems with hearing act as his (and thus perhaps the series') *religious* crisis, since it is, in effect, a crisis of faith. As Schmidt suggests, 'The story of modern hearing loss, it seems, can hardly be told any other way; it is always, finally, a story of religious absence' (2002: 29).

I think I can justify this connection in relation to Grissom, despite the fact that he is presented specifically as somebody who is not spiritual, by examining the way in which he is simultaneously (if contradictorily) presented as a religious figure. It is made clear in the series that Grissom's role as a CSI is a vocation (not a career) and, while he 'only *believes* in the evidence,' his position as 'father' to the CSI team and his adherence to his science as a 'faith' (and indeed his general abstinence from sex), make him priest-like. This aspect of Grissom's character is made abundantly clear in the second season episode 'Alter Boys' (2:6) where he is, in narrative terms, doubled with a Roman Catholic priest (and, surprise, surprise, revealed to be a lapsed Catholic himself). The plot of 'Alter

Boys' involves an appropriately biblically inspired framing of one brother by another for several murders. In the course of the episode, while the forensic evidence all points to the younger brother, Benjamin Jennings (Corbin Allred), having committed the crimes, it is revealed that it is the older brother, Roger (Jeremy Renner), who is guilty. In fact, it emerges that Benjamin had only tried to help his older brother Roger by burying the bodies for him and has thus, inadvertently, ended up by 'carrying the blame,' literally, as there is physical evidence on both his hands and clothing.

Evidence as to the real character of each brother is revealed during the course of the episode. Benjamin is revealed by the priest to be a 'good boy', who keeps bad company but continues to attend mass regularly. In contrast, Roger Jennings is revealed to be a convicted violent criminal who is seen working in the kitchen of a pizzeria (called 'Dante's' – another in-joke).[4] By the end of the episode, Grissom and the audience know that Benjamin is in fact innocent, but there is nothing Grissom or his team can do to save him from prison or to prevent Roger from walking free.

The most significant sequence in relation to my argument comes at the very end of the episode. At the beginning of this sequence, Catherine and Grissom are exchanging information concerning the two different cases featured in the programme. As they talk, the audience and the characters hear a commotion located (initially off-screen) in the cells in which we know Benjamin is incarcerated. Once Grissom realises something is seriously wrong, he rushes to the cell to discover that Benjamin, unable to face his forthcoming jail sentence, has committed suicide by biting his own arms to rip open his arteries. He bleeds to death. At the climax of the sequence, and once it is clear that Benjamin has died, Grissom collapses back into the corner of the cell with blood on his hands. Initially, there is great deal of noise in this sequence and we hear shouts and grunts, the concerned murmur of the guards and paramedics, as well as gasps and gruesome gurgling from Benjamin as he dies. Aside from the blatant visual cue – of 'blood on his hands' – which indicates that Grissom is guilty in a biblical sense, more significantly, all of the *sound* is wiped for the last twenty to thirty seconds of the episode. Thus, the audience watches in total *silence* as Grissom gazes in horror at his hands. At the very moment in which Grissom is forced to realise the limitations of his belief in science and 'hard evidence' (since he has failed to save the innocent), he and the listening audience are 'deafened'. Clearly, I don't think this can be a coincidence. In fact, I would suggest that there is, in this sequence, a direct reference to the importance of 'hearkening'.

Following Levin's model, I have suggested that this mode of listening involves a reconfiguration or a destabilising of the 'figure and ground' in relation to the self and the world. And clearly Grissom's certainty – his world view – is shaken by this event. The absence of sound in this sequence is key, since hearkening, as I've suggested, could also be understood as a willed or enforced 'deafness'. Thus the enforced silence serves to remind both Grissom and the audience that the rational, scientific process of a 'skilful listening' facilitated by machines (and as championed in the series by Grissom) has its limitations in the messy, relativistic and chaotic world of men and gods. For Grissom, then, the crisis his deafness represents is not simply related to his potential inadequacy as a scientific investigator or to his infrequent fallibility as an erotic human subject (who, if sexualised, might become distracted from the 'truth'). What it also suggests is that, despite his belief in the 'evidence' and the rational certainties of his pre-modern scientific practice, he is never entirely able to escape the humanity of the victims and perpetrators of the crimes he investigates. Grissom's deafness – a recurring interruption in which he is perhaps forced to 'hearken' to the mysterious, spiritual realm – reminds him (and the audience) that it might be a mistake to repress this spiritual aspect and the messy and irrational aspects of both his and others 'humanity'. Yet to overtly or consistently acknowledge this would be a problem for Grissom (and the series), since to include them would threaten the certainty of the pre-modern science practised and celebrated in the programme. It is therefore not surprising that this narrative thread is rather abruptly and conveniently disposed of at the end of Season Three, at which point, Grissom is operated on and his deafness 'cured'.

Nonetheless, I think it intriguing that the religious and erotic aspects of sound are so important in *CSI*. As I have argued, in almost every aspect of the soundscape in the programme there is a play – or tension – between the sounds of technology and machines with sounds that provide an organic or spiritual element (whether this is a ghostly human voice, a human touch on the piano, or silence itself). Thus, however much the activities of the CSI team seem to be able to tidy up, or rationalise, our messy human business, there is frequently a ghostly presence or a human touch which haunts us, disturbing the fantasy of seemingly infallible investigators who apparently need only to look at the evidence to find the truth. *Listening* to the evidence, however, sometimes proves a less rational or satisfactory activity. This is not surprising since listening, and the ear itself, have been seen historically as problematic for an enlightenment project that had hoped to bring order to the mess and chaos of nature and, equally, to repress those 'otherworldly voices'. Indeed, as Schmidt suggests, for those who sought to champion the enlightenment project and to critique the mystical aspects of religion, the ear was a suspicious organ, for 'The ear was mystical; the ear was female; the ear was obedient, timid, exploitable, weak, and untrustworthy' (2002: 251). CSI registers this suspicion in a variety of ways; through story, of course, but more consistently and covertly by what can – or can't – be heard.

:10:

THE QUINTESSENCE OF CON

The Las Vegas
of *CSI*
Lucia Rahilly

Cherubic children who kill their kin; a transgendered mask-maker who stages suicides; a casino tsar who dies playing dress-up in diapers – the Las Vegas of *CSI* is the quintessence of con. In Vegas, simulation is sin. And on *CSI* it seems science is the solution.

Like many TV crime dramas, *CSI* is infatuated with facts: evidence, Gil Grissom assures us, 'only knows one thing: the truth' ('Friends and Lovers', 1:5). What is particular about the series is its process – its faith that science, expertly deployed, can combat the confounding power of the spectacular. From the get-go, *CSI*'s preoccupation with process springs to the surface: 'Process the vic,' Grissom commands his acolytes, 'Process the car. Process the suspect.' But at a structural level, too, the series is predicated on the scientific approach: *CSI* essentially plots the scientific method. The programme's narratives assume textbook form: assess the evidence; formulate a hypothesis; test, falsify, and revise until reaching a coherent, fact-based conclusion. Again and again, season after season, crack crime-fighters truffle out facts, devising an initial proposition ('You want to call it?') and undertaking multiple iterations – flashback-style reconstructions of the criminal act. And then, finally, verification: the perp concedes guilt. Hew to format, and repeat: on *CSI*, the scientific process leads almost invariably to truth.

CSI, then, presents a kind of Enlightenment-inflected antidote to postmodernism at its most pernicious. Cops, lawyers, politicians, the press – all are prey to the prejudice and power dynamics that lead to deception. And the denizens of Vegas, particularly, specialise in semiotics: they've mastered the superficial signs that, in our visual lexicon, convey the salient features of identity. Take transsexuals, for example. With the proper combination of hair removal, gait modification, hormone pills, and vocal alteration – the protocols for passing, according to an MTF workshop agenda – a man born as Walter can beguile thousands of spectators as a showgirl named Wendy Garner (Sarah Buxton). Add a dash of sweetness and some faux menstrual blood, and Wendy manages to ensorcel a live-in fiancé ('Ch-Ch-Changes', 5:8). But to Team CSI? In the context of the lab, the notion of passing is implausible at best. A nail clipping, a sample of saliva, even the merest mote of epithelia can blow the most carefully constructed cover. Wielding only a sloughed-off speck of skin, the CSI science squad can distill the essence of 'what you are,' in Grissom's words, in the twinkle it takes to test for DNA ('Unbearable', 5:14). And postmortem, faced with a fleshless skeleton? Gender is 'all in the hips' ('Who Are You?', 1:6).

Of course, *CSI* is about science and, as Grissom reminds us, scientists must never judge. Ostensibly, what's at issue to the fact-ferreting criminologists is not the ideological construct of transsexuality but, rather, the deceptive potential of display. In a legibly tranny social space – a bar, say – a six-foot siren might pucker her painted moue and deploy her archest come-hither coquetry. Yet, to Nick Stokes and Grissom, the transparency of her masquerade also minimises her threat. The crime-fighters, confident that they can classify her correctly, watch her drink up, hook up, and shoot up (silicone – it's good for the cheekbones) with the wry detachment of forensic *flâneurs*. Grissom even issues a few philosophical scraps on the construction of gender norms, recalling a poem about the sex of amoebas, for instance, and citing a species of hermaphroditic oysters that might suggest, in his words, that 'being born with just one sex is a mutation' ('Ch-Ch-Changes'). But, inevitably, *CSI*'s evidence-obsessed project is at loggerheads with the subjective premise of transsexualism. To the science squad at CSI, the semiotics so critical to incorporating another gender seems dangerously close to a swindle. As Catherine Willows instructs Grissom, transsexual dancers might be able to pass as showgirls, but never as strippers, because 'you can't cheat the full monty'.

Catherine's remark, with its reference to nudity as truth, highlights a central paradox in *CSI*'s scientific process. On the one hand, the team suspects what they see: Las Vegas is the city of surfaces and sham. In fact, even the unclad form is unreliable; as David Phillips (David Berman), the assistant coroner, observes, 'You'd be surprised at how many women I get with fake parts.' Ever wary of appearances, therefore, the criminologists train their UV flashlights on minutiae indiscernible to the naked eye. Oscillating between high tech and high camp, they don brightly coloured goggles, unfurling tossed-away towels to illuminate week-old semen residue. Purposefully squeezing their plastic spray bottles, they conjure blood spatter on floorboards bleached seemingly spotless. And, back at the lab, they busy themselves with microscopes and pipette sets, often accompanied by music intended, apparently, to sex up what might otherwise seem a somewhat sophomoric science montage. Unlike most detectives, the sleuths of *CSI* – armed with their standard panoply of misters, dusters, and cotton swabs – are surprisingly likely to perceive, say, a smidgen of earwax as the proverbial smoking gun.

On the other hand, ironically, in turning their focus toward the internal, the impalpable, and the infinitesimal, the criminologists not only assert the truth of what's visible but effectively expand the scope of visibility. Burrowing into the byways of the body – following the trajectory of a bullet into the chest, for example, or zeroing in on some succulently damaged piece of soft tissue – *CSI* renders the anatomical interior viable visual terrain, inverting *Sin City*'s emphasis on the external. In lieu of the louche allure of cosmetically enhanced exotic dancers, masochistic illusionists, and the garish accoutrements of casino culture, the series visualises viscera: livers being puréed, entrails being punctured, bile burbling in a spasming windpipe. And when Grissom, in his attempts to suss out the scenario beneath the surface, makes forays into the operating theatre of the gimpy, perpetually pessimistic coroner – in those sequences, *CSI* starts to veer toward morgue porn. The medical *mise en scène* functions like the articles in *Playboy*; it provides legitimising context for instances of unusual somatic exposure – in this case, scientific, quasi-educational gravitas to rationalise grotesqueries. Suddenly, in the name of the fact-finding process, both the inside and the outside of the body are on display.

So, science is the solution – but it's also, ultimately, the same old, same old. So much so, in fact, that what's elided from the process-centred plot begins to become more titillating than the chronicle and confession of the crime itself. Certainly, Grissom's injunction simply to gather and evaluate evidence – to 'chase the lie until it leads to the truth,' rather than to pursue particular criminals or, more broadly, an ideology of justice or retribution – beats a steady tattoo as the series progresses

('Fahrenheit 932', 1:12). Ditto the caveat against the contaminating taint of human interaction: on CSI, love and sex almost invariably lead not to the self-obliterating pleasure of *le petit mort* but to actual fatality – either to prurient, psychopathic murder or, as is often the case in the opening scene, to *coitus interruptus* caused by the discovery of a corpse. For several seasons, the criminologists themselves seem likelier to have more use for latex gloves than for their prophylactic counterparts. As *CSI* progresses, however, evidence of the scientists' personal lives start to thaw and leak into the antiseptic environs of the lab – and those traces, rather than the penumbra of a thumbprint or the discovery of a stray spot of spittle, take on the qualities of intrigue. After all, who would have imagined Grissom, the venerable reciter of koans and quoter of Shakespeare, Emerson, Aristotle and various niche entomology journals, admitting to Catherine that he missed working with her – and obliquely confiding that he 'even missed your tush' ('King Baby', 5:15)?

:IV:

FORENSICS

Theoretical Positions

:11:

READING
THE TRACES

CHARLIE GERE

My aim in this chapter is to look at some of the ways the work of Jacques Derrida might be useful in understanding *CSI: Crime Scene Investigation* and also perhaps to think how *CSI: Crime Scene Investigation* might be useful in thinking about the work of Derrida. To write an essay about a programme such as *Crime Scene Investigation* for a book entitled *Reading CSI* is itself to undertake a kind of forensic investigation in which the evidence, the 'trace', left by the programme is 'read' so that what it really means can be revealed.

Perhaps the first part of this hermeneutic process is to decide what kind of programme *Crime Scene Investigation* is, and to which genre it belongs. According to Derrida's formulation of the 'law of genre', which states that 'genres are not to be mixed' (1992: 223), *Crime Scene Investigation* must be assigned to the genre of television fictions about the law. In other words it is a detective story, or police drama. As such it descends directly from a tradition of stories about detectives solving crimes or mysteries through the exercise of high intelligence and minute observation. (For the purposes of this essay, and out of personal preference, I refer only to the original *Crime Scene Investigation*, set in Las Vegas.) With his quasi-academic interests and achievements, and his celibacy, Gil Grissom is one of the many heirs to Sherlock Holmes. But the drama is also about the collective efforts of a department, and as such follows on from programmes such as *Hill Street Blues* or *NYPD Blue*. (Though it does not resemble those police drama series centred on a single main character, such as *Columbo*, *Kojak* or *Ironside*. In such programmes the other characters were solely there for the benefit of the lead figure, which is not the case in *Crime Scene Investigation*. The lead figure in each of the series is clearly of great importance but by no means indispensable. Even though the team in question is comprised of forensic scientists, they seem to operate, improbably, like detectives or police officers, and have an unlikely, but perhaps dramatically necessary, degree of involvement and interaction with suspects and the public.

That one of the most important genres on television concerns the law is highly appropriate. The concept of genre itself is not just subject to a law, that 'genres are not to be mixed,' but brings with it the very question of the law itself. 'As soon as the word genre is sounded, as soon as it is heard, as soon as one attempts to conceive it, a limit is drawn. And when a limit is established, norms and interdictions are not far behind: "Do," "Do not," says "genre," the word genre, the figure, the voice, or the law of genre' (Derrida 1992: 224).

But, as Derrida points out, the claim to general applicability of a law of genre is confronted, as is all law, with the singularity of each case in which it is supposed to apply (1992: 187). For the law, any sort of law, to be universal, it must continually confront the singular, in that each and every case needs to be judged, and to be subject to a decision that exceeds the programmatic machinery of the law:

> ... a decision, if there is one, cannot take place without the
> undecidable, it cannot be resolved through knowledge... As to
> a decision that is guided by a form of knowledge – if I know,
> for example, what the causes and effects of what I am doing
> are, what the program is for what I am doing, then there is
> no decision; it is a question, at the moment of judgment, of
> applying a particular causality. When I make a machine work,
> there is no decision; the machine works, the relation is one of
> cause and effect. If I know what is to be done... then there is
> no moment of decision, simply the application of a body of
> knowledge, of, at the very least, a rule or norm. For there to be
> a decision, the decision must be heterogeneous to knowledge as
> such... Otherwise there is no responsibility... Even if one knows
> everything, the decision, if there is one, must advance towards
> a future that is not known, that cannot be anticipated. If one
> anticipates the future by predetermining the instant of decision,
> then one closes it off, just as one closes it off if there is no

anticipation, no knowledge 'prior' to the decision. At a given moment, there must be an excess or heterogeneity regarding what one knows for a decision to take place, to constitute an event (Derrida 2002b: 231–2).

When I judge *Crime Scene Investigation* to be a particular example of a universally recognisable genre of television drama, I am making such a decision, however obvious it might actually appear to be. In fact, of course, *Crime Scene Investigation*'s belonging to the genre of the law is not as obvious as it might appear at first, given that, as already pointed out, Grissom and his team are not police officers, or detectives, or even lawyers, but scientists. Thus *Crime Scene Investigation* exceeds what would seem to be one of the limits of the genre of the law, that the main figures should be recognisable as belonging to the apparatus of the law. Of course the crime scene team work *for* the law, but the fact that they are scientists already points to something that exceeds the programme's inclusion within a particular genre. This tension in relation to the genre of the programme itself resembles the complex structures of law, authority, singularity and universality that also constitute the content within the programme.

It is instructive here to compare *Crime Scene Investigation* to another successful programme involving similar questions of investigation and truth. *House*, starring Hugh Laurie, takes place in a hospital, rather than a police department. Nevertheless it is evidently a detective story, albeit involving medical rather than criminal evidence. Dr Gregory House himself is clearly modelled on Sherlock Holmes, down to the homophonic chain that connects their names (House - Home - Holmes). Like *Crime Scene Investigation*, *House* is a detective story not just because it involves detection but also because, in both cases, science, whether medical or forensic, stands for the law in both its claims for universality and for its application to the singular.

The tension in science between its claims for universality and in the singularity it continually confronts manifests itself in its modes of inscriptions and in the technologies it uses. However much a scientific finding might be deemed to be universally true, it also requires some means of singular material inscription: air pump, test tube, cyclotron, or DNA sample-testing apparatus. As the work of a number of recent historians and philosophers of science has shown, however universal a claim to truth scientific research has, it is still based on singular instantiations in specific apparatus and in particular contexts.

The forensic technologies used in the programme, which are a staple of each episode, are crucial to the process of crime solving in *Crime Scene Investigation* and constitute one of the great, if not the greatest, pleasures of the programme. These take a number of forms, from the high-tech materials and devices used at the crime scene, to the improbably efficient computer databases, the searching of which produces compelling visual spectacles, through to all the different laboratory processes for testing substances. I have a strong conviction that this aspect of *Crime Scene Investigation* was inspired, or at least influenced, by similar scenes in the film *Manhunter* (1986), the first and lesser known, but far superior, Hannibal Lector film. The film also starred a much younger William Peterson as a detective with a particular empathy for the minds of serial killers; a role which anticipated that of Gil Grissom in *Crime Scene Investigation*, and which features a number of highly effective scenes of forensic investigation.

Watching *Manhunter* again to confirm my earlier insight about its possible influence on *Crime Scene Investigation*, I was struck with what was initially a banal thought; how much younger William Peterson looked in the film than in even the earliest of the *Crime Scene Investigation* episodes, and how much younger the cast of *Crime Scene Investigation* appear in those episodes than later. This brought to mind one of the more uncanny aspects of watching material of this sort, the sense of a certain haunting implicit in any kind of recorded media. In an interview with Mark Lewis and Andrew Payne, Derrida observed that:

> Contemporary technologies like film, television, telephones, live on or off of, in some way, a ghostly structure. Film is an art of the ghost, which is to say, it is neither image nor perception. The voice on the telephone also has a ghostly appearance. It is something neither real nor unreal, something which returns, is reproduced – finally, it's the question of reproduction. From the moment when the first perception of an image is linked to a structure of reproduction, we are dealing with the ghostly (Derrida 1989: 68).

Similarly, Derrida describes the 'spectral effects, the new speed of apparition (we understand this word in its ghostly sense) of the simulacrum, the synthetic or prosthetic image, and the virtual event, cyberspace and surveillance, the control, appropriations, and speculations that today employ unheard-of-powers' (Derrida 1994: 54).

The presence of such spectral technologies allows *Crime Scene Investigation* to transgress the law of genre and be contaminated by another genre; that of the ghost story, though not in an explicitly occult sense. It is through these technologies that the dead crime victims come to haunt the living and are able to continue to speak, to the forensic scientists of *Crime Scene Investigation* at least. Sometimes they are literally able to speak, through a recording of some sort. At other times it is the results of the forensic investigation through which the dead address the living, whether in the form of material trace at the scene, DNA evidence, or fingerprints. It is through this kind of address from the dead to the living that the programme becomes a meditation on the problem of hermeneutics. The question in each episode is always whether it is possible to understand what the traces of the dead mean.

This notion of spectrality also has an interesting relation to the choice of Las Vegas as the location for the first instantiation of *Crime Scene Investigation*. Las Vegas is a place built purely for gambling. Its location, in the Nevada desert, makes no sense in terms of natural resources or trade. It is a place devoted to the circulation of money, the most spectral of commodities. By being dedicated to gambling, Las Vegas also invokes the idea of luck and contingency, and it is the contingency of death, its apparent randomness, that the forensic scientists are expected to counter with their hermeneutic skills.

The haunting in *Crime Scene Investigation* goes in many directions, including via the information technologies which feature so frequently in the forensic investigations. It is also not just that the apparition appears to us, but, with what Derrida calls the 'visor effect', also surveys us (this is a reference to the ghost of Hamlet's father, who appears in armour). In a series of televised interviews with the philosopher Bernard Stiegler, Derrida remarks, with specific reference to television as a spectral technology, that:

> The specter is not simply someone we see coming back, it
> is someone by whom we feel ourselves watched, observed,
> surveyed, as if by the law: we are 'before the law' without any
> possible symmetry, without reciprocity, insofar as the other is
> watching only us, concerns only us, we who are observing it (in
> the same way that one observes and respects the law) without
> even being able to meet its gaze (Derrida and Stiegler 2002:
> 120).

Thus the presence of information technologies in *Crime Scene Investigation* can be seen as more than merely aspects of the forensic science that the show seeks to represent. These spectral technologies can stand, more generally, for our relation with the television upon which we watch *Crime Scene Investigation*, and which allows spectral emanations from the outside, from the other, into our private space, and which also seems to survey us. They also stand for the implacable and asymmetrical capacity for surveillance of the law. These technologies can both be looked at and also look, remorselessly, at the evidence with which they are presented. Take, for example, the many scenes in which the fingerprint database is employed (at improbable speed). The computer appears to see the image of the trace of the fingerprint and compare it to others in its database, until a match is made and a suspect is singled out. Unlike the detectives, subject to doubts and misdirection, these machines seem to brook no disagreement or comeback (or even to offer any means by which they could be disagreed with).

Derrida explicitly refers to the facelessness of the 'visor effect' in his essay 'Force of Law,' in which he writes that the police do not consist simply of 'policemen in uniform, occasionally helmeted... By definition the police are present or represented everywhere there is force of law' (2002a: 278). He continues that the police is a:

> figure without face or figure, a violence that is formless... As
> such, the police is nowhere graspable... In so-called civilized
> states the specter of its ghostly apparition is all pervasive...
> And still, as this formless ungraspable figure of the police,
> even as it metynomizes itself – spectralizes itself – as the police
> everywhere become, in society, the very element of haunting,
> the milieu of spectrality (2002a: 279).

The police come to embody the aporia of the 'mystical foundation of authority'. The authority that is able to enforce a law must have been established through an act of violence that, necessarily, could not have authorised itself by any anterior legitimacy.

> Since the origin of authority, the founding or grounding... the
> positing of the law cannot by definition rest on anything but
> themselves, they are themselves a violence without ground...
> This is not to say that they are themselves unjust, in the sense
> of 'illegal' or 'illegitimate'. They are neither legal nor illegal in

> their founding moment. They exceed the opposition between founded and unfounded, or between any foundationalism or anti-foundationalism. Even if the success of performatives that found a law ... presuppose earlier conditions and conventions ... the same 'mystical' limit will re-emerge at the supposed origin of said conditions, rules or conventions, and at the origin of their dominant interpretation (Derrida 2002a: 242).

The distinction between the violence that founds the law and the violence that preserves it, and is needed to uphold it, needs continually to be policed, and it is the police who constitute the border between the two. As such the police do not simply uphold the law; they make the law, not least through modern technologies of repression and surveillance. Derrida suggests that 'modern technologies of communication, of surveillance, ensure the police absolute ubiquity, saturating public and private space, pushing to its limit the coextensivity of the political and police domain' (2002a: 279).

These technologies can be seen to stand for the machinery of the law in a number of senses. They are the literal means by which, increasingly, the operations of the law take place. They are also metonyms of the idea of law as involving the application of processes, procedures and rules. Following that, they can also stand for the idea that the law, as opposed to justice, is itself programmatic. Because *Crime Scene Investigation* uses these devices it is perhaps more effective at showing this than more conventional programmes about the law.

At the same time, *Crime Scene Investigation* suggests the need to go beyond the programmatic application of the law. One of the principal features of many *Crime Scene Investigation* episodes is a series of different reconstructions of a crime, as the evidence mounts up, changes or is reinterpreted. These are represented through what appear to be flashbacks (which appear as a kind of haunting, involving the use of an uncanny visual style of camerawork), but which are also provisional in that throughout the course of each episode they change in accordance with the mounting evidence. In the end, contrary, possibly, to the spirit of philosophical hermeneutics, some kind of final and absolute truth about an event is usually arrived at. Nevertheless, the successive reconstructions do invoke anxiety about whether it is possible to definitively arrive at some final truth, about the events in question, or about anything at all.

To some extent, *Crime Scene Investigation* can be regarded as a meditation on the relationship between writing (taken in an expanded sense to include any kind of trait or mark, including those left by the dead or revealed through the forensic machinery described above) and interpretation. One of the names for evidence gathered at a crime scene is 'trace'. This is also the term most famously used by Derrida to denote the way that writing (and thus all signification) operates as a system of differential relations that cannot be subsumed into either element in the binary opposition of presence and absence. The trace both is and is not. This is bound up with how writing is always predicated on the possibility of the (radical) absence of both sender and receiver and thus with death. As Derrida put it in his famous essay 'Signature Event Context' (an essay he refers to as SEC, a telegrammatic rendering which is reminiscent of *Crime Scene Investigation* being truncated to 'CSI'):

> In order for my 'written communication' to retain its function as writing, i.e. its readability, it must remain readable despite the absolute disappearance of any receiver, determined in general. My communication must be repeatable – iterable – in the absolute absence of the receiver or of any empirically determinable collectivity of receivers. Such iterability... structures the mark of writing itself, no matter what particular type of writing is involved (whether pictographical, hieroglyphic, ideographic, phonetic, alphabetic, to cite the old categories). A writing that is not structurally readable – iterable – beyond the death of the addressee would not be writing (1988: 7).

Less obvious is that what is true about the receiver is also true about the sender.

> What holds for the receiver holds also, for the same reasons, for the sender or the producer. To write is to produce a mark that will constitute a sort of machine which is productive in turn, and which my future disappearance will not, in principle, hinder in its functioning, offering things and itself to be read and to be rewritten... For a writing to be writing it must continue to 'act' and to be readable even when what is called the author of the writing no longer answers for what he has written... (ibid.: 8).

Derrida suggests that these traits are 'valid not only for all orders of "signs" and for all languages in general but, moreover, beyond semio-linguistic communication, for the entire field of what philosophy would call experience...' (1988: 9). One of Derrida's major points is that, in order to continue to function as writing beyond the radical absence of either producer/sender or receiver, writing must not 'exhaust itself in the moment of its inscription,' but instead carry a 'force with it that breaks with its context' (1988: 9). It is impossible for the meaning of any mark or trace to be fully controllable or saturable, or entirely enclosed within a particular context.

In that it deals with marks that continue to be productive of meaning after the death of their producers, or at least those who bear them, *Crime Scene Investigation* would seem to literalise Derrida's sense of writing, and mark-making more generally, as uncanny. In *Crime Scene Investigation*, the dead continue to haunt the living, without any need for supernatural agency. Fortuitously for this chapter, another term that Derrida uses to allude to that which exceeds the binary oppositions of presence and absence is 'hauntology' (which in French sounds like 'ontology', of which it is intended as a critique).

Derrida writes about what he describes as one of the aporiae of the relation between justice and the law, which he names as the 'haunting of the undecidable'. This follows on from his distinction between the programmatic and the decision, discussed above. This distinction is precisely applicable to the question of law and justice in that, for a decision to be just, to be a judgment, it must go through the 'test and ordeal of the undecidable'. Without this process, the judgment would not be free. It would only be 'the programmable application or the continuous unfolding of a calculable process. It might perhaps be legal; it would not be just' (2002a: 252). But nor does the process of coming to a decision assure that a judgment is just:

> Once the test and ordeal of the undecidable has passed (if that
> is possible, but this possibility is not pure, it is never like an
> other possibility: the memory of the undecidability must keep a
> living trace that forever marks a decision as such), the decision
> has again followed a rule, a given, invented or reinvented, and
> reaffirmed rule: it is no longer presently just, fully just. At no
> moment, it seems, can a decision be said to be presently and
> fully just: either it has not yet been made according to a rule,
> and nothing allows one to call it just, or it has already followed
> a rule – whether given, received, confirmed, preserved or

reinvented – which, in its turn, nothing guarantees absolutely; and, moreover, if it were guaranteed, the decision would have turn back into calculation and no one could not call it just. That is why the test and ordeal of the undecidable, of which I have just said it must be gone through by any decision worthy of this name, is never past or passed..., it is not a surmounted or sublated... moment in the decision. The undecidable remains caught, lodged, as a ghost at least, but an essential ghost, in every decision. Its ghostliness... deconstructs from within all assurance of presence, all certainty or all alleged criteriology assuring us of the justice of the decision, in truth the very event of the decision. Who will ever be able to assure and ensure that a decision as such has taken place, that it has not, through such and such a detour, followed a cause, a calculation, a rule, without even that imperceptible suspense and suspension... that freely decides to apply – or not – a rule? (2002a: 253).

The undecidable haunts *Crime Scene Investigation*. The programme is predicated on the tension between the known and the unknown, and on the decisions that need to be taken in relation to the crimes it depicts. Grissom may be capable of uncanny insights, the rest of the team may work with great efficiency and skill, and the various technologies may produce improbably speedy and definite results. But if these were all to produce nothing but certainties then the programme would not be so compelling. It would also be only about the law and not about justice. It is the points at which the forensic scientists go beyond the obvious and the known that the real pleasure of *Crime Scene Investigation* lies.

There are numerous examples in every episode, series and version of *Crime Scene Investigation* to demonstrate the above, so I will cite just one, from the first season of the original Las Vegas series. In 'Fahrenheit 932' (1:12), Grissom receives a video from a man convicted of arson and murder, who begs him to re-examine his case. The man has been convicted and found guilty of starting a fire in his house in which his wife and child perished. Grissom decides to do so, despite the fact that it has been apparently solved by Conrad Ecklie (Marc Vann), a fellow CSI scientist, with whom Grissom has had a number of problems in previous episodes. From the evidence gathered by Ecklie it would seem that the conviction is safe. The convicted man was seen running away from the scene, and traces of propellant are found in the cupboard where the fire started.

In classic *Crime Scene Investigation* style, Grissom works through the evidence to show that Ecklie has got it wrong, and that another, better, explanation is right. I will not spoil the pleasure of watching the episode for anybody else by revealing what and how Grissom demonstrates this. For the purposes of this essay what is more important is Grissom's motivation in reopening the case. Unlike Ecklie, who is clearly simply content to have produced apparently adequate evidence to secure a conviction, Grissom appears motivated by the need to see genuine justice, which in turn leads him beyond the limitations of the programmatic interpretation of evidence and into the unknown. Above all, he is obliged to take decisions beyond what is obvious and known. Thus Grissom's actions, in this episode and others, manifest precisely the aporia between the law and justice.

Of course, *Crime Scene Investigation* is an entertainment programme and not a seminar on the ethics of deconstruction, so in the end another truth is established. Nevertheless, by refusing what seems the obvious reading of the evidence, Grissom suggests the need for a kind of ethics of reading (the evidence), which must remain open to new contexts and meanings. There is a certain reflexivity in making this point about *Crime Scene Investigation* in a book about different interpretations of the meaning of *Crime Scene Investigation*. It might seem that learning how the characters read the evidence in *Crime Scene Investigation* can teach us not just how to read the programme but how to read altogether.

:12:

HORATIO CAINE'S SUNGLASSES AND THE CRIMINALIST VIEWER

'Looking' and 'being looked at' in *CSI: Miami*

Patrick West

The website CelebrityGlasses.com lists CSI Horatio Caine Sunglasses for $19.95. This desire to see the world as Horatio sees it – where does it come from?

What stymies any straightforward response to this question is the complexity of the way 'looking' itself operates in *CSI: Miami*. For as much as Horatio, conventionally enough, looks at the world (and for and at us, the television public) through his sunglasses, he is equally looked at: by us, and by the world. While the (worn) sunglasses of many other screen stars have become sutured to the iconic images of their faces – it's hard to picture, for example, the Blues Brothers without their shades on, even at night!, or a sunglasses-less Jack Nicholson in the front row at the Academy Awards – what is remarkable in Horatio's case is how very often we see him putting on and/or taking off his sunglasses.

Replayed in episode after episode, as well as figuring prominently in the 'Cast/Characters' section on the *CSI: Miami* official website, Horatio's nervous shtick suggests an almost compulsive repetition of that scene in *Cool Hand Luke* (1967; a movie the show's writers seem to enjoy referencing) where a prisoner on the chain gang uses the excuse of constantly removing and replacing his sunglasses to steal looks at a pretty girl – the sexual/visual politics of this version of looking will concern us more shortly.

Horatio's constant fiddling with his sunglasses draws attention to how 'looking' works because, crucially, it suggests *the disassociation of looking from the looker*. It inserts difference into our everyday understanding of looking in that sunglasses with no eyes animating them intimate a *non-human* form of looking. That is, no other character takes over the role of being the wearer of Horatio's sunglasses. Rather, the sunglasses take on a presence of their own, which suggests a 'residue' of looking – one directed, in fact, towards Horatio himself. To jump a little ahead in our argument, Horatio's accessory 'partakes of some strange life-essence that makes it transcend its material status' (Franses 2001).

My argument in this chapter is that *CSI: Miami* packs such a huge cultural punch within today's 'societies of surveillance' because it interlocks its concern with criminality with the way various operations of looking serve to create subject positions – positions of power and (ambiguous) pleasure – for its viewers. Thus, the show contains a seductive double (visual and cultural) audience interpolation; but, at the same time, it sounds a warning note about the excesses of 'looking' demanded by the current escalation of paranoia about criminality. In my conclusion, I ask whether the forms of looking, and of identity, that *CSI: Miami* offers up for us might not also be a prison-house for our selves; and, if so, how might we use these same televisual representations to reinvent ourselves?

The most noticeable type of looking in *CSI: Miami* is the (masculine) gaze at the (feminine) body. In its simplest form, this involves the voyeuristic enquiry of the camera as it 'speed shifts' its attention from body part to body part of an otherwise undifferentiated critical mass of women/woman. Of a great many possible examples, the opening scene of the episode 'Blood Brothers' (2:1) excites attention for its rapid sequence of sexualised images of catwalk models at a fashion parade.

All the main elements of Laura Mulvey's classic analysis of the gaze in 'Visual Pleasure and Narrative Cinema' are to be found in this scene. Quite obviously, the frisson of this scene is scopophilic, and involves 'taking other people as objects, subjecting them to a controlling and curious gaze' (2000: 240). In this scene, the women bear an 'appearance coded for strong visual and erotic impact so that they can be said to connote *to-be-looked-at-ness*' (2000: 243). More than this, however, the televisuality also suggests an individualised and private voyeurism, much as, in Mulvey's terms, the cinema creates spectatorial conditions (darkened auditorium; lighted screen) that encourage a cinéastic 'peering through a keyhole'. *CSI: Miami* achieves this effect by closing in so tightly on the women's bodies (frequently against a blue-screen backdrop that even suggests the pre-diegetic 'primal condition' of the production of the image itself) that the audience, much of the time, is excised from the shot; the scene is (apparently) for me alone.

Except not quite. For, apart from the fact that the other 'looks' emanating from the audience can never be completely forgotten (if only for the human noise factor), there are also three shots of camera image-captures in this scene, one by a man and two (interestingly, fleetingly, almost subliminally) by women. The first of these instances aligns with Mulvey's analysis, in that another man acts as the 'screen surrogate' of the (masculine, generally male) audience gaze (2000: 243). The second and third instances, involving women, are more problematic from a patriarchal viewpoint, and point towards the 'resistances' in the CSI: Miami text to (masculine, male-centred) scopophilia. What this scene also suggests is the close connection between looking and crime in the show. In the background to, and intercut with, the fashion parade, such that the second and third of the image-captures mentioned just now might be reacting to it as much as to the catwalk models, an altercation takes place as prelude to the episode's before-the-credits homicide.

The episode 'Spring Break' (1:21) similarly presents an instance of the (masculine) gaze at the (feminine) body in a way that reflects the terms of Mulvey's analysis, and yet also stretches the boundaries of her theory. Vacation time in Miami finds hordes of young men using video cameras, mobile phones and the like to film more-or-less obliging young women for amateur stag films with titles like Babes on Break (fictitious title). Here, again, we find a plethora of surrogates for the (masculine) gaze. Following the storyline blueprint of the series, a crime has been committed, and CSI Calleigh Duquesne arrives on the scene, followed by a persistent teenager through whose camera viewfinder we view her – as with the use of the blue-screen environment discussed above, the red REC display emphasises the intensity of the looking. 'Hey Blondie. You're hot. Flash me. Why don't you show me something? Come on, flash me now. Flash me. Flash me. You know you want to.' At this last affront to her very identity, Calleigh does flash something, opening her suit coat to reveal, under the curve of her right breast: her gun. 'Is this hot enough for you or you want to see my weapons permit?' The man backs off, saying 'Hey, I didn't mean anything.' Thus, his words make clear the loss of power (even identity?) that results from such a reversal of the look. From looking down the 'barrel' of his camera, the man (almost) looks down the (masculine, even phallic) barrel of Calleigh's gun. Here, a woman has taken possession of the (masculine, not always male) gaze.

Mulvey's path-breaking theory of cinematic scopophilia is thus highly relevant to an analysis of the televisual modes of looking prevalent in *CSI: Miami*. From a slightly different but clearly related perspective, Karen Lury argues that 'pornography, if not always explicit within any one storyline, does seem to me to imbue the visual aesthetic of the show in general' (2005: 56). I would modify Lury's claim to read that, while parts of the show do seem to imitate pornographic sub-genres (as, for example, in the near up-skirt shot that begins 'Blood Brothers') this is balanced by the self-consciously artistic framing, lighting and *mise en scène* of, for example, the meeting in the episode '10-7' (3:24) between Horatio and Agent David Park (Lance Reddick) in an atrium-like corridor. Here, the 'arty' aesthetic is nothing like pornography, in its play of shadows, depths and volumes, such that the human figures seem to become wholly blended into their surroundings. All this is a world away from the explicit focus on body parts characteristic of pornography. Thus, for me, 'looking' in *CSI: Miami* works in a wide variety of ways across the show. And while Mulvey's work is frequently relevant, Jacques Lacan's theory of the gaze is a necessary supplement to it.

In its barest terms, Lacan's theory of the gaze is the reverse of Mulvey's. For Lacan, the gaze is a matter of being looked upon rather than looking, a concept which he begins to explain in an anecdote recounted in *The Four Fundamental Concepts of Psycho-Analysis*. In his anecdote, a young Lacan is slumming it with a family of fisherman off the Brittany coast, 'waiting for the moment to pull in the nets,' when a certain Petit-Jean 'pointed out to me something floating on the surface of the waves... a sardine can... It glittered in the sun. And Petit-Jean said to me – *You see that can? Do you see it? Well, it doesn't see you!*' (1978: 95). The joke is lost on Lacan, however, and he asks himself why. He decides that the can 'was looking at me, all the same' (ibid.: 95). To the extent, that is, that Lacan – a budding intellectual amongst these people of the land and the ocean – 'looked like nothing on earth. In short, I was rather out of the picture. And it was because I felt this that I was not terribly amused at hearing myself addressed in this humorous, ironical way' (ibid.: 96). In other words, Lacan felt *self-conscious* in the strongest possible sense of this term.

In the helpfully titled article 'In the Picture, But Out of Place: The Lacanian Gaze, Again,' Rico Franses provides an exegesis on Lacan's tale, starting with the gaze/look distinction that underpins Lacan's complex psychoanalytic theory. 'If the gaze of film theory [in Mulvey, for example] is that element which grants the looker power, the Lacanian gaze is everything in the visual field except the look of the person looking' (Franses 2001). Just as Horatio's sunglasses without eyes peering through them suggest a looking without a looker, so in Lacan's theory 'even if there is no one else present, as long as one is looking, one is also subject to the gaze, [which] does not reside in someone else's looking at the looker' (ibid.). Franses concludes: 'On the side of things, there is the gaze, that is to say, things look at me' (ibid.).

Clearly, Lacan does not *literally* mean that some flotsam on the ocean was gazing at him. Rather, his theory concerns the way in which we construct ourselves as human subjects, which, for him, is crucially to do with language acquisition: 'I identify myself in language,' Lacan claims in one of his keynote slogans, 'but only by losing myself in it like an object' (1977: 86). Transposing this back into the visual terms of the present discussion, we could say that to 'identify myself' (that is, to look) is simultaneously to 'lose myself as an object' (that is, to become the object of the gaze – 'things look at me' [Franses 2001]). Identity is thus a double-edged sword: our sense of self comes at the cost of an alienation of self, to the extent that our identity is a *linguistic* one. Born into language, we have already died a little bit.

Extrapolating upon this logic, Lacan insists that our identity has the form of *desire*, desire being by definition unsatisfiable ('a continuous force... essentially excentric and insatiable' [Sheridan 1977: viii]). Taking this idea further, Lacanians make the argument that desire is the desire of the Other, where the Other stands for the field of language, within which we both find and lose our selves. To look is to be gazed at, because looking is an assertion of identity, and this same identity is fundamentally alienated through the desire of the non-human and indifferent Other, which means the field of language and, in this case, the visual field. Lacan feels looked at by the sardine can because he feels 'out of place' amongst the fishermen – alienated in his (linguistic) desire – identified within Petit-Jean's words, but also made uncomfortable and self-conscious by them (Franses). For Franses, drawing on Lacan's text, 'It is [Lacan's] sudden self-awareness of... sustaining himself in the function of desire that makes him feel out of place in the picture, and it is this sudden visibility he feels in the self-consciousness of his desire that is the gaze' (ibid.). And for Lacan himself, crucially, 'The gaze... is, not a seen gaze, but a gaze imagined by me in the field of the Other' (1978: 84).

To the extent that the show's visual field contains an equivalent dialectic of the look and the gaze, I suggest that *CSI: Miami* is an exemplary text of this same drama of identity formation, only blending it with a sense of how our contemporary identity construction is interwoven with the fact of our forced and/or chosen participation in a (criminalist) 'society of surveillance'. That is, Horatio's sunglasses are Lacan's sardine can. But do these have anything in common besides being random objects representing the gaze of the Other? Franses suggests that those specific objects that attract our look are, like the looker him or herself, alienated in the field of desire, too. The significance of this is that they present to the looker as some thing that might heal the wound at the heart of his/her split identity.

In the context of Lacan's theory, this is what is so interesting about Horatio's playing with his sunglasses. On his face, looked through without being looked at, they intimate a unified identity of 'seamless sight'; off his face, however, they suggest the missing link of identity: the potential 'putting back together' of sight and self. Strange as it may seem, the popular culture text of *CSI: Miami* appears to call Lacan's theoretical bluff: Horatio's sunglasses, in that they *can* be worn, can also make us whole. (In a sense, then, Horatio's sunglasses could be said to trace a retreat from Lacan's alienating visual field into the terrain of Mulvey's gaze, as the buttress of a certain form of patriarchal power.)

For Lacan, however, and Franses, following closely in Lacan's footsteps, such objects are *necessarily* mere decoys of complete and consistent selves. In technical terms, Horatio's sunglasses and Lacan's sardine can constitute the *object petit a*. This portmanteau term signifies a connection of the *object* to the Other of desire (*a* stands for 'autre' or 'other' in French), while the modification of the adjective *petit* ('small'), along with the use of the lower case for *a*, suggests that what we are dealing with here is ultimately only an abjected or 'trashed' element of the Other of our desire. To this extent, the *object petit a* suggests the (in Lacanian terms) impossibility (but can we still insist upon the possibility?) of the reconstitution of the self in *non*-alienated desire. Franses sums it up thus:

> It is the object retroactively posed by me as being that element I was in possession of when I did not know where I ended and the rest of the world began, when I was still conjoined with the world, and still experienced jouissance, although of course I did not know it at the time, because this *object a* which I believe I still had, I possessed before I became a subject, when I had only being, and before I sacrificed this being for knowledge (Franses 2001).

The importance of the *object petit a* within my upcoming reading of certain scenes from *CSI: Miami* lies in its status as a *potential* 'cure' for our identity ills. I give the *object petit a* a more positive spin than Franses does, using for my inspiration Juliet Flower MacCannell's suggestion that 'It is literally the switchpoint, the turning-point not only for the analytic cure, but for the power culture has over us – *and our resistance to this power*' (italics mine) (MacCannell 1986: 167). This last phrase is crucial, I think. How does *CSI: Miami* contribute to such 'resistance' in its own concerns with looking, criminality and identity formation? Attention to the television text itself – working variations on all the theories of 'looking' outlined in this chapter – reveals modes of interpolation, and also modes of resistance.

The Quentin Tarantino-directed double episode of *CSI: Las Vegas*, 'Grave Danger' (5:24 and 25), arriving on our television screens complete with cinematic pretensions, opens with one of the clearest correspondences across the franchise of this link between the Lacanian gaze and criminality. CSI Nick Stokes is lured to a faked crime scene and abducted, but before we first see his antagonist seeing him, the scene itself takes on the function of the gaze, directing it at Nick – and at us, given our diegetic investment in Nick as the protagonist of this scene. Slavoj Zizek identifies the same irruption in the visual field of the *object petit a* in Alfred Hitchcock's *Psycho*. When Lila walks towards Mrs Bates' house near the film's conclusion, Hitchcock juxtaposes 'the subjective view of the approaching object with an objective shot of the subject in motion' (Zizek 1999: 15). Zizek suggests that 'What we have here is precisely the dialectic of view and gaze... : the subject sees the house, but what provokes anxiety is the uneasy feeling that the house itself is somehow already gazing at her, from a point which escapes her view and so renders her utterly helpless' (ibid.: 15). CSI or Crime Scene Investigation indeed; here, the scene itself – in the mutually reinforcing context of criminality – 'investigates' Nick/us, creating for him/us an identity, but one constructed through his/our alienation in the visual scene, which is the field of the desire of the Other.

To this reading, however, a (for us enabling) caveat must be appended. Zizek points out that Hitchcock is exemplary in his refusal to 'subjectify' the gaze of the house:

> As soon as we try to add a subjective shot from the house itself
> (the camera peeping out tremulously from behind the curtains
> of the approaching Lila, perhaps), we descend to the level of the

ordinary thriller, since such a shot would represent not the gaze
as object but only the point of view of another subject (1999:
note 5, 34).

Tarantino's low-level long shot across the parking lot feels both objective
and subjective; the gaze back at Nick is non-human (objective) and
human (subjective). Thus, 'Grave Danger' might be said to 'sully' the
theoretical purity of the Lacanian perspective on the gaze. But that's all
to the good. Building on Lacan's theory through our reading of *CSI: Las
Vegas*, we can notice how resistance to the (objective) gaze is 'built into'
Tarantino's version of it. Identity formation here is woven through both
the alienated field of the desire of the Other *and* through the desire of
Nick's criminal antagonist, making the ensuing battle of wills something
like an exchange between fully formed individuals rather than a trial,
as such, of identity formation. In other words, in this case the text of
the *CSI* franchise responds to, and also works variations upon, feminist
and psychoanalytic theories on looking and what they might signify for
identity formation in the context of criminality.

Something similar occurs in the *CSI: Miami* episode 'Identity' (3:15).
All manner of things to do with looking are going on here, which plays
riffs across the boundaries where Mulvey's and Lacan's theories give
onto the space of the 'free play' of the televisual text itself. At these
intersections, what exactly happens to identity? Let's have a look.

The relevant scene in 'Identity' is the one where Horatio confronts
Clavo Cruz (Gonzalo Menendez) on the Miami waterfront. Clavo is
a louche playboy who exploits his status of diplomatic immunity to
(literally) get away with murder. Clavo's just taken delivery of a 'brand
new Lamborghini', the last one being 'no good to [him] anymore' after
'some puta [whore or bitch in Spanish] painted it red.' The interaction
between Horatio and Clavo begins a few moments before this snatch of
dialogue, however, when Clavo first steps into his freshly delivered car.
As he does so, we see Horatio's face, complete with sunglasses, perfectly
framed in Clavo's near-side mirror. This is followed by a reaction shot of
Clavo, also wearing sunglasses. (We thus exactly share Clavo's perspective
on the world in the first shot, in that he must be seeing what we are
seeing: Horatio in the mirror. That is, Clavo is a classic 'screen surrogate'
in Mulvey's terms (2000: 243).) Next thing, Clavo gets out of his car
and walks up to Horatio: 'Lieutenant Caine', Clavo says; 'Clavo Cruz',
Horatio bats back.

What this early part of the scene does, I suggest, is very firmly implant the two male subjects in the scene within the matrix of identity construction as it is triggered by visuality. They see each other, and then represent each other – *by name* – in language. (Interestingly, the conventionally attractive 'to-be-looked-at' woman in the scene never speaks herself; she is only ordered around, by Clavo mainly, but also by Horatio. Her role is little different from that of the Lamborghini's: to be beautiful but mute.) Thus, in that the two men look at each other – more precisely, are subject to the depersonalised gaze of *each other's* sunglasses – Lacan's theory of the visual field and identity construction informs this sequence. Horatio and Clavo, we sense, feel 'looked at'. This interpersonal effect is strongest when one looks at someone else wearing *mirror* shades; however, the fact of looking at ordinary sunglasses, with all their cultural connotations of authority, disdain and so on, also produces it – as is the case here. At the same time, the way Horatio and Clavo 'face off' from behind their sunglasses also recalls Mulvey's notion of the (masculine, usually male) gaze that attempts to control the world. This is particularly so in that the two men are here very much engaged in an aggressive power struggle. The content of their interaction over a criminal matter is reflected in its form.

Horatio has tracked Clavo down for his part in the murder of the 'puta' Clavo ran over in his previous car. Interrupting their scene on the waterfront is a flashback to the murder. Returning to the present, this is the point at which Horatio, in typical fashion... takes off his sunglasses. It is also the point at which the theories of Lacan and Mulvey begin to lose their purchase on this scene as frameworks for its interpretation, for what happens between Horatio and Clavo from now on serves to unsettle both their gazes (Mulvey) and their participation in the (visual) field of desire alienated in the Other (Lacan). That is, 'looking' is still a prime element of the scene, but its analysis takes us away from a normative understanding of identity construction, and towards new identity possibilities.

What strikes me as significant is that after Horatio takes off his sunglasses, so does Clavo – almost in imitation of Horatio. We should put to one side the question of Clavo's sunglasses as themselves an example of the *object petit a*, because this takes us into the incoherent (in Lacanian terms) territory of a multiplication of the *object petit a*. Instead, the interesting reading here, I suggest, concerns the actual interaction between the two men, and what that means for identity. Without their sunglasses, identity construction through their own gazes, or in relation to the Other via its singular anonymous gaze, is no longer primary. In a way that recalls the passage traced within Tarantino's crime-scene shot of Nick Stokes (both objective and subjective), here we have intimations of possible identity reformation in the slippage from the Other to a particular 'other' in the social/cultural field. At this level of interpretation, the nuances of the scene are important. While Horatio takes off his sunglasses entirely, and then puts them back on at the end, Clavo only slips them part way down his nose for a few seconds. It is as if tropes of 'looking' are being played with in this section of the text. While Clavo's female companion in the scene neither talks nor wears sunglasses, Horatio and Clavo occupy a variety of positions within the visual field that – if Mulvey's and Lacan's theories have anything to say about identity, and they do – must intimate a set of new permutations of identity, available for deployment by (only male?) viewers in a criminalist context. Meanwhile, sunglasses-less and unspeaking, the unnamed woman is stuck with the one identity – in Clavo's terms, perhaps she is just another 'puta'...

My final examples come from the episode 'Hard Time' (2:3). Here, once again, identity is constructed through visuality, but also deconstructed in a way that 'gives the slip' to the restricted range of identity positions available in the perspectives of Mulvey and Lacan. The linked scenes I analyse seem to reflect the importance of 'looking' in the extra-diegetic world of today's 'societies of surveillance' for the criminalist viewer, while also sounding a note of caution about the traps for identity contained in such a world. Put simply, the representations of looking I will now sketch out are both negative and positive.

To the sounds of ethereal music, the pre-credits segment of 'Hard Time' opens with a similarly dreamy cinematographic excursus that lingers over the natural beauty and stylish architecture of Miami. Soon enough, however, we are swivelled, at greater speed, into a designer-label condominium with to-die-for views. A pale 'Grecian' female face seems to peer out from a mirror-like object on a cabinet by the bed. The rising camera looks through the anamorphic distortion of a fish bowl, before closing in on a conventionally attractive young man, in jockey shorts, caught in the act of unwrapping the plastic cover from a pornographic magazine. On the point of sexual arousal, he slides beneath the bed sheets, opens the magazine, and (we're encouraged to picture this) begins to masturbate. A blonde woman's face stares out from the cover of his magazine.

We seem to hear the strange munching sounds before the man himself does. But then he does hear them, and the music shifts abruptly into a sequence of sinister, extended tones. We read his mind: what is that sound? From searching to left and right, his eyes slowly rise towards the ceiling. A white light-shade like a huge eyeball glares down at him. Standing up on the bed, the man eyeballs *it*, then reaches up to investigate with a hand. We are as stunned – nauseated even – as he is, when a squirming mass of maggots falls out. And now the camera fires up through the ceiling and into the condominium above, where a badly battered woman, Peg Donovan (Eden Rountree), lies on the floor, maggots infesting a wound in her skull.

Before seeing what happens in this following scene, however, let's consider what we have so far. Once again, Mulvey and Lacan are relevant to the interpretation, but ultimately inadequate to an analysis sufficient to the actual complexity of this scene. Without doubt, this is a scene structured initially around the male gaze in Mulvey's terms. The man acts as the surrogate of a masculine (presumably male) viewership in his enjoyment of the images of the women that are 'dead' on the pages of his magazine. And all the more so in that we don't see these images ourselves, only his response to them. We might also want to argue that the diegetic sound of the maggots triggers the Lacanian gaze. All of a sudden, the man is wary, unsure of himself, looking around to see what might be looking at him. From controlling the scene (Mulvey) it has started to control him (Lacan). The light-shade above looks down like a giant eye, concealing, behind its implacable gaze, the knowledge yet to be so horribly discovered... the pricking of male sexual passion.

Complicating this twin reading, however, are those elements that take us beyond a simple correspondence of the scene to the theory. For as well as being the subject of the gaze, as Mulvey describes it, this young man – buffed, barely dressed and beautiful – is also potentially its object, most particularly for female and gay audiences. Furthermore, if the light-shade has something of the *object petit a* about it, this assignation does not survive its transformation into a receptacle of writhing abjection. But, most of all, Mulvey's and Lacan's notions are equally found wanting courtesy of the various ambiguities of 'looking' going on here – so very much and varied looking, in fact, given that there is only one actual set of eyes in the scene. Above all, the 'Grecian' female face adorning the bedside cabinet seems to hover between the states of reflection and object-hood. Is it more 'looked at' or 'looking at'? Might it even be simulacral: just a reflection, without any original to be seen? Tantalisingly, it suggests an uneasy presence of 'looking', one that will turn out to be an anticipation of the disruptions and resistances of visuality present in the scene to follow.

So, back to that injured woman on the floor above, with maggots in her skull. We have gone a little forward in time, as medical examiner

Alexx Woods arrives to examine the body. Other members of the CSI team, Horatio included, are also present. It's all quite routine, until Alexx comments: 'the corneas aren't clouded; beautiful green eyes.' 'OK Alexx, wait a second, shouldn't those be clouded?' Horatio follows up. Agonisingly, Alexx is about to puncture the woman's skin to check the liver temperature as a better guide to the time of death, when Horatio stops her. 'Hang on a second, this woman has perspiration on her. Check her.' Alexx can hardly believe what she's managed to miss: 'Oh my god.' 'Alexx,' Horatio tells her, 'she's still alive.' The theme music bursts in and the credits come up.

My point here concerns the relationship of 'looking' to identity construction. Unable to tear our eyes away from the repulsive-but-fascinating sight of the maggots in her skull, this crime victim is firstly the object of our gaze (similar to the 'dead' pictures in a pornographic magazine). But then, dramatically, she proves to be alive, in a transformation hardly less stunning than if the 'Grecian' female face from the previous scene had suddenly blinked. And, crucially, it is her eyes that signify her status as alive. In a sense, she turns the tables on our looking, going from being an object ('just' a body) to being a subject, with all that that implies; from an eye to an 'I'. Some alliance of the 'looking eye' with the body in its status of 'to be looked at' is formed in this scene, with the effect of challenging the usual ways in which identity is formed through engagements within the field of visuality. In under three minutes of screen time, we have gone from one end of this spectrum of identity construction to the other. A man's eyes gaze at the 'dead' images of women in a pornographic magazine, triggering a chain of events that introduces a woman whose own eyes (the apparatus of her looking at the world) are the clue to her sudden leap – back into subjecthood, back into language, back from 'the dead'.

All one need do is look around to notice that the postmodern world is a 'society of surveillance'. From 'If You Can't See My Mirrors I Can't See You' on the back of a van, to the ubiquitous scoping of a million CCTV cameras at the local mall, we inhabit a culture of 'looking', a culture very frequently associated with criminalist discourses of person and property. Into this milieu comes *CSI: Miami*. This show speaks to our desires to create ourselves as subjects through the operations of visuality outlined in the theories of Laura Mulvey and Jacques Lacan. However, it also sounds a note of warning about the dangers of such identity construction in a world – like ours – where visuality is always already a powerful element in the *mise en scène* of criminality. Might not the very means by which our identities are formed be suffering from our ongoing participation in criminalist discourses? Paranoia about crime would seem to be making our visual identity formation insular and restricted, while identity formation through 'looking' suggests a counter-trend prejudicing and skewing our conceptions of criminality. It is the question of this crossover between identity construction through modes of 'looking' and 'looking' as it operates in today's criminalist context that *CSI: Miami* addresses at a range of levels.

For example, in the reading of the episode 'Hard Time' I have just concluded, we appear to be invited to tarry over the parallel between the way a crime victim is looked at and the male gaze as a component in the formation of (masculine) identity. The resistance to this unpalatable comparison occurs when the victim 'comes alive' through her own way of looking, as if the patriarchal power of the male gaze were itself being called to account. Similarly, the 'gaze from outside' of Lacanian subject formation is interrogated via its televisual equivalent in the low-level long shot across the parking lot at Nick Stokes in 'Grave Danger'. Curiously enough, in terms of identity formation, this scene actually operates to mollify the Lacanian alienation and paranoia of our initiation into language-based subjecthood through the gaze of the Other. That is, it replaces the Other with an 'other' – an 'only' human antagonist for Nick. In the same way, it also mollifies paranoia about crime as a 'face-less' and un-opposable force.

So, once more, what of those CSI Horatio Caine Sunglasses, listed for $19.95 at www.CelebrityGlasses.com? This desire to see the world as Horatio sees it – it comes from our much theorised desire to form an identity through looking. But, in the same breath, it comes from our entrapment within a 'society of surveillance' and the consequent diversion of our identity desires through a criminalist domain. The saving grace of *CSI: Miami* is that, as much as it panders to our sometimes dubious investments in the pleasures and powers of looking, it also offers a range of transgressive suggestions for 'seeing' ourselves otherwise. Though in some ways a prison-house for our selves, *CSI: Miami* might just also unlock the door of our becoming as twenty-first century identities.

:13:

'THE BULLETS CONFIRM THE STORY TOLD BY THE POTATO'

Materials without Motives in *CSI: Crime Scene Investigation*
SILKE PANSE

'You don't have to talk to us. He'll talk to us.'
Gil Grissom to a murder suspect, referring to the corpse.
('Alter Boys', 2:6)

'You don't believe me?' asks a suspect.
'Right now, we believe the evidence,' Grissom replies.
('A Little Murder', 3:4)

Grissom: 'The bullets confirm the story told by the potato.'
('And Then There Were None', 2:9)

CSI: Crime Scene Investigation is the first crime series to reject a plot driven by psychological motivation in favour of one that moves forward solely by the accumulation of empirical evidence. Unlike other forensic dramas that still rely on understanding the criminal's motive or even on the emotional involvement of the investigator, as in, for example, the British series *Silent Witness*, in *CSI* it is the dead bodies that speak. The importance of the (direct) word has shifted to that of the (processed) image. Personal testimony, brought forward in language and in the first-person singular, 'I swear' has been replaced by visual evidence that has no subject; or, as Grissom says, 'A case has no face' ('The Execution of Catherine Willows', 3:6).

The emphasis on the image as a means of determining the truth, however, does not mean that the evidence is immediately visible or directly accessible; it has to be read, processed, deciphered or translated. *CSI* makes the invisible visible. It is not what we see with the naked eye that counts, but what we literally see in the different – ultraviolet or infrared – light of forensic processes. The emphasis on secondary processing applies to the use of procedures in the programme as well as to the use of digital images in the making of the programme. In *CSI*, the term 'procedural' receives a more literal interpretation than the mere focusing on the larger plot unit of a trial to the exclusion of character development. *CSI* is about the procedures of processing, with respect not only to the logistics of crime, but also to the processed images of the series itself.

Of the three *CSI* franchises, the original *CSI*, set in Las Vegas, focuses the most on the science of materials to the exclusion of characters' testimonies. Objects, not subjects, 'tell stories'; bullets and potatoes are deemed more reliable than witnesses. Grissom's rational mind does not deal with the irrational and immaterial that motivates psychoanalysis and religion and instead only works with materials. In Grissom, modernist and scientific emotional detachment is coupled with a caring personality and a methodology of working from raw data to conception of the crime, rather than imposing an idea top down. A negative example of how one should not work is provided by Grissom's superior, and nemesis, Conrad Ecklie (Marc Vann), about whom he judges: 'Ecklie doesn't have a scientific bone in his body. He starts with the answers he wants and then devises the questions to get them' ('Mea Culpa', 5:9). Suspects and victims are treated as carriers of surface traces, instead of as mysterious characters. The cases are forensic jigsaw puzzles or riddles rather than character-based enigmas. *CSI* does not pursue linear motive-driven character narratives, but material evidence arising out of fragments. A multiplicity of singular details is pieced together to form the bigger picture, like the pixels of its medium. The investigations in *CSI* thus stand in contrast to crime stories structured around a cop or a detective. In *CSI*, it is not the narrative of a unified character that counts, but that of a method based on the accumulation and analysis of a multiplicity of material facts. The body has literally become that of evidence and has ceased to be whole. The bodies as well as the interpretive tools have to be assembled. The internal focus is not emotional, but visualised as a material one that often depicts internal spaces.

Gilles Deleuze wrote of electronic images that they 'no longer have any outside' and are 'the object of perpetual reorganization, in which a new image can arise from any point whatever of the preceding image' (1989: 265). In *CSI*, not only do new images arise from 'any point whatever', but also new evidence arises from any of the points of the image and new conclusions are drawn from any point of the evidence. Deleuze's observation about a loss of the hierarchies of space to a constantly varying omni-directionality can be applied to a welcome loss of the hierarchies of criminal analysis. The material context indicts the suspects, not their psychological motivation. Materials do not have a motive.

GRISSOM, THE INTERPRETER

'It's all about interpretation' maintains lab technician Jacqui Franco (Romy Rosemont) in 'Play with Fire' (3:22). In *CSI*, the spectacle of fragmentation stages an interpretation. Fragmentation is an analytical tool. Viewing a story of an investigation is always the reading of a reading; a reading of hermeneutics – the interpretation of the crime. The crime is a text that is judged negatively: the author of the crime has to be found in order to be punished. When the CSIs begin their work of interpretation, they do not know what their 'text' is, where it ends or where it will lead them. They do not know if an object is arbitrarily there, 'innocent' and without significance to the outcome – a death – or if it is a clue and has been 'written' as part of the crime. They have to determine the boundaries of the text as well as the signature. Sometimes Grissom has to decide if several crime 'texts' are 'written' by the same 'author' (as in 'The Strip Strangler', 1:23).

In *CSI*, the image and text are not separated into story and illustration, but the images become the text. The story is written following the visual detail, not language. Like the hearing-impaired Grissom, the viewer is supposed to be able to understand the story without hearing the characters speak. Director Danny Cannon explains: 'Our philosophy was that if the sound on your TV set went out, you should still be able to know what the story's about' (*The Hollywood Reporter* 2004: 5). However, what *CSI* also does is treat images like a language. In a sense, the images 'internalise' the excluded verbal language. Typical hermeneutical tasks undertaken by the CSIs involve isolating and matching visual formations, discrete segments of their visual 'texts', for comparative purposes, such as comparing fingerprints through the AFIS (Automated Fingerprint Identification System) or bullet striations under the 'comparison microscope'. Bernard Stiegler argues that the 'analogico-digital image is the beginning of a... grammaticalization of the visible' (2002: 148–149). In the case of *CSI*, it would be a grammaticalisation of the naturally invisible.

CSI manages to evoke (and evade) rivalling models of textual interpretation, those of French post-postmodernist philosophers Deleuze and Jacques Derrida, and that of Anglo-American cognitive neo-positivists. Both were critical of Freudian psychoanalytical readings based on unifying metaphors and rejected an overarching Theory, but these may very well be the only similarities. Like positivism in the nineteenth century, cognitive approaches to film came about as a reaction against 'meta-physical abstractions' (Comte 1988: 3). They were developed in the 1980s (Bordwell 1985) explicitly against the psychoanalytic film theory of the 1970s which explored the irrational, choosing to focus instead on the rational and the visible. Following a post-positivist philosophy of natural sciences, rather than of humanities, cognitive scholars argue for a scientific pursuit of film theory using empirical methodology. Instead of looking at larger and less graspable areas such as psychoanalytical subjectivity (Carroll 1996: 58, 59), their research focuses on chains of cause and effect that begin with small and visible areas of enquiry, such as the optical point-of-view shot. The mechanical subjectivity of the camera is then often backed-up with examples imported from human psychology.

However, unlike filmed, indexical images, computer simulations 'do not come with an inherent visual point of view' (Wolf 1999: 286) With CGI, the point of view 'is not visual or perceptual, but conceptual and theoretical', and 'refers to the programs, theories and assumptions controlling the simulation' (ibid.: 287). Images of the insides of objects cannot be researched through direct and commonsensical viewing patterns. In the often computer-generated CSI image, the point of origin is more important than the point of view. While CSI's emphasis on material science can be seen to be in line with a positivist tradition, in contrast to neo-positivist cognitive film theory, it is about the rational invisible. Whereas cognitive 'post-theory' equates rationality with common sense, the forensic science in CSI is there to make up for the inadequacies of (the cops') common sense, and those of the human eye. Contrary to cognitive approaches, the empiricism of the natural sciences, as represented in the non-scientific artistic product that is CSI, is often concerned with proving how the fragments come together in a non-commonsensical way. Sometimes the cause and effect chains discovered in the diegeses are arbitrary and do not even have a conscious perpetrator.

In describing the changes in the relationship between the human eye and optical technology, Jonathan Crary outlined that:

> During the seventeenth and eighteenth centuries that
> relationship had been essentially metaphoric; the eye and the
> camera obscura or the eye and the telescope or microscope were
> allied by a conceptual similarity, in which the authority of an
> ideal eye remained unchallenged. Beginning in the nineteenth
> century, the relation between eye and optical apparatus
> becomes one of metonomy: both were now contiguous
> instruments on the same plane of operation, with varying
> capabilities and features. The limits and deficiencies of one will
> be complemented by the capacities of the other, and vice versa
> (1990: 129).

With the use of CGI, this relationship has changed again, and the eye
now is the deficient one. *The Journal of Forensic Science*, which is frequently
quoted by the CSIs, maintains that 'assessments from images should be
approached with caution since there are inherent limitations of the naked
eye in identifying morphological changes in certain skeletal features'
(Sitchon and Hoppa 2005: 793). Whereas Auguste Comte, the founder
of positivist philosophy, objected to any technological mediation, such
as the microscope and preferred direct observation instead (Wolf 1999:
275), the positivism of *CSI*, by contrast, is founded on indirectness.

TRACING THE DETECTIVES

Catherine Willows: 'Don't touch me, I'm evidence.'
('A Little Murder', 3:4)

What in previous detective drama has been dealt with in psychoanalytic
terms of repression and displacement, in forensic television is objectified
as material trace: 'The basic principle on which forensic science is
founded is that a criminal always takes something to the scene of a
crime and always leaves something there, or, more simply, in the words
of [French founder of forensic science] Edmond Locard, "Every contact
leaves trace"' (Gardner Conklin et al. 2002: 278).

Derrida introduced the word 'trace' into the post-structuralist canon,
arguing that there are always traces of an absence in what is present.
The signified and the signifier are never entirely separated as one always
leaves marks in the other. Derrida opposed a 'metaphysics whose entire
history was compelled to strive toward the reduction of the trace' (1974:
71). Grissom would probably agree. Given the prominence of trace and

the protagonists' indirect interpretations of the inscriptions of a crime, CSI seems to lend itself to a Derridean interpretation. His suggestion that a mark always needs another for it to make sense is literally realised in the puzzle work of the CSIs, who also read their 'text' indirectly. The crime story has to be deduced from its aesthetics. Blood spatter and bullet holes indicate the choreography of a crime, which is only available to us through processing, reconstructions and computerised renderings. Even the image itself can serve as evidence to identify the camera that 'shot' it.

The point of departure in CSI is always the end of a life and the absence of the killer. It begins posthumously after the signified, that is, the life of the victim, is gone and only the signifiers, the corpse and trace, are left. The death of the signified allows the play of the signifiers. This play of signifiers is made manifest in 'Bad Words' (4:19) where a champion of a game similar to Scrabble has literally been made to eat his word by a rival. CSI, like Derrida (1979), focuses on textual signifiers and associates trace with simulation. But, whereas Derrida found meaning in play without a function, the CSIs only go through their aesthetically pleasing play with the fragments of a text in order to get closure. Unlike Grissom, Derrida was against scientific objectivism. In CSI, textual crime-scene dissemination in the end leads to only one interpretation. Whereas trace is that which is not present for Derrida, trace is the only thing that is left from the absent criminal for the CSIs.

In his application of Derrida, Bernard Stiegler argues that we cannot experience an image in the present without inscribing our memories in it. Equally, there is no memory that is objective and without images (2002: 148). Instead of the inscription of memories on the present, CSI emphasises the material presence of the traces, such as the dusting for fingerprints or tape-lifting fibres. In a sense, only tracing, the indexical form of processing, makes evidence visible. Still, to bring evidence to 'Trace' always involves an announcement by the protagonists that they would do so. In a programme famous for its CGI 'CSI-shots', indexical trace is highlighted. It is as though the CSIs are emphasising what the absent trace is in computer-generated television – the older medium of indexical trace, celluloid. The excessive references to trace and traces *in* the image might compensate for the absence of trace *of* the image; the content of the programme for the lack of its medium. Paradoxically, a trace, of course, always already indicates an absence. In a medium – digital video – into which no traces can be physically inscribed, the tendency of programmes has been to increasingly focus on the physical traces on and of our bodies, both in the medical action dramas of the last decade and the contemporary forensic crime series. The dead bodies with indexical traces on digitally processed sites might be those of celluloid.

THE UNRELIABLE EYEWITNESS

The effect of the emphasis on processing in this procedural show, the so called 'CSI effect', has been that jurors have ceased to believe the direct observations of the eyewitnesses and circumstantial evidence, in preference of forensic evidence such as DNA or fingerprints. In an interesting counterpoint to this, CSI has integrated the critique of its emphasis on empirical evidence into its dialogues. In a court case in 'Secrets and Flies' (6:6), an entomologist colleague of Grissom's presents a video of the gestation of blowfly pupae on a decaying pig. This experiment seems to establish a time of death of the victim which otherwise runs counter to all circumstantial evidence. Ecklie asks Grissom to evaluate the tape and is unusually understanding: 'Jurors might be more receptive to video documentation than books.' Grissom is able to prove that even though the video was correctly recorded, the experiment itself was manipulated.

CSI consigns to history what Derrida maintained – and critiqued – a few years earlier: 'people will continue to prefer, even if only naively, supposedly living testimony to the archive' (2002: 98). In another manifestation of his critique of the apparent 'authenticity' of speaking, Derrida predicted: 'One will continue to have more confidence in testimony than in the archive and in evidence, while naturally neglecting all that can intervene, even in the most sincere of authentic testimony' (2002: 98). However, Derrida already described the beginnings of a slippage from testimony to evidence, as when a recording of a testimony in court assumes the status of evidence. Grissom has already listened to Derrida lamenting the ignorance of the juridical discourse about the complexities of a mistaken witness, who can nevertheless be true to himself (2002: 98). Still, whereas the consequence for Derrida was to keep the text open, Grissom, of course, seeks to close the case. And even Derrida was against purely textual evidence: 'The technical archive, in principle, should never replace testimony' (2002: 94).

In contrast to the emphasis on processing as the method of obtaining truth in the computer-generated images of CSI, in forensic journals, digital images are regularly seen as a source of deception.[1] The forensic investigation is geared towards ascertaining the originality of an image: 'The use of digital photography has increased over the past few years, a trend which opens the door for new and creative ways to forge images...

This poses a need to verify the authenticity of images originating from unknown sources' (Peterson 2006). Manipulation, writes Stiegler, 'is the essence, that is to say, the rule of the digital photo. And this possibility... inspires *fear*' (2002: 150).

CSI calms this fear in a double operation: the forensic experts determine the criminal originators of the crime scene, and they do so with digital imagery that, in a sense, has no original. The successful procedures of the CSIs also soothe the anxiety of being overwhelmed by information. In contrast to the evocations of memory that the cinematic image carries – that is, the exposed celluloid is always already a 'remembered' trace of a past event – television 'can be missed and mis-remembered', is 'easily forgotten or simply stored and never watched' (Lury 1995–1996: 114).

This is also because there is so much of it. Frequently the CSIs also have to process what seem to be infinite amounts of data. In 'Chasing the Bus' (2:18), Sara Sidle articulates the potential of being snowed under by material when confronted with the apparently indistinguishable debris on a motorway after a bus accident: 'This stuff could have been from any vehicle.' Eventually, however, the CSIs will always separate the meaningful from the meaningless. Thus the anxiety of the viewer is calmed by the content of the programme, transmitted through the very medium by which it is triggered.

POSTMORTEM RELIEF

There have been other forensic detectives on television, such as Jack Klugman in *Quincy M.E.* in the 1970s, and Dick Van Dyke's physician in *Diagnosis Murder* in the 1990s. But the rise of postmortem television series poses the question of why they have become far more prevalent at this particular moment in time? In the hospital television dramas of the 1990s, such as *ER*, the body was in trauma and all action was geared towards preventing death. Forensic series, post 9/11, however, begin with the dead body. The body already being dead, in a sense, brings a soothing quality with it. The struggle to avert death is over. When Grissom encounters a corpse, there is a certain relief. As a corpse, one is in safe hands with him.

The 'relief' of the postmortem state is also expressed in the ambient mood of the programme, in which the reflective atmosphere is both mentally and aesthetically tangible. *CSI* is aesthetically as defining for forensic crime series as *ER* has been for hospital drama. The emblematic images of *ER* were the back-lit X-rays stuck to the light boxes of the trauma rooms. With the X-ray, 'the subject was forced to concede the limits of the body, erasing the limit against which it claimed to be inside and outside' (Lippit 1999: 67). The defining image in the definitive medical drama of the last decade was an indexical image of the inside. The X-ray made the permeability of inside and outside visible. Its undynamic simultaneity was compensated for, in the earlier seasons of *ER*, by the fast pace of the Steadicam and the action-driven medics, both of which generated a furious activity that could only be executed by a non-permeated body. The film camera contained the porosity of the X-ray images displayed as part of the *mise en scène* by excessively circling around them like a guard dog encircles its sheep.

The hectic Steadicam shots emphasising the doctors' direct action in *ER* is, in *CSI*, replaced with 'indirect' computer-generated images that match the indirectness of the analytical deductions from the forensic scientists (notably there is only one letter that distinguishes 'CGI' from 'CSI'). The epitomising images of *CSI* are computer-generated process shots travelling along a given corporeal route, such as blood cells in arteries, or a peanut into the stomach, or following a bullet creating its own path through the body. Tracking the trajectory of a bullet had been one of the aesthetic directives for the series by its creator, Anthony E. Zuiker. In these process shots, for which the series is now renowned, the camera traverses layers of a body or other matter like a bullet. It is only through mediation that we can access reality – again. The CSI's material is generated democratically, and empirically, from the bottom up, and their enthusiastic work of control through the use of simulations is experienced as a relief.

SIMULATED OBSERVATION

CSI caters for the myth of a deeper truth in the metaphorical sense, by literally getting closer and deeper. Getting closer used to mean more accurate indexical observation and thus better visual evidence. Previously, in film, the image of science was upheld in the surface view of observational documentary. In the 1960s, the documentaries by Direct Cinema directors were infused by a scientific ethos that was based on not intervening or inventing. Only non-intervention produced 'direct images'. These documentary aesthetics influenced the style of hospital dramas such as *ER*, where events were filmed as though they were discovered and 'the increased mobility of the televisual frame was expressive of the attempt to catch up with the events as they happened' (Jacobs 2003: 55). Cop series, too, such as *Dragnet, Z Cars, Homicide: Life on the Street, NYPD Blue, Hill Street Blues* and *The Cops*, adopted the grainy and shaking style of observational documentary for an impression of realism. This realism, however, then led to the reproach that crime series often reinforce a dominant reality (Buxton 1990). The 'CSI-shots' belie this accusation. Not only are the images in CSI highly stylised – more so than those of other forensic drama series such as Silent Witness or Bones – but also the microscopic insides of objects and bodies are not sites that constitute our daily experience; they are recognisably outside the realms of realism. CSI does not 'represent a "real" world of recognisable identities, places, times and events in which stories unfold in familiar ways' (Casey et al 2001: 45) as has been attributed to cop shows in the past. At a time when documentary as a style is further and further removed from documentary as evidence – with many fictional films and television programmes adopting and/or parodying documentary as style – the images in CSI represent evidence when they are the least observational and the most processed. In CSI, the immediacy of documentary realism has been substituted by the flaunting of the effect. What had been 'visible evidence' for documentary, in CSI is invisible evidence. The state-of-the-art laboratory of the set mirrors the advanced technology with which the series is produced. CSI does not evoke a desire for more police power, as has been the criticism of earlier cop shows, but for more equipment and knowledge.

The emphasis on the evidential in CSI resonates with the recent popularity of documentary. However, usually an image becomes evidential by being indexical; that is, it is evidential because the representation has been caused by what it represents, like a documentary image on television. The representation and its referent share the same level of indexically referenced reality. In CSI, by contrast, the evidential imagery is often represented by generated, non-indexical computer-generated images and is therefore separated from the referential level of its potential causes. The indexical tracing by the CSIs within the diegesis is detached from the indexical images of its televisual representation and even further removed from the non-indexical images processed by the computer. What we see on the screen is not indexical evidence. It is a dramatised simulation, an illustration. With CSI, the aesthetics of science have changed. The status of the evidential as external, attained through indexical observation, has been surpassed by the 'insider's view' of data generated according to the laws of science and computer simulation. The inherent qualities of computer imaging are remarkably well matched to the CSIs' task of reconstructing past events: 'Unlike infrared, ultraviolet, or even X-ray photography, computer imaging involves more interpretation and often must reconstruct objects or events in order to visualize them' (Wolf 1999:

280). Computer simulations also allow working with multiple options and parameters that can be analysed from any point of view, human or material.

Interestingly, Mark Wolf argues that computer images become indexical the more they are simulated: 'As a simulation is constructed, and the data set becomes larger and more comprehensive, its indexical link to the physical world becomes stronger, until the simulation is thought to be sufficiently representative of some portion or aspect of the physical world' (1999: 280). In a reverse trajectory to that of evidence gathered through non-interventional observation, in *CSI*, the more interfering, the better the evidence; the more fictionalising, the more realistic. *CSI* shows how, the more microscopic it gets, more of what is shown is outside of our direct grasp, and the more we have to use deductive methodology to reconstruct a whole picture. The image, in fact, is not 'enhanced', it is created. Moreover, the path from simulation to evidence is padded with default data filling the gaps of a specific case: 'The substitution of a generalised, 'standard' computer model for a specific existing object is common throughout computer simulation' (ibid.: 283). In the diegesis of *CSI*, too, the move from one piece of the puzzle to the next – the causal chains presented as evidential – is often invented for the series. One forensic scientist, for instance, finds '*CSI*'s worst scientific leap' to be 'when they recover one fibre and link it to one carpet manufacturer and then trace it back to one store and then to the person who purchased it (Palmer 2003: 1). In both cases, there is recourse to non-specific data (either generic or originally made up). The fallacies in the content of *CSI* complement those of its form.

UP CLOSE AND IMPERSONAL:
THE MICROSCOPIC 'CSI-SHOT'

'This is your fault. Your nose is so far down a microscope, you got no idea what your people are doing.' Capt. Jim Brass to Gil Grissom
('Who Are You?', 1:6)

In 1947, the film critic André Bazin wrote that 'word is getting out that microbes are the greatest actors in the world. Next year we will ask them for autographs' (145). Whereas fiction film accentuates the outdoors action spectacle of, say, visible explosions and floods dwarfing humans, *CSI* looks at animate and inanimate material fragments of what is invisible inside. As *CSI* producer Carol Mendelsohn points out: 'One of the things we did from the start that was unique was that we didn't go big, we went small. We took a fiber and made it look like a redwood forest' (Richmond 2005: 5). When cinema takes on the perspective of the miniature, it is about depicting humans as a whole looking small in comparison to their environment, like in *The Incredible Shrinking Man* (1957), *The Incredible Shrinking Woman* (1981) or *King Kong* (1933, 1979, 2005). Even in *Fantastic Voyage* (1966), which Cannon lists as an influence, a surgical team is miniaturised and inserted into a dying man. But in *CSI*, we are not asked to experience the world from the perspective of a corpuscle or a bullet. There is no anthropomorphising of the microscopic or sharing of its subjectivity; as Grissom advises Warrick Brown: 'There is no room in this department for subjectivity' ('Pilot', 1:1). Empathy with particles or bugs does not get us anywhere.

CSI convincingly and jubilantly turns objects into images. Stiegler spoke of 'image-objects', which, in contrast to mental images, are always inscribed in a technical history (2002: 147). With image-objects, the signified and signifier cannot be separated from each other. In a sense, *CSI* demonstrates this: the story grows out of the images of objects. The content arises out of form. Only in retrospect is there transcendent narrative content – the completed puzzle – that serves to bind the multiple pieces. This applies to the epistemological process of the CSIs in the diegesis as well as to the preceding conception of each series. Executive producer Ann Donahue describes the gestation process of an episode as such: 'One of the things we did at the beginning that was unique was that anytime Danny [Cannon] wasn't directing, we'd drag him into the writers' room and tell him, "Talk to us about how we can visually tell this story." And he would sit there and fill in us writers; that spurred us to begin to write visually, which isn't necessarily what TV writers are trained to do at all' (Richmond 2005).

However, Stiegler was referring to images as objects, not to objects as images. *CSI* 'objects' are details of animate organisms such as blood particles, of inanimate items such as a baseball bat, or of an event such as a sneeze. The close link between objects – and not subjects – and their images, what I call 'object-images', in *CSI* is usually visualised in close-ups of interior sites. Whilst evidence is treated within a framework of positivism in *CSI*, and even though subjects – or rather traces of subjects – are objectified, the objects that make up the 'CSI-shots' are simulated and visually subjectified. They are not depicted from an external position, but from a site of interiority, even though they represent objective evidence.

The subjective point-of-view of the eyewitness is replaced by the macro-shots of object interiority. Whereas a shot of, for instance, a train going through a tunnel is a metaphor that merits a psychoanalytical reading, in *CSI* no language stands in for objects. Instead of a psychological, invisible subjectivity, interiority is visualised more literally. Subjectivity is materialised in prosthetic or simulated tracking shots traversing the insides of arteries or drainpipes. The introspection is not geared towards the mind, but literally delves into, for example, an ear. In the '*CSI*-shot', it is the image that travels sometimes literally with a periscope camera penetrating an artificial body in what *CSI*'s Visual Effects Supervisor Larry Detwiller calls a 'prosthetic event' (2004), but most likely through a combination of different simulations and reconstructions, both computer generated and indexical. Medical and forensic dramas have accentuated the proximity to interiority by being predominantly set not only indoors, in the operating theatre, the autopsy room or the laboratory, but also by their preoccupation with the body's interiors. So far, *CSI* has driven this impulse of interiority furthest, with the images depicting not only the inside of the visible body, but the inside of what is invisible in the body, travelling down the natural body canals for food or blood. In their quest to go 'where no camera has gone before', as *CSI*'s CG Supervisor from Stargate Digital (Hatton 2004) declares, the *CSI* starship reaches new microscopic galaxies of the interior.

Television has fostered telescoping both in the metaphorical sense of taking an event or a detail out of its discursive and historical context, as well as literally in the form of the close-up. The close-up epitomised television with a linkage between the cosiness of the private space and the intimacy of the frame (Jacobs 2000). The close-up in early television personified intimacy as it usually tightly framed the face. It has been identified with realism and emotional closeness even if the intimacy of the televisual close-up was deemed to be 'one that is always observational'. In contrast to the cinematic close-up, which elicits identification, on television we observe a mind, but do not identify with it (ibid: 118). The observational, not simulation, was associated with the microscopic (ibid: 130).

In *CSI*, by contrast, the microscopic close-up is associated with scientific distance instead of intimacy and with stylisation in the place of realism. In line with the properties of the televisual, *CSI* takes details out of their context and enlarges them. These, however, are smaller, material and essentially invisible segments, rather than the larger, visible, units of a whole face or even an event. Jason Jacobs located an 'intimacy of scale' with few characters and reduced crews in early television (ibid: 129). The connection between the small and intimacy has been disconnected in *CSI*. What we cannot get 'intimate' with, even as we get close to them, are, after all, corpuscles. *CSI* pushes the disappearance of distance associated with television to its limits by visualising the invisible.

The shot of the otherwise invisible detail in *CSI* works in a similar way to a telescope designating a viewpoint in a landscape (even if the scenery is visible to our unaided eye, and particles are not). There, perhaps, the site only becomes attractive to us as tourists because something is made visible that we would not be able to see naturally. What used to be the close-up of a face in television promising access to emotions promises access to knowledge in *CSI*. A face as an expressive whole does not reveal any evidence, but a speck of dust does. The materials have 'stolen' the televisual close-up. The sight of the internal detail gives us, as tourists of knowledge, the impression of insight. The short glimpses of an internal view have to be mastered by the mind. If this is a spectacle of the detail, it is one that triggers the desire to grasp what exactly it is we are seeing, not merely to indulge in visual pleasure. With *CSI*, knowledge has a glossy aesthetic, simulation makes up evidence, the invisible assumes visibility, the internal is externalised, and object subjectivity replaces the subject's psychological perspective.

:14:

MAC'S MELANCHOLIA

Scripting Trauma, 9/11 and Bodily Absence in *CSI: NY*
JANET McCABE

Empty sky, empty sky
I woke up this morning to an empty sky.
'Empty Sky', Bruce Springsteen from *The Rising*

Detective Mac Taylor will not rest. So dedicated is he to duty, the integrity of the crime lab he leads, the New York City denizens he serves, that he cannot slumber. Personally anguished, almost manically obsessed with tracking down the serial killer who 'locks in' his victims – bodies paralysed, left only to dream – he does not sleep a wink the entire pilot episode. It soon transpires, though, that his insomnia is not the price paid for determination, but lingering grief for the wife he lost in the Twin Towers on 11 September 2001.

Confessing his exhaustion to Jane Doe (Jewel Christian), Mac tells how his wife Claire perished on 9/11. ('No one had seen it coming.') How he had thrown out everything that reminded him of her. Too painful. Except a beach ball she had blown up. 'One thing I couldn't throw away was that beach ball,' he says. 'Her breath was still in there.' Enough said. Leaving the Angel of Mercy Hospital, he hails a cab. The lights of the city that never sleeps reflect in the taxi window. Mac looks out. Mournful, tormented – shattered. An aerial view follows him out of the car and up to the Ground Zero site. Profile shot as the camera comes alongside him. His face pained. Hand showing his gold band rests on the fencing. His body crucified. Three shots abruptly pull back. The yawning abyss – of unbearable grief, of aching loss, of cavernous space. Panning up into the vast, empty night sky.

Extraordinary.

After six seasons speculating on the chemistry between Gil Grissom and Sara Sidle, and three seasons wondering what the deal is with Horatio Caine and his supposedly dead brother, I am overwhelmed to know so much about Mac so soon.

But that's it. Personal details become sparse, doled out sparingly, if at all, from here on in.

So why so much so soon?

This chapter contends that *CSI: NY* is based on the founding trauma of an absent body; and the

series – formulaic narrative, generic patterns, aesthetic forms, thematic concerns, cultural politics, industrial conditions – participates in rituals of re-remembering and forgetting 9/11. At the same time, it *is* a melancholic text, constituting a space verbosely concerned with trauma and recovery. Bodily absence tangles with the public stories and cultural memories of those traumatic events in September 2001; and, in its obsession with wanting to know *everything* about the corpse in establishing truth and restoring order (until the next episode at least), the *CSI* franchise is bound up in this complex cultural work. But, in setting the latest *CSI* spin-off in the city where so many lives were lost, and where attempts to make sense of the impact of such a catastrophic event fraught with intense grief, *CSI: NY* endlessly repeats personal (and social) trauma involving the body and recuperation. Guided by recent thinking on the ways in which new media technologies respond to and make sense of contemporary history, and indebted to screen debates on trauma, I consider how *CSI: NY* puts trauma and recovery into a discourse for a post-9/11 America – why these stories and why tell them now (Elsaesser 2001).

9/11 AND TELEVISION

9/11 occurred in the modern era of digital and satellite electronic media, making it technologically possible for a global (rather than primarily national) audience to watch the north and south towers of the World Trade Center collapse in real time. People around the world 'experienced' 9/11 as it happened – instantaneous and 'live' – through the medium of television; and those television images have turned out to be central to the history of 9/11 and how it is remembered.

Frank P. Tomasulo, describing our increasing reliance on technologically mediated evidence to describe and 'authenticate' contemporary history, argues that 'our concepts of historical referentiality (what happened), epistemology (how we know it happened) and historical memory (how we interpret it and what it means to us) are now determined primarily by media imagery' (1996: 70). Academic thinking on how real-life events are created and made sense of *in* and *through* media forms and imagery builds on a historical and media scholarship influenced by post-structuralist formulations, deconstructionism and Derridean analysis. Such work seeks to theoretically prove that no historical realities and 'facts' exist beyond a field of visual mediation and other mediating discourse. No historical event simply exists, but instead it is 'written' into a discourse, or what Hayden White (1978) has called 'emplotment' – a form of historical storytelling in which a narrative is imposed on actual historical occurrences. In one sense, the narrative of 9/11 was 'written' before it happened; it was inscribed, for example, in Hollywood disaster movies, from *The Towering Inferno* (1974) to *Die Hard* (1988) and *Die Hard 2: Die Harder* (1990). Emerging from the rubble was a discourse of American heroism, of courageous individuals battling Armageddon, of ordinary folk made exceptional by extraordinary circumstances. Argued here is how, to some extent, a narrative was imposed on 9/11 as it occurred, but, and more importantly, it is in and through discourse – its rhetoric, language, aesthetics – used to complement and/or revise reality that we understand and 'experience' the event.

Never before has such a colossal historical moment happened on the doorstep of major broadcasting corporations. The simple fact that cameras were ubiquitous and the entire globe *was* watching the live coverage provided by the main satellite and network broadcasting companies confirms to a large extent what Guy Debord said about how a technological culture 'experiences' its historical time as if 'everything that was lived directly has moved away into a representation' (1983: 1). Viewing quotidian historical events on television – as they happen in real time, not long after they have taken place, and/or replayed over again – may lead to what Thomas Elsaesser has described as 'a new authenticity … in the making' (1999: 6). When we say we remember, he argues, are we not really saying that we remember watching it on the TV, 'until we could no longer tell the television screen from our retinas' (ibid.)? Suggested here is how contemporary media culture often transforms momentous 'historical' events into spectatorial 'experiences' determining individual subjectivity in relation to them.

Considering the role of television in the 'constructive process of histories' (1997: 6), Marita Sturken claims:

> Television is coded, like all electronic technology, as immediate and live. It is about the instant present, in which information is more valuable the more quickly we get it, the more immediate it is. *Television allows for an immediate participation in the making of history; it produces 'instant history'*. When television images become 'historic' images ... *they retain some of the cultural meaning of electronic technology, connoting the instant and the ephemeral*. Their low resolution, slightly blurred quality allows them to retain a sense of immediacy, *as if they were presenting the unfolding of history* rather than its image set in the past (125; emphasis mine).

Highly portable imaging technology, from professional camera portapacks and personal camcorders to digital cameras and mobile phones, gave 9/11 'a shape, an identity, and a texture' (Elsaesser 1996: 146). It created in effect a kind of electronic vérité. Raw, uninterrupted footage, long-take aesthetics (sporadically disrupted by out-of-focus images) and single, continuous shots (sometimes filming nothing, with often only disembodied voices and/or sounds audible) created a strong sense that the spatio-temporal continuum was somehow being preserved – the photo-realist style, in fact, championed by André Bazin (1967; 1971) which communicates historical temporality most closely related to our perception of lived experience.

Each piece of film, every single still photograph, is assumed to offer fragments of clues to what happened that day. But in ceaselessly replaying and endlessly dissecting filmed and photographic images, as if each holds within them some definitive answer as to why and how what happened did, and in continuously presenting and re-presenting the historical trauma, the media resists closure for the historical narrative. Taking this idea a step further, Elsaesser reasons that film and electronic media images may actually prevent us from being able to stop obsessing about an event: 'an activity closer to therapeutic practice has taken over, with acts of re-telling, remembering and repeating all pointing in the direction of obsession, fantasy, trauma' (1996: 146).

Whereas the electronic vérité has *become* the event, and with the very materiality of mass media and its take on history, according to Elsaesser, inhibiting closure, the experiential impact of what was captured in images troubles and even forecloses meaning. No public inquiry, no television commentary, no print media in fact, can adequately explain the raw footage precisely because the narrative of national trauma and emotional loss overshadows any empirical attempts to do so. The instant the American Airlines Flight 11 ploughed into the north tower, a chance moment caught on a FDNY training video, is what has become scripted as the moment when a nation changed, when America went from being formidable, impenetrable and secure to being vulnerable, infiltrated and mutilated.

'History is *not* a text, not a narrative, master or otherwise,' argues Fredric Jameson. 'History is what hurts' (1981: 35, 102). Irrevocable loss – bodies obliterated, never recovered – has prolonged national mourning, plunging the American nation into a profound state of melancholia. As a psychological category, melancholia is a form of narcissism; it is the depression caused when the lost object was loved as a mirror of the self. Perhaps it is plausible to link melancholia with its return in contemporary American television fictions like *CSI: NY*. In accordance with Venziano's theory of quantum physics that Mac Taylor applies to his investigations, 'Everything is connected.' Mac's nightly vigil may explicitly reference the public rituals of mourning the dead,[1] but my interest rather is with how melancholia is inscribed *in* and *through* the *CSI: NY* text as it ceaselessly repeats trauma and recovery. The central issue for me is to account for why *now* this television text – its aesthetics, its forms, who utters it (and the positions and viewpoints from which the protagonists speak); the institutions (both in and beyond the text) that prompt it; and how it 'puts into discourse' (Foucault 1998: 11) trauma involving that which refuses easy representation, textual blockages, and the compulsive need/pleasure to repeat driving the series and the *CSI* franchise.

CONVERSATIONS WITH THE DEAD (1):
TRAUMA THEORY AND RECOVERY

E. Ann Kaplan, extending Sigmund Freud's 'linking of trauma to fantasy', argues that at certain historical moments particular aesthetic forms emerge 'to accommodate fears and fantasies related to ... historical events' (2001: 202, 203). Focusing primarily on melodrama, and understanding this generic formation as repeating the traumas of both class and gender struggle, she argues that 'melodrama would, in its very generic formation, constitute a traumatic cultural symptom ... [and that,] taken up by cinema, it arguably continued to repeat, while concealing cultural traumas too painful to confront directly' (ibid.). Could we not say that *CSI: NY* recycles a diverse range of media memories to perform a comparable task? It makes sense that certain generic traces, narrative evocations and aesthetic residues become displaced forms, turning trauma into television fantasy, 'where it could be more safely approached or remembered but also forgotten, in the peculiar manner of trauma' (Kaplan 2001: 202).

Series creator Anthony E. Zuiker decided on New York as the home for his newest *CSI* 'because he had never shaken the memory of how moved and impressed he was "watching the fortitude of New Yorkers after 9/11"' (Carter 2004: S13, 4). It is said that he wanted 'to exploit New York's deep

potential for storylines, including the lingering effect of September 11 on the city's police' (Guzman 2002: 37). I am reminded here of arguments made by Alison Landsberg, who describes the ways in which the somatic properties of the mass media enable people to experience, as memories, events in a 'personal, bodily way' (1997: 75), to produce 'sensations' which 'might actually install in individuals' "symptoms" through which they didn't actually live, but to which they subsequently have a kind of experiential relationship' (1996: 23). What intrigues me is Zuiker's comment about how the 'sensations' he experienced while watching the coverage created the empathetic identification that inspired the show, as does what he could not forget as a consequence. It is not the 9/11 of visceral spectacle and the 'unseen' – its horrors, its real human bodies – but of redemptive narrative involving stoical New Yorkers struggling to keep going in a fractured and traumatised city that lingers long in his mind; and it is this recovery of the living amidst death that CSI: NY brings to the television screen.

Marita Sturken usefully claims that 'those who have lived through traumatic public events testify through the very presence of their bodies ... to the materiality of memory' (1997: 12). CSI: NY opens with a montage sequence evidently meant to bookend the closing one described above. A smouldering red sun dawns over Manhattan. Landmarks like the Empire State and Chrysler buildings are visible; but the cityscape bears the unmistakable gash left by the collapse of the Twin Towers. Three abrupt edits disrupt the aerial panning shots of Gotham, before focusing on a church nestled between the skyscrapers. Viewed from the air its distinctive cruciform floor plan is discernible. Dissolve to a Madonna's head; cut to Mac Taylor. Alone and pained, he is clearly a troubled soul. His mobile phone rings. He is called away from the solitude of pious meditation, leaving his sanctuary and driving into the new day. A young woman's body has been found. Initial inspection reveals she was dumped. Picking up her cold, dead hand, he spots her wedding band. Wearily he rises. Looking out, and with grim anguish, he says, 'Someone out there is missing a wife.' Panning around, the camera reveals the Brooklyn Bridge and the scarred Manhattan skyline. Disparate bodies – a statue of the Madonna, a female corpse, bodies obliterated – may not yet make sense. (The true trauma is revealed later, and then *only* through viewing the entire episode.) Whatever else, for now Mac is established as the subject position of bearing witness to crimes committed against the body. If, as Michel Foucault has said, 'the injury that a crime inflicts upon the social body is the disorder that it introduces into it' (1991: 92), then does it not follow that Mac, invested by societal law, will not rest until order is restored? He cannot – will not, in fact – forget the harm done here. Credits roll.

This is not the first time we have met Mac Taylor. Leaving the shimmering golden tones of Miami, Horatio Caine heads for New York in the CSI: Miami crossover episode ('MIA/NYC Nonstop', 2:23) on the trail of a killer who has inexplicably slain a middle-aged couple. (After all, Horatio did make a promise to their daughter.) Residues of 9/11 toxins found in phlegm at the crime scene have led him to a seedy apartment in the Bowery where an undercover cop is found dead and his identity

missing. The first exchange between Mac and Horatio immediately
evokes a much longer history of the lone troubled male hero.

Horatio: Caine. Miami. I'm investigating a double murder.

Mac: Mac Taylor. New York City Crime Lab. Detective
              First Grade. I'm listening.

No small coincidence that media traces of the *noir* detective, internally
divided and intensely, almost manically, committed to the job, can be
found in their representational DNA. Unattached, and engaged in grim
work that condemns them to a solitary life, these forensic criminologists,
like their filmic and television predecessors, are single-minded in their
dedication to 'the unravelling of obscure crimes' (Houseman 1946-1947:
162). Given the 'cultural and historical "relevance"' of the 1940s male
figures who were derived, argues Frank Krutnik, 'from the ways in which
they served as a generically-regulated response to the various upheavals
of the wartime and postwar era' (2004: xiii), it seems to me, at least, no
surprise that this male type again becomes 'relevant' at another moment
of historical trauma and cultural transformation.

Gone, however, are the days when these protagonists are 'alienated
from the culturally permissible (or ideal) parameters of masculine
identity, desire and achievement' (ibid.). Desire maybe, but not identity,
and certainly not achievement. No longer does the hero exist on the
margins of the law; he is, in fact, always inside the law and subject to its
strict rules, codes and procedures: he *is* the law and often quite literally
lays it down. Whereas the 1940s private detective had, according to John
Houseman, 'no discernable ideal to sustain him – neither ambitions, nor
loyalty, nor even a lust for wealth' (1946-1947: 162), his latest television
incarnation is as an honourable public servant fuelled by a strident moral
mission to find answers for victims of violent crime. Season Two, and
Mac discovers that Aiden Burn has broken a seal on the evidence bag
related to the Regina Bowen (Elizabeth Ann Bennett) rape case ('Grand
Murder at Central Station', 2:2). He tells her that there are three things
he will defend at any cost: 'the honour of this country, the safety of this
city and the integrity of this lab'. Handling evidence is a solemn trust.
Lives hang in the balance. Never mind that she did not actually tamper
with the evidence. She broke the seal. She broke faith. She's dismissed.
Post-9/11 America has no room for negligence and a shoddy disregard
for exacting procedure. It is largely as a force of legal justice – but, more

importantly, moral idealism – which Mac, as an honest patriot and as someone who accepts this responsibility as a sacred duty, is invested, and from which his power to discipline derives its source, justification and rules. It is *his* power to judge and punish that banishes Aiden to narrative purgatory. (Only for her to reappear as a corpse, burnt beyond recognition in 'Heroes' (2:23).)

Scientifico-legal procedures for managing the formless evidence are key to justifying intervention and the legitimate right to do so. It gives the crime lab final responsibility; and it allows Mac and his team to take custody of the cadaver and absorb it into various procedures of knowledge – of empirical scientific evidence, of the law and judicial system, of a television narrative. What prevails is the absolute conviction in the ability of science, the technology, the forensics – the autopsy, DNA sequencing, 'polymerase chain reaction' (a process that allows for small amounts of DNA to be cloned), toxicology, trace evidence – to render all human remains identifiable. (And, certainly, the real New York CSI crime lab has 'continued to deal with the burden of 9/11' [Hayes 2004: 38].) Standing grimly over the female corpse found in Brooklyn Heights, Mac tells Dr Sheldon Hawkes: 'I want to know everything about this woman' ('Blink', 1:1). He means it. This dead body, as do the others on a weekly basis, enters into powerful scientifico-legal machinery that endlessly makes it subject to meticulous observation, infinitesimal analyses and perpetual examination. 'No crime committed must escape the gaze of those whose task it is to dispense justice,' wrote Foucault (1991: 96). Scene after scene has the team painstakingly going over the evidence. From the gross exam to peering through the comparison microscope, nothing goes undetected or unseen. Such processes involve an empirical gaze; rituals of observation that make it possible to take charge of, take possession of as it were, the body by a discourse that seeks to permit it no anonymity, no secrets.

CSI bodies speak volumes about the crime; but they are only ever an 'effect and object of power, as an effect and object of knowledge' (Foucault 1991: 192) over which someone else has the right to speak about them. The examination leaves behind it a mass of documentation constituting a detailed narrative. Accumulating evidence, marshalling what is fragmented and incomplete, allows Mac to organise it and project a story onto it. Constructing a fixed narrative of what occurred, in fact, works far more efficiently when its agents are no longer alive, allowing for narratives of completion to stand. Identifying the deluded Russian, Dr Bogdhan Ivanov (Vitali Baganov), as responsible for locking in one female victim, and unintentionally killing the others, Mac confronts him over the interrogation table. Faces appear out of the sepia gloom, shot in profile, as Ivanov must admit his offence against these women's bodies, against the social body – he is nothing less than a 'monster'. Mac reconstructs the crime using DNA evidence as irrefutable proof. He talks of lost innocence and trust betrayed. Science imposes a Manichean order over narrative proceedings; and the binaries of a past cold-war geopolitics – America vs. Russia; good vs. evil; democratic justice vs. totalitarian wickedness – are re-remembered and replayed in the present.

Week after week, files containing pathology reports and forensic evidence are slammed on the table: case closed, end of story. E. Ann Kaplan has written that 'The repetition of certain stories may betray a traumatic cultural symptom ... closure, seals over the traumatic ruptures and breaks that the culture endured' (2001: 203). From one week to the next, the same drama is destined to be played out over and over again. Homicide may be random, shockingly brutal, sudden even, but the investigation is predictably routine. Embedded right into the procedures – of empirical science, of forensic police investigation, of the television serial format – as they are used, is an enabling discourse aiming to master trauma committed against real bodies as well as the social body at large. Its intent may establish the truth about a murder, identifying its perpetrator, but pleasure comes from seeing the strict exercise of scientifico-legal power – nothing evades it, nothing can resist it – to restore order; as Zuiker said, his aim for *CSI: NY* was to 'capture the essence of human drama by showing *American heroes who work very hard to bring peace of mind and closure to survivors*' (Hayes 2004: 38; emphasis added).

CONVERSATIONS WITH THE DEAD (2): MELANCHOLIA, LATENCY, FORGETTING

CSI is a franchise for our post-9/11 times. It has no truck with ambiguity, with the grey areas of moral relativism. Only clean, neat and unequivocal resolutions are acceptable. Parallel possibilities of how the crime *could* have been committed are offered to the viewer before being briskly and categorically closed down by the irrefutable scientific evidence. So indisputable is the data, so incontrovertible the proof, that the person behind the murder has little choice but to admit their guilt. When presented with the DNA evidence, for example, Ivanov sings like a canary. He immediately admits to having a sexual relationship with Zoya Pavlova (Ana Alexander) and to his dastardly medical experiments. He isn't the only one. Why try to lie when forensics will establish the 'truth' beyond any reasonable doubt? But what lurks beneath this obsession for justice, this fixation with the sacred honour of handling evidence, this absolute belief in the science to bring about resolute closure? In short: does not this text protest too much?

Each episode (similar to others in the franchise) is highly ritualised and self-contained, making carryover storylines difficult while lending broadcasters much needed scheduling flexibility. Ironclad scientific evidence may bring about absolute narrative closure, but there is something intriguing, troubling even, in the compulsive drive to weekly repeat trauma and recovery that, in turn, leads to particular forms of remembrance and forgetting in *CSI: NY*. Describing contemporary historical events as essentially 'modernist', Hayden White writes that 'modernist techniques of representation' (1996: 32) better provide depictions for events so unprecedented in scale that historians and the public at large find them difficult to 'master'. Extending White's premise still further, Thomas Elsaesser claims that the very properties of audio-visual media may, in fact, be responsible for preventing closure and triggering symptoms in the spectator, 'of the memory of events which live in the culture because of images they have left ... too painful to recall, too disturbing not to remember' (1996b: 146).

Susannah Radstone (2000) insightfully claims that memory takes specific forms at particular historical moments, principally as a means of making visible, and keeping in check, specific ambivalences and slippages concerned with identity and cultural values. In recent times, she argues, equivocations have become manifest in fabrications, subjectivity and fantasy. I am reminded of the *CSI: Miami* crossover episode, in which viewers watch as melancholia descends over the *CSI* aesthetics. Crushed blue hues replace the dazzling golden brightness of Miami; and New York is transformed into another fantasy-scape, this time of nostalgia and menace, of 'silvery buildings and silvery air, the city a grid of pale skyscrapers and dark canyons' (Hayes 2004: 39). *CSI: NY* is invested in an idea of New York City that draws as much upon a repertoire of past mediated media memories – notably, the brooding atmospherics of 1940s *film noir*, the gritty realism of a longer television history of procedural police dramas as well as the apocalyptic spectacle of recent disaster movies like *The Day After Tomorrow* (2004) – as it does upon creating new ones. Made visible here is a city of aftermath, a place where survivors are left and the spectre of unfathomable loss still looms large. A cool palette of ice blues, dull browns, metallic silvers and slate greys give a visceral quality to the urban gloom. It is an experiential landscape, a *mise-en-scène*, in fact, of profound mourning and melancholy the viewer feels possessed by. Abrupt edits and virtual traces replace the spatio-temporal continuum of 9/11, conveying a broken and fractured dreamscape; and beguiling aesthetics and television fantasy supplant electronic *vérité*. *CSI: NY* thus appears engaged in putting in place a new consensus for remembering (and forgetting); and, at the same time, in repeating these images of a city permanently scarred, week in and week out makes it almost impossible for us to forget.

Despite debuting as one of the USA's top ten shows in September 2004, *CSI: NY* started to lose its audience. Ratings became as bleak as the grim storylines and the harsh New York City streets. 'We were going much too dark in the tone of the show, too aggressively, and there's no doubt we lost some viewers in that patch,' show's creator Zuiker is reported to have said in response to the plummeting figures (Healy 2005: E1). Giving his account of why *CSI: NY* was failing in *The New York Times*, Patrick Healy wrote, 'The multiple homicides, the gore, the spectre of terrorism, the blue tint in daytime scenes and the pitch black night ones all cast a melancholy spell over the city and the show's lead detective Mack (sic) Taylor ... whose wife was killed in the twin towers' (ibid.). In short: it all got too depressing for prime-time. Edicts apparently came down from top CBS executives, asking the programme-makers to literally lighten up: 'Go beyond the dark underbelly of downtown and capture more colourful and vibrant tales of the city' (ibid.).

Season Two finds the team moving out of their dismal, subterranean offices, and away from the pristine chapel morgue with its white subway tiles and crotch-vaulted ceilings, into modern, light and airy new premises. Sheldon Hawkes, who in the aftermath of 9/11 had apparently taken to sleeping in the morgue – a room filled with death – leaves the medical examiner's office to join the team out in the field; and Mac loses the tie and starts sporting open necked shirts, and even goes on a date. No more talk of 9/11; and ratings start to stabilise.

Maybe so, but I am prompted here by what Marita Sturken has said about how 'cultures can also participate in a "strategic" forgetting of painful events that may be too dangerous to keep in active memory' (1997: 7). Is this turning away not an example of what Milan Kundera called 'organised forgetting' (quoted in ibid.), and does not trauma keep returning but in displaced and/or re-remembered forms?

YOU MUST REMEMBER THIS:
9/11, DISPLACEMENT AND RESOLUTION

At Season Two's end, Mac and Detective Don Flack attend a homicide in the West Village ('Charge of this Post', 2: 24). Soon after entering a multi-storey office block on the trail of clues, an enormous explosion shakes the building, blowing out windows and doors, and filling the street with ominous plumes of dark smoke. Recovered memories of his time in the military, when a bomb destroyed the US Marine barracks in Beirut, are re-remembered when Flack sustains life-threatening injuries. Mac is forced to tie off a major arterial bleeder in the detective's chest with a shoelace, repeating a procedure he had performed on a wounded soldier years before. Mac may have lost someone in Beirut, but he does not want to lose someone else in New York City. Memories of past traumas are relived and re-remembered in the present day as the deluded Dean Lessing's (Eion Bailey) rejection from the military sends him on a bombing spree of the city. Lessing may be insane but his warning is stark: New York remains vulnerable; law enforcement agencies are not ready; and America must be vigilant.

It is not too much of a leap to suggest that this relatively unspecified Middle Eastern skirmish remembered by Mac is a displacement for the conflict in the Gulf (and the failure to resolve the first Gulf War is widely seen as precipitating 9/11). When this episode aired in 2006, America had been fighting in Iraq for three years. It was no longer the shock-and-awe campaign of the first Persian Gulf War; it was, instead, increasingly looking uncomfortably reminiscent of Vietnam. It seems clear that what is lost to Mac – his colleague, his capability for saving lives, his ability to bring closure – is symptomatic of a displacement of a greater loss: the displacement of that which can hardly be named, those who perished in 9/11. Flack's recovery may go some way to resolving the past losses Mac has sustained, and his recuperation may bring resolute closure to both the episode and the second season, but Mac's wife remains lost, as does Aiden. Given that different versions of what is lost are deeply inscribed into the very media forms used, it is impossible not to remember and re-remember each week. 9/11 is not easily forgotten – it haunts the *CSI: NY* text as much as it does our media-mediated cultural imaginings; and besides, the franchise needs trauma to continue.

Media participate in fast confining any historical event to the past; and in this regard *CSI: NY* is no different. But it does, at the same time, participate in remembering 9/11; and a television text is once again central to the making of that history. Returning to where I began, Ground Zero: the *CSI: NY* production team were the first to be granted permission to film at the site after the tragedy. The footage of Mac walking up to Ground Zero taken at night, filmed in 2004, is another site of remembrance; its slippery integration of fantasy, invention and the real creates a media memory of what the site looked like that night in 2004. Given that Ground Zero is forever changing, always transforming, as the rebuilding continues, the closing moments of the pilot emerge as a form of commemoration capturing a specific moment lost in time.

... And melancholia once again descends over the text as it embeds itself in the form.

:V:
DNA
Industry and Reception

:15:

FIVE'S FINEST

The Import of *CSI* to British Television
SIMONE KNOX

INTRODUCTION

In common with other US television programmes of recent years that have been grouped under the (admittedly loose) label of 'quality television', such as *ER*, *The Sopranos* and *Desperate Housewives*, the forensics crime drama *CSI: Crime Scene Investigation* enjoys commercial success on a global scale. Similarly, the *CSI* franchise has been attracting scholarly attention, such as the present collection, for its distinctive visual style, issues of representation and the programme's production and consumption contexts. While these are important approaches, I will use a different methodology in this chapter, to explore how, within their global success, US imports like *CSI* are distributed, broadcast and consumed within specific television channels, broadcasting contexts and countries, eventually entering debates within scholarly discourse. Like other scholarly work on US television programmes, this collection is itself situated within a British context, featuring contributors – myself included – largely from British academic institutions; thus, the experience of watching *CSI* first as an import on British television, rather than on its US home network CBS, is likely to be at the heart of this volume.

To point out that US programmes on British television are imports might seem unnecessary, but it is an important, and frequently unacknowledged, distinction, because it means that audiences (including scholars) in the USA and Britain are dealing with different dimensions of a television programme's manifold identities. The 'CSI' we consume and receive in Britain is not exactly the same as the CSI as it appears in other countries (including the USA), marked as they are by particular distribution and broadcasting processes, including those concerning acquisition policies and practices, as well as the scheduling, promotion and reception of imports within specific national television cultures. I want to unpick the CSI that appears on British television (especially terrestrial channel Five) and explore its macro-textual role as an important US import on British television (see also Rixon 2003). I choose the term 'macro-textual' rather than the perhaps more obvious 'extra-textual', because extra-textual unhelpfully implies something outside of and surplus to 'the text', and I mean to move away from the notion of an imported programme as a discrete text or 'programme proper' (Gripsrud 1995: 131–33). Not only is the imported programme part of particular trans-national broadcasting contexts and processes, but these are also part of the imported programme: as this chapter will explore, CSI is not simply exported (and thus becomes part of these processes), but is produced to be exported and exportable; thus these processes are part of, and shape, CSI from the very beginning.

What also motivates this chapter is the struggle that the academic study of television in Britain has experienced in addressing the presence, role and significance of imported US television programmes for British television. As Paul Rixon remarks, 'It is as if domestically made programmes are British television while American programmes are mere interlopers.' (2003: 49) With much mass media discourse traditionally concerned with cultural imperialism and Americanisation, Television Studies is slowly shifting towards addressing how US imports might form a part of British television's institutional processes, production practices and reception contexts. This shift needs to be encouraged and furthered because, if the focus within the study of British television were to remain so exclusively on British productions, the very real success and significance of US imports like CSI to recent British television would be in danger of being overlooked in future work on British television around the turn of the millennium.

IMPORT/EXPORT SCENE INVESTIGATION

I will begin by looking at the particular processes and practices that came into play when CSI became available as a potential import at the international television market in 2000. The international television market consists of several annual events at which new programming is sold and bought, co-productions are set up and partnerships consolidated. The key trade shows include MIP-TV and MIPCOM (both held in Cannes), as well as the US counterparts, NATPE and the LA Screenings, which focus more strictly on US product. At an event like the ten-day LA Screenings, several hundred overseas programme buyers get their first chance to view the pilots of the new autumn prime-time shows that major studios and independent production companies are producing for US television. It hardly seems surprising that, when the CSI pilot was screened at the event in May 2000, the series proved to be an attractive proposition. CSI has pedigree credentials: Jerry Bruckheimer's attachment as executive producer not only brings a reassuring track record of success – his credits include films such as *Beverly Hills Cop* (1984), *Top Gun* (1986) and *Enemy of the State* (1998) – but in particular promises high production values and the slickness of Hollywood for the smaller screen of television. This is certainly fulfilled by CSI in a number of ways. In terms of casting, CSI offers a film star in the lead role (*Manhunter*'s William Petersen) and several actors known from quality television shows in the ensemble cast (e.g. *ER* and *China Beach*'s Marg Helgenberger, and *ER* and *The West Wing*'s Jorja Fox); a format that has been followed by the CSI spin-offs. CSI's high production profile and quality aspirations show themselves especially in the programme's glossy *mise-en-scène*. That this should make CSI attractive to British buyers, because it is something that British productions usually do not and/or cannot compete with, is encapsulated within the following press article comparing one of the CSI spin-offs to a British crime drama:

> CSI: Miami [...] opened with a widescreen shot of David Caruso
> bombing around the Florida Everglades on a hovercraft,
> wearing designer shades and a nice suit. *Murder in Mind* [...]
> opened with a close-up of Gary Kemp snuggling down under
> a blue floral duvet. There you have the difference between
> American and British crime dramas in a nutshell. (Smith 2003)

The high production values and cinematic slickness of CSI not only work to make it a desirable buy, as they tend to attract sought-after audience groups, but also signal that CSI, as noted earlier, is produced to be exportable. Producers of US television are aware that this slickness gives them an advantage internationally and is expected by overseas buyers. Simultaneously, however, US producers are only able to produce (and undertake the financial risk involved in) such expensive programming, because, as Fletcher (2004) suggests, it is underwritten by both national syndication and international exportation. This is thus a circular process, in that the very thing that helps to export the US programme is also that which makes it dependent on exporting.

With this sketch of some of *CSI's* textual qualities, it seems straightforward that *CSI* would have appeared an attractive proposition for overseas, including British, buyers. However, this is complicated by (1) *CSI* being only one of thirty new shows showcased at the LA Screenings that year; (2) that *CSI* was not bought for British television for several months; and (3) that, when *CSI* was eventually bought, it was not by one of the established competitors for US imports. In May 2000, *CSI* was presented to overseas buyers alongside fifteen drama and fourteen comedy programmes, including the dramas *Boston Public*, *Dark Angel*, *Deadline*, *Freedom*, *The Fugitive*, *The Lone Gunmen*, *Madigan Men*, *Special Unit 2*, *The Street* and *Titans*. As the relative obscurity of many of these programme titles suggests, most of these (then newly launched) offerings did not go on to achieve export success. The question is then why it was *CSI* that would become such a success? This question is not an idle one, given that many of the discussed textual reasons for the attractiveness of *CSI* are also evident in several of these programmes. For example, several have pedigree credentials in the form of producers with successful track records (e.g. *Deadline* was executive produced by *Law & Order's* Dick Wolf), Hollywood connections (e.g. *Freedom* was executive produced by *Lethal Weapon's* Joel Silver), starry casts (e.g. Gabriel Byrne in *Madigan Men*), and high production values (e.g. *Special Unit 2* reportedly had 'a *Men in Black*-like visual feel' [Guider 2000]).

Most of these programmes did not become successful imports because, for a number of contextual reasons, they were not (deemed) successful (enough) on US television in the first place, and were thus cancelled or not renewed. This is another possibly obvious, but important, distinction, the consequences of which need to be untangled. US imports have a dual status of being both programmes in their home market and imports in foreign television landscapes, with their success as imports being – at a very basic level – dependent on their success in the US, which, despite extensive development and audience research, remains a volatile market with a high turnover of shows. However, in May 2000, all of the newly presented programmes were 'equal' in the sense that they had promising attributes and had not yet failed in the USA. Therefore, it is likely that several of these shows were bought by overseas (including British) buyers, before they were pulled in the US, and that the leftover fragments of these shows were then not broadcast by the importing channel. This idea of 'invisible television', that British television is host to a number of failed US programmes that are bought but not shown, presents a methodological challenge, as its presence lies in its absence and thus beyond direct accessibility; tantalising ghostly traces marking British television through their absence.[1]

What must have been particularly reassuring about *CSI* as regards the dual challenge of success at both national and international level is that the series inflects the long-established cop show genre with a focus on forensics, which no high-profile show had done since *Quincy*. These connotations of freshness and, simultaneously, of reassurance – that it was 'slightly different in the crowded genre of crime' (Ford 2006)[2] – gave *CSI* the edge over the likes of *Titans*, an Aaron Spelling soap centring on the unlikely problems of the ultra-rich, which was perceived as a throwback to Spelling's *Dynasty* years. Moreover, while most high-profile US drama series tend to have a polished look, what makes *CSI* (and, latterly, *24*) stand out is its distinctive visual style. With its use of hyper-kinetic 'snap-zooms' (Lury 2005: 44–56), *CSI*'s strong visual signature style certainly cuts through the clutter of the televisual flow and gains product differentiation in the over-supply of US programmes.[3]

Overall, what gave *CSI* an edge over its (inter)national competition and promised reassurance that it had ongoing potential, is that the show has a particular combination of textual features. However, this only makes it more surprising that *CSI* was not actually snapped up by a British buyer in 2000. That import/export processes are not as straightforward as 'an appealing programme is acquired because it is an appealing programme' needs to be understood in terms of the distinction between text and context. Whilst there are, of course, contextual factors for *CSI*'s success in the USA,[4] I will focus on the contextual reasons why and by whom *CSI* was (not) bought for British television, which concerns trade practices and market conditions of supply and demand. As Five's then-Director of Acquisitions Jeff Ford suggests: 'It's all about the environment of 2000: what was going on, who had what [and] the negotiation between buyer and seller' (2006).

Trade events like the LA Screenings also represent an opportunity for the completion of contractual agreements between sellers and buyers. These (often long-term) output deals mean that not every series is available for open bidding, potentially marked with a first refusal option, or already sold (even 'by default') as part of a wider package. Interested buyers may not be able to bid for a programme, because, within their channels' regulatory quota restrictions, their own budgets and/or schedules are already committed. While *CSI* itself was not sold as part of a deal, this certainly goes towards explaining why *CSI* was not purchased immediately, and why it was not purchased by the then main British competitors for US imports. To contextualise briefly, the current main competitors for US imports in Britain do not include the two largest broadcasters, BBC One and ITV1, which, scoring ratings success with prime-time US imports in the 1970s and 1980s, have since moved away from acquired programming (with the exception of feature films) towards using domestically produced drama in prime-time. It is the minority channels BBC Two, Channel 4 and the cable/satellite channel Sky One that have established themselves as the major competitors for US imports. For these channels, which cannot afford to fill their schedules with home-produced drama, US imports have represented a key way to establish their channel identity in an increasingly competitive and fragmented market, targeting audience groups not catered for by BBC One and ITV1. That these major competitors did not buy *CSI* is partially explained by, for example, Channel 4's expensive long-term output deal with Warner Bros. that had secured the rights for its hit programmes *Friends* and *ER* and provided them with series like *The West Wing* by default (see also Smith 1996). Thus, in 2000, Channel 4 – which was also preparing to bid for *The Simpsons* in 2002 – possibly did not have sufficient budget or scheduling space for another series with the potential of several seasons' worth of twenty-plus one-hour episodes. Similarly Sky One, which easily obtains Fox programming through its corporate connections, may already have had its schedule committed, while BBC Two, whose channel identity is not defined by access to recent US series, tends to take its time with showing imports and thus does not need much new imported programming.

The competition for US imports is also marked by increasingly narrowly targeted individual acquisition preferences. Thus, similar to their success in the USA depending on contexts of scheduling and audience demographics, US shows are selected by overseas buyers according to whether they are perceived as the right programme type for an identified scheduling slot, target audience and channel identity. Already suggesting that acquisition and scheduling are intertwined activities, this cautious 'You've got to find the right key to open the right lock' approach (distributor quoted in Westcott 2002) means that it might take longer for US programmes, such as *CSI*, to get sold (and also that *CSI* in 2000 was competing against programmes launched in previous years).[5] With BBC

One and ITV1 defining their public service commitments in such a way as to focus on bringing audiences British productions in prime-time, the major competitors BBC Two, Channel 4 and Sky One did not buy *CSI* not just because they were already tied up, but also because they may have perceived *CSI* as not fitting their particular channel needs in terms of scheduling slot, target audience and channel identity. Channel 4, for example, had established a reputation for quality US television, whereby quality was often defined by a serialised focus on characterisation (e.g. *Six Feet Under*), and, while *CSI* is quality television, its quality pertains more to its visual style (see also Bignell, forthcoming); while Sky One was, at that time, employing fantasy and sci-fi programmes to target teenage audiences.

Even for Five, a channel that had previously been unable to bid for certain US shows because of Channel 4's output deals and was not committed to any output deals itself, but was in need of a hit show, this 'right key for the right lock' approach stopped it from purchasing *CSI* immediately: Ford recalls that he thought *CSI* 'very exciting and very different in the use of camera [and that] it has a hipness to it' (Ford 2006) but, despite recognising its potential as a breakthrough show, he could not purchase *CSI* in May 2000, because Five's schedule lacked a suitable slot. It was only six months later, when Five reassessed the ratings for their Saturday night prime-time slot, that Five decided it had the 'right lock' for which *CSI* might be the 'right key', and bought it:

> When I saw *CSI*, I knew it was fantastic and that we gotta have this. [...] It was all circumstances: knowing we had to change our Saturday strategy, because it wasn't working, knowing that we had to move on and get into more series. (Ford 2006)

That *CSI* had not been purchased during this six-month interval is to be understood also in terms of the seller's perspective. Banking on *CSI*'s potential, Canadian distributor Alliance Atlantis, which co-owns *CSI* with CBS, was holding out not only for the right price,[6] but also for the right offer: while Channel 4, for example, may have considered, or even tried, buying *CSI*, it was Five who could and would promise the desired, and in Britain elusive, prime-time slot with a terrestrial broadcaster. As the then Director of Programmes, Kevin Lygo, commented: 'The reason why we got *CSI: Crime Scene Investigation* is because we told the distributor we'd look after it [...]. C4, for example, pushed *The West Wing* to a late-night slot. What we can do is air these shows at 21.00' (quoted in Lipscomb 2001).

'AMERICA'S FINEST': *CSI* ON FIVE

Having explored the key processes and practices involved in the acquisition of *CSI* for British television, I will now consider how a US import like *CSI* is used by, and functions for, a British television channel. *CSI* premiered on commercial broadcaster Five on 9 June 2001 at 9pm. Immediately noteworthy is Five's scheduling strategy in placing *CSI* in a Saturday night prime-time slot, which the *CSI* franchise has occupied ever since. When *CSI* premiered, competing programmes included a themed evening devoted to texting on BBC One, a repeat of a pop-culture nostalgia programme on BBC Two, a talent contest and a repeat of a variety special on ITV1, an edition of *Big Brother* and a repeat of a pop-culture nostalgia programme on Channel 4, as well as a youth home video show on Sky One. This line-up is indicative of how Saturday night prime-time on British television at the time was dominated by light entertainment programmes, then trendy nostalgia programmes and reality TV. With BBC One and ITV1 aiming at a broader family audience, BBC Two, Channel 4 and Sky One competed for a younger adult audience with more youthful formats. As the newest and least established terrestrial, Five's reading of the preceding Saturday schedules must have found that the opposition was playing it safe with repeats on this difficult summer weekend night, that drama, and especially US drama, was noticeable for its absence, and that certain audience groups were thus being underserved and ready to be 'peeled away'. The scheduling of *CSI* is therefore a textbook example of a 'strategic hit' (Ellis 2000), providing an attractive alternative that looked very different to the more inexpensive-to-produce light entertainment shows.[7] That Five was able to place *CSI* in this Saturday prime-time slot – a slot which had facilitated its acquisition of *CSI* – was only possible because it abandoned one of its regular film slots, around which its schedule had previously been moulded. Because its film slots had been expensive, attracted inconsistent ratings, and could not build viewer loyalty and channel identity in the same way as a long-running series, Five would ditch more of them over the subsequent years.

With the start of *CSI*'s second season in February 2002, Five cemented its Saturday slot by scheduling it back-to-back with *Law & Order* at 10pm. This long-running Emmy winner had already been shown with limited success on late-night BBC, but proved successful when paired with *CSI* on prime-time, complementing the more stylish *CSI* with its grittiness and acclaim. With *CSI*'s ratings climbing from an initial (for Five sizeable) average of 1.5 m to over 2 m and an 11 per cent audience share in Season Two, Saturday night was established as a Five cornerstone. Five's next long-term scheduling strategy was to establish a foothold on another night of the week: while *The Shield* had premiered on Sundays, Five would manage to gain entry on Tuesday evenings, when, with the start of *CSI*'s third season in January 2003, it moved *CSI* to 9pm Tuesdays (followed by new acquisition *Boomtown*) and filled the Saturday *CSI* slot with *CSI: Miami* (still followed by *Law & Order*). In this Tuesday slot, *CSI* has achieved a weekly average of over 3.5 m viewers and a 16 per cent audience share since Season Four. This strategy of 'ridgepoling' (see Saenz 2004), whereby a show from a successful block is used to 'break into' another evening's schedule, worked because *CSI*, unlike *The Shield*, was already a banker that could be relied upon to provide a ratings result for Five. With its increased acquisitions portfolio, the channel could further swap individual imports between Tuesdays and Saturdays as and when needed; however, Five always schedules the more established *CSI* (including repeats and spin-offs) first as the lead-in (Saenz 2004) to guide audiences towards new programmes such as *The Shield*, *Boomtown*, *The Lyon's Den* and *Law & Order: Criminal Intent*.[8]

Making use of a strong sense of flow marked by programme affinity, similar demographic appeal and discourses of US quality television within these strands, Five has simultaneously been using commissioned documentaries, arts shows, football, light entertainment and tea-time soaps in its schedule. The significance of this broader range of commissioned programming is that, while stripping US quality programmes gives Five shape and a channel identity, it helps it as a terrestrial broadcaster, which lacks a major prime-time British drama, to distinguish itself from narrow-casting cable channels whose schedules are stripped with US imports.

The Tuesday prime-time success suggests that Five recognised it could peel away underserved viewers from BBC One and ITV1 with US dramas at times when Channel 4 was not already doing so. With Channel 4 having established import strands on Wednesday, Friday and, intermittently, Monday nights, Five removed itself from head-to-head import competition with Channel 4, competing fruitfully against Channel 4's successful light entertainment/reality Tuesday slot (e.g. *Wife Swap* or *Ramsay's Kitchen Nightmares*) with methods similar to those Channel 4 had been using against BBC One and ITV1 for years. Perhaps more importantly, Five's successful move into Tuesday night also illustrates that *CSI* is not just successful on British television when scheduled judiciously as the only drama on Saturday nights. On Tuesdays, the (by then more established) *CSI* would regularly compete with high-profile British prime-time dramas on BBC One and ITV1, including *Red Cap*, *Cutting It* and *Bad Girls*.

That *CSI*, even when repeated, would fare well in its ratings against these British productions, some of which (e.g. *Cutting It*) are arguably glossier and aimed at younger audiences than many British productions, strongly suggests that imports like *CSI* have particular discourses of quality television and audience appeals that continue to distinguish them from British productions. Despite what BBC One and ITV1 frequently claim in order to justify not acquiring US imports for prime-time, *CSI*, shown on the least established terrestrial channel, proves US imports can compete successfully with prime-time British drama; they simply need to be handled carefully and given time to establish themselves: '[*CSI*'s success] has been five years in the coming, because Five had taken the journey and come out the other side.' (Ford 2006)

The presence of *CSI* on British television has been given further shape and meaning by Five's advertising and marketing strategies. Five marketed the initial double bill of *CSI* and *Law & Order* as 'Partners in Crime', a promotional overtness about its scheduling that suggests the intertwined nature of scheduling and promotion, and with which Five's promotion of its US imports has continued. In 2003, Five introduced the now famous 'America's Finest' campaign, whose promotional idents initially featured familiar cop imagery set in an urban context. Using muted colour schemes, prominent sound effects of police sirens and hand-held camera, these trailers for Five's crime imports contained a rawness that not only emphasised the grittier aspects of the slick *CSI* to link it with *Law & Order*, but, especially through the documentary-style use of camera, further linked Five's crime dramas to previous quality cop shows like *NYPD Blue*. Within a year, however, Five had replaced these idents with a visually much more striking promotional trailer for its 'America's Finest' campaign: it begins with a close-up of a torch flashing at the screen and then turning sideways, before a bullet is fired from it. The camera follows the bullet as it travels along the torch's beam across a background of elegant blue and green colour schemes, passing under a magnifying glass and smashing through glass plates, sending shards flying.

Referencing forensics imagery – the screen is scattered with ballistics data – this promotional trailer specifically mimics the hyper-kinetic visual signature style of *CSI*. Similar to *CSI* cutting through the televisual clutter of competing (US) programmes, this arresting trailer not only cuts through Five's own flow and draws attention to its imports, but also, by extension, together with *CSI*, helps Five cut through the televisual clutter of the multichannel environment. Underscoring that *CSI*'s discourse of quality very much concerns a visual quality, the trailer's expensive spectacularity draws attention to the promotion itself, whereby, in a circular process, the quality of the trailer both references and 'proves' the quality of CSI (as a programme that is worth investing in), as well as, by extension, the quality of Five (as a channel that is committed to, and invests in, quality US programming). Initiating this promotional strategy once it had a significant amount of CSI product on its schedules, Five ties in the programme brand of CSI with its channel identity to establish a brand identity of (visual) quality for itself.

Branding itself with discourses of (visual) quality was imperative to Five because of the channel's troubled history. Having launched in Spring 1997 with a skeleton budget of £110m as the fifth terrestrial broadcaster in the UK, Five's – then Channel 5's – initial promise of 'modern mainstream' was soon replaced by what Five's former Chief Executive Dawn Airey infamously called 'films, fucking and football'. Five's acquisition of CSI is situated in the context of the channel's move away from cheaper programming from 2000 onwards.

To explore how Five makes use of CSI for its branding, it is useful to recall the work of Janet McCabe (2000) on the use of US imports by British minority channels in the 1990s. McCabe suggests that Channel 4's institutional discourses produce programme identities for its US imports in a way that mobilises and manages specific knowledge about its imagined viewer. This argument helps to illuminate how Five gives shape to a field of knowledge about its imports and understands CSI's visual signature style in a way that asserts and renders highly visible an audience with which Five had not previously been associated; namely a quality audience. This process of mobilising knowledge about its imagined viewer is evident not only in the conspicuous trailer, but also in other promotional material, such as statements in newspaper articles, which draw attention to Five's scheduling of CSI et al. With BBC Two and Channel 4 having attracted criticism in public discourse for their treatment of US imports (e.g. sudden rescheduling and inconsistent time-slots), Five has repeatedly stressed that it takes care of its imports by giving them a regular prime-time scheduling slot. While this promise 'to put it in the right place and protect it and look after it [...] and be committed to build a show' (Ford 2006) is one of the reasons why distributor Alliance Atlantis would sell CSI to Five, it asserts a quality audience that appreciates, deserves and is elsewhere denied quality scheduling for quality programming. This serves Five's institutional needs (by creating viewer loyalty), reaffirms Five's own quality identity and, in turn, justifies Five's financial investment in its US imports.

Also noteworthy regarding Five's 'America's Finest' campaign is that, with Five's promotional emphasis on quality scheduling already making a comment on its competition, the slogan further comments on the US imports shown by British competitors. Jonathan Bignell points out how the naming 'references not only the slang designation of the police force, but also the claim that these programmes represent the highest quality prime-time imports' (forthcoming). However, claiming to have the 'finest' imports also entails that the imports on competing channels are less 'fine'. Five here taps into the state of US imports in the early 2000s, when there was a brief sense of an end of a wave of quality US television from the 1990s, with several US shows (e.g. Channel 4's *Friends* or *Sex and the City*) coming to an end or being perceived as having outstayed their welcome (e.g. Channel 4's *ER*).[9] Steadily establishing *CSI* just before the next clutch of successful US imports (for example, Channel 4's high-profile *Desperate Housewives* and *Lost*), Five made use of this brief 'lull' to announce its intention to take over from, or at least share with, Channel 4 the 'responsibility' of bringing British quality audiences the best US acquisitions.

However, the process of an imported programme like *CSI* being ascribed a particular (quality) programme identity by Five and being used to help brand Five is also shaped and made complete by reception processes. *CSI* was the first programme on Five to receive positive attention from the British national press, specifically the 'quality' press (i.e. broadsheets such as *The Guardian*, *The Observer* and *The Independent*), which had previously tended to neglect or deride the channel. This nod of approval completes and reinforces *CSI*'s and Five's quality identities. Promotion and reception are thus intertwined – Five has used quotes from broadsheet articles in its press releases – and, in this case, have helped Five to attract a quality audience, namely 'a younger and more upmarket audience, which is always the dream' (Ford 2006). This desirable ABC1 demographic has generated significant revenue for Five by attracting advertisers and sponsorship deals such as that of the 'America's Finest' flagship strand by Toucan, makers of high-end telecommunications items.

That it was only through *CSI* that Five could successfully signal its turnaround[10] suggests that the text itself is still central to the interrelated processes of scheduling, promotion and reception. Five had started to reposition its programming profile in 2000 (e.g. poaching tea-time soap *Home and Away* from ITV1 or commissioning more arts programmes), and *CSI* was by no means Five's first US import – within its quota of acquired programming at approximately forty-five per cent, Five had previously screened US fantasy dramas such as *Charmed*, *Xena: Warrior Princess* and *Hercules: The Legendary Journeys*, which had achieved only relative niche successes. Nevertheless, it took the prestigious and visually distinctive *CSI* for Five to make a high-profile signal of its turnaround, with both Five and the broadsheets constructing *CSI* as symbolic of the Five brand change. (It is apt that Five should use the visually striking *CSI* to transform its brand, given that Five had also suffered from inferior picture quality due to transmitting problems.) Therefore, it is not surprising that, through deals with Alliance Atlantis, Five secured the rights for the entire *CSI* franchise, thereby enabling the channel to maximise the strong branding potential inherent within the franchise, all branches of which share the same basic formula and variations of the visual signature style.[11]

At the time of writing, *CSI* continues to be an integral part of Five's schedule, promotional strategies and brand identity. The 'America's Finest' campaign has been updated with a new 'white look' that moves away from *CSI*'s visual signature style in favour of a brilliant white background against which characters/performers from Five's US imports appear in close-up. With its fresh whiteness and understated piano score, this stylish campaign moves beyond the police procedural to link together different genre programmes (e.g. the *CSI* franchise and *House, M.D.*) and identify them within the broader category of quality television, which it links to Five's rebranded white logo; the white campaign's tagline, 'This much we know: simply great dramas at 10pm', affirming a unity of programmes, channel brand and imagined quality audience. With Five's acquisitions portfolio increasing, and *CSI* coming into its sixth season, the now more established Five is still making use of *CSI* – it remains Five's highest-rated drama – but simultaneously moving beyond its reliance on the show: Five both needs, and needs to need, *CSI* less. Incidentally, the white campaign's focus on characters expressing the words 'This much I know' taps into *CSI*'s increasing serialised focus on characterisation. While its relative lack of seriality made it well suited to ad hoc repeating, *CSI* seems to be, as creator Anthony E. Zuiker puts it, 'going more to character' (quoted in Morris 2001). While this move will affect *CSI*'s repeatability, it will not only enhance audience involvement, but also make it utilisable for a wider range of promotional strategies.

CONCLUSION

It has been my focus in this chapter to examine *CSI*'s impact on British television programming, to explore how 'that show was and is transformational for Five' (Ford 2006). The import of *CSI* to British television has been the result of the right combination of textual features, which have worked with a set of contextual processes, to succeed at the two 'hurdles' of the US and international television market. Screened within a flow of US and domestic programmes on British television, the nascent macro-textual meanings of *CSI* acquire a particular set of discursive ones within a specific broadcasting context. On Five, *CSI*'s specificity as US quality television defines the meanings of *CSI* for Five – *CSI becomes* 'America's Finest'.

By using *CSI* to instigate change, Five has established itself as a serious competitor for US imports. The channel's high-profile and costly purchase of *Friends* spin-off *Joey*, following its unsuccessful and expensive bid for *The Simpsons*, underlines that, in this more competitive British market, US shows remain central to the competitive edge of British television. Despite the fear of failure, British channels will continue to compete fiercely for the 'right' US programmes, and, with the proliferation of digital off-shoots, particularly for the exclusive rights to these shows: Five's ratings and branding strategies for *CSI* have been weakened by the fact that *CSI* and *CSI: Miami* are also shown on cable channel Living TV.

Finally, one crucial observation about Five's use of *CSI* is that the channel has repeatedly highlighted the centrality of its US imports to the channel (see Revoir 2003). Here, Five differs from many British channels, whose use of US imports is often marked by the concern that they will be *perceived as* dependent on these imports. While this is not surprising with regards to BBC One and ITV1, which define their public service commitments around British programming, it is somewhat surprising with Channel 4 and Sky One.[12] These channels' brand identities are intertwined with their offering prestigious US imports, yet these are also an admission of some kind of 'defeat'. While reasons for this final unease about imports involve fears of Americanisation and the loss of a distinctive British television drama culture, US imports are problematic for British broadcasters and, as mentioned earlier, academic accounts of British television, because of their fundamentally liminal status: they are both self and other, part of British television and (somehow) not. It remains to be seen whether Five will become more 'schizoid' about US imports once it moves into domestically produced prime-time drama. Of course, *CSI* emerged on the cusp of changes within British broadcasting, facilitated by digital technology, towards, as Rixon (2003) points out, more individualised forms of consumption. Exactly how the relationship between British television and US imports is likely to be affected remains to be seen. However, with high-profile US programmes likely to respond to these changes and continuing to be produced to be exportable to overseas audiences – an exportability which suggests that self and other are never fully complete on their own, depending on each other for their definition and meaning – it looks set to remain a very special relationship.

ACKNOWLEDGEMENT

This chapter is one of the outcomes of the research project 'British TV Drama and Acquired US Programmes, 1970–2000', funded by the Arts & Humanities Research Council and based at the University of Reading. I would like to thank Jeff Ford, formerly Five's and currently Channel 4's Director of Acquisitions, for giving his time to be interviewed. I would also like to thank Five's Tamara Bishopp and Louise Bowers for their help.

:16:

RTÉ AND THE
CSI FRANCHISE

DERMOT HORAN

I first saw the original *CSI* (without the 'Las Vegas' tagline) as a pilot at the Los Angeles Screenings of 2000. It was presented by Disney as one of their drama shows for international licensing. However, what I did not know at the time was that the distribution deal with the producers was not yet signed. Most US network shows are financed to the tune of at least $1.3 million dollars by a network licence fee, but a glossy show with high production values will cost more than that. In the case of *CSI*, some half a million dollars per episode, or $11 million per series, was the deficit between what CBS were willing to pay for the series and what it was going to cost.

Following the LA Screenings, Disney's distribution division felt the deficit was too high, considering that the market for US series internationally was quite depressed at the time. It pulled out of the deal. Alliance Atlantis, the Canadian media group, came in and took what was at the time a very considerable risk and agreed to distribute it. It was particularly risky, as Alliance Atlantis did not have the leverage of having a catalogue of new blockbuster movies, which the US major studios all have. This, coupled with a tendency at the time among the main European broadcasters to put US drama series out of peak time, and replace them with local production, meant that Alliance went into the marketplace on the defensive.

Or that is how it appeared. Of course, what happened was that the original *CSI* became an overnight success for CBS. It combined with the reality show *Survivor* to take on the 'Must See TV' shrine that was NBC on Thursday nights, and won. No network for the previous ten years had been willing to take on NBC's powerhouse, which had included *Friends*, *Frasier* and *ER* in its line-up. Arguably, the scheduling of *CSI* on a Thursday night at 9pm actually destroyed NBC's strongest night and, in doing so, destroyed NBC's reputation as the network of choice for upscale 18–49-year-olds. NBC's loss was CBS's gain, as the veteran network shed its old-fashioned image, gaining younger audiences (whilst not alienating its loyal viewers) and reaping the rewards in more lucrative advertising.

Thus, Alliance Atlantis had a bone fide hit on their hands and set out to exploit that success. As a smaller distributor, they were able to focus on this one series and do all it could to support its success in each territory to which they sold it. The US majors are often selling such large amounts of programming to territories that they cannot offer this bespoke service for one series. One sale led to another and, once a large network in Europe had scheduled it in prime-time and gained a large audience, Alliance Atlantis would pass on this intelligence to other broadcasters, daring them to play the show in the middle of the evening, where most European broadcasters were just playing local production.

In late 2006, American dramas are once again featuring in international broadcasters' prime-time schedules. Much has been made of the *Desperate Housewives* and *Lost* factor. Yes, they have helped, but the first show to do this in the twenty-first-century was *CSI*. Two years later, and CBS took a leaf out of NBCs book and launched a second *CSI*, this time in Miami. NBC had spawned a second *Law & Order*, called *SVU*, which had been working well for NBC, and still does.

CBS felt that by relocating the crime scene investigations to another city, with strong casting they would be able to do the same thing. David Caruso, whose movie career had faltered since leaving *NYPD Blue*, returned to the small screen to lead the Florida team. His slightly ageing, craggy looks, which had not helped on the big screen, were box office on the small screen.

In 2004, the latest of the franchise, *CSI: NY* arrived with another movie star, Gary Sinise. Arguably, this has been the least successful of the franchise, but has still held its own on the schedule. It also demonstrated that the viewer can just about tune into three shows per week, but no more. Recent *Law & Order* spin-offs like *Law & Order: Trial by Jury* have not worked, and this is in the main due to same-theme overload. From an international perspective, the franchise roll-out to three shows has worked, with the original buyers of the franchise also buying the next two. Alliance could garner higher licence fees for the next two, based on the success of the first. The broadcaster could almost guarantee itself another ratings success.

The other key advantage to the franchise is the fact that each episode is self-contained. Every investigation is solved within the hour. Thus, if you are a busy person, and so many are these days, you can afford to miss an episode and come back to the series the following week none the worse for missing it. This is not the case with the many serial dramas on the networks' schedules these days. Series such as *24*, *Prison Break* and *Lost* demand that the audience come back, week-in, week-out. This is a powerful proposition if millions of viewers are hooked. However, there are now so many of these serials that viewers must make a choice as to which 'appointments to view' they must make. Statistically, the schedules can probably only sustain one or two of these per network, and even that is pushing it.

CSI can ignore this trend. In many ways it harks back to the earlier days of television, when nearly all crime drama was self-contained. Of course we can all remember the odd serial success like *The Fugitive*, but there are so many more self-contained successes – *Starsky and Hutch*, *Magnum P.I.*, *Ironside*, *Columbo*, *Cannon*, *Murder She Wrote*, to name just a few.

The other useful tool to a broadcaster with a strong self-contained series is that you can drop the show from the schedule to run a one-off event, such as live sport and the viewer will return the following week. This cannot happen with the serialised drama. In Ireland, for example, RTE interrupts *CSI* midweek with Champions League soccer, and the series does not suffer. Having self-contained shows like this are invaluable to a scheduler's stock of programming. Equally, if a one-off hole appears in a broadcaster's prime-time schedule, and there is an onus to maintain the share and rating, an episode of *CSI* in any of its forms usually does the job.

In summary, *CSI*, in its three forms is a very valuable franchise to any broadcaster. Its production values are second to none. It is set in America, but could be located in any major city. It resolves each case on a weekly basis. It is a scheduler's dream, due to its self-contained nature and the flexibility which this gives.

:17:

DISSECTING *CSI*

The View from the Trainee and the Professional
DARYL VINALL AND SHELLEY ROBINSON

CSI FOR THE NEW FORENSICS GUY
BY DARYL VINALL

The first time I laid eyes on the *CSI* team I was hooked. Whether on the scientific method used to achieve results, or the high-octane drama of many of the episodes, I couldn't tell. But as time goes by, and I learn more about the reality of forensic investigation, I seem less and less interested in the drama and more fascinated by the reality.

For example, reviewing the pilot episode after my first year of training, I can see basic mistakes. The first thing any forensic investigator would do on entering a crime scene (especially one where a man is found in hotel bathroom with a gunshot to the head, wrapped in a sleeping bag with a recorded suicide note) is to make sure that nobody has entered the scene or disturbed anything. Next they would don their PPE (Personal Protective Equipment), consisting of a coverall, shoe covers, hair net, latex gloves, facemask and goggles. This is to say nothing of breathing apparatus to protect against noxious fumes in case of clandestine drug labs or chemical spills, or even specialist equipment for biological hazards or airborne toxins.

Gil Grissom would surely and instantly lose any sex appeal if he donned a hair net and shapeless coverall. In fact, all he does in this scene is to put on a pair of latex gloves, remove some tweezers from his kit and remove a stage three larval pupae from the body. He may confidently declare that this guy has been dead for three days, but in reality this could not be confirmed until a doctor or coroner is present to declare death. Only then can a body be moved. In truth the only time a Scene Of Crime Officer (SOCO) can assume that a person is dead is if the head is completely severed from the body. This is the case even if there is too much blood lost for a person to survive.

The biggest problem with learning forensic science and watching *CSI* is that, even though the programme sparked my interest (and I am indeed one of the many reported that rushed to sign up for a course due to the popularity of the programme), as time goes by and I learn more about laboratory techniques and crime scene examinations, I watch less and less of the programme itself. Not that it no longer interests me to see a dramatic version of forensics. But the deeper I get into the course the more I think, when I see the *CSI* teams in action, that we would do things differently and better, knowing that often their methods aren't accurate.

How did my journey begin? Well, I was sitting on my bed one evening watching *CSI* and my mum came in to have 'a talk'. While we were chatting, we couldn't help watching *CSI*, and I remember saying something like 'That must be a cool job to have, I'd love to do that.' She said, 'Well, go and do it then.' My honest response was that I did not think I would be able to do it, as it always looks far too complicated. But she insisted, 'You can, you've always liked science and you can do it if you really set your heart on it.' So I looked up forensic science courses. I was surprised that I could actually take a two-year BTEC course in forensic science before embarking on a full degree, and set up an interview for the summer.

On my arrival, I found that there were a lot more people wanting to sign up and, of course, not everyone would get in. While waiting, I started talking to a few of the people in the queue and, like me, a lot of them had seen *CSI* and wanted to work in a cool job. Unlike me, however, most didn't understand that there would be a lot of boring repetition and that *CSI* is not necessarily anything like the real job. I hear you asking, 'Could this be the reason so many students are dropping out of courses?' Well, I honestly don't know. There are lots of students dropping out: at the beginning of my first year, the class had twenty-five pupils; by the end we had only sixteen. That is a large number of students to lose for a course that, when it started, was oversubscribed. We could have had at least a few more people who were serious about learning forensics. Not to say it doesn't make it better for us this year, but it would be nice to know that people go in with open eyes instead of a romantic fantasy of what it could be.

Of course if you honestly went into forensics only because of watching an episode of *CSI* then you would deserve to be disappointed. Criminals, after all, are reported to learn more from *CSI* than a prospective forensic officer. The main problem is that, as in all dramatisations, it is the tedious side of the job that is left out. Meticulous calculation of the gap between furniture and walls, measuring of evidence in relation to walls and furniture, exact specifications of a room and where the exit and entry points are – hardly riveting TV. There are staggering amounts of paperwork for every piece of evidence, especially if it is to be presented in court. The attention paid to detail and the preparation of thorough paperwork is key to having a watertight case, especially if it is based heavily on forensic evidence. Why? Because otherwise the defence can query any and all evidence and make it seem less reliable in a juror's eyes.

It may seem that I no longer enjoy the programme and all the excitement of a good conclusion – even if nowadays I can often work it out much earlier than I could before I took the forensics course. This is not the case. What I am saying is that while you are watching this delicious piece of drama you must remember that the job is, in fact, nowhere near as glamorous as it seems. As is always the case in television drama most of the mundane side of life is left out. It would not be a compelling programme if, for a half an hour, Grissom went over the reports for the day and filled in scene descriptions without ever entering into dialogue with another person, as is often the case in the real world.

But don't let my extremely dreary explanation of forensics put you off for one moment. Trying to pass a course means that I am totally caught up in the realities, rather than the drama, of forensic science. Some of the best times over the last year have been the actual practical side of the course such as recreated crime scene searches and the laboratory experiments to do with blood, DNA, chromatography and spectroscopy. I still love wearing my forensic lab coat, which is pale blue with elasticised arms (to prevent contamination). It makes me feel like a real forensics guy and makes a huge difference to how I feel about the job. Having my own coverall and shoe covers (which, to this day, I love the look of), despite the fact that they are hot, stuffy and generally uncomfortable, makes the reality that one day I shall be doing this for a living instead of learning all the closer. In fact, looking the part is still as exciting as it was the first time – even though I have to admit that, once the original novelty had worn off, I could not bear to look at the coverall, let alone wear one! On the other hand, I can still remember the first time I wore one: I felt like a small child on Christmas Eve, that slightly sick anxious feeling you get waiting to open the presents and spend the day finding a hundred ways to have fun with them.

The best thing about *CSI*, though, is that it has the basis of scientific principles entwined with a dramatic plotline in which each episode is almost always just as delectable as the last. The reality is that, despite all of the tedious attention to detail and paperwork, the rush I get from solving a problem is like no other feeling in the world; it satisfies like no other and is definitely comparable to the rush of the drama that is *CSI*.

CSI ON THE (REAL-LIFE) PATHOLOGY TABLE
BY SHELLEY ROBINSON

'Why don't you just do DNA on it?' Thus went the dinner-party conversation. The topic was the identification of human remains. As a practising forensic pathologist, I am accustomed to the expectation that I will provide gruesome stories at social functions. This time, I just sighed and said, 'It's not that simple,' rather than launch into the complex scientific data that forms the basis of DNA comparative studies. I am at a loss to explain why people so avidly digest the gory details of murder and mayhem along with the entrée. I find horticulture and architecture much more interesting. But my friends and fellow dinner-party attendees have been watching *CSI*, and similar shows, and they are keen to practise their newly acquired crime-solving knowledge. After all, they have seen how it's done and it looks pretty straightforward.

These people are part of the community who expect a simple solution. The way we go about solving crimes is public knowledge as a result of these shows. Long gone are the days when a certain amount of mystique, and even fear, surrounded the work of doctors, scientists and law-enforcement agencies. Our work is now prime entertainment, and what better entertainment than to combine the satisfactory closure of the old police shows with the community's morbid interest in behind-the-scenes medicine and science? I think that this lies at the centre of the huge popularity of the criminal investigation show. But, now that everyone knows how it is done, their expectations of those of us who work in the area have changed. They are not going to be fobbed off with 'laboratory tests have shown...' or 'autopsy findings revealed...' They want to see the tests done, interpret the results, catch the suspect, ensure that justice is done. Unfortunately, it doesn't quite work like that in real life (or death).

Take, for example, the technology. There are lots of complicated-looking laboratory instruments, complete with flashing lights, digital displays and multicoloured screens showing graphs and charts, all at the touch of a button. 'Let's run it through analysis,' says the police officer, handing the scientist a test tube of evidence that has just been scraped up from the crime scene or collected from the body being autopsied. The scientist dutifully plugs the sample straight into the machine, which beeps obligingly then, thirty seconds later, prints out the result. And not just any result. It's the critical clue that is going to identify the dangerous criminal. My department doesn't have that particular laboratory instrument. The specimens collected from the autopsy and the crime scene must be processed according to standardised procedures that include multiple labelling and documentation steps. This is necessary to maintain a 'chain of custody' to avoid allegations of tampering that may be made later should the case go to court. The specimens often need to be refined or extracted before being placed in the analyser and this process may take hours to days. There are standards to be run, quality control to be maintained. But the viewing public doesn't see all this time-consuming stuff. They just see the instantaneous results.

And what fabulous results they are. Never wrong, rarely inconclusive, they usually provide the vital clue, the missing piece of the puzzle that leads to the apprehension of the perpetrator. So what is stopping the police from rushing out, kicking the door down and arresting the suspect? In real life, the results aren't always helpful. Sometimes the test hasn't worked at all and we are left with nothing. At best, the results may just be one tiny piece in the body of evidence being amassed against a suspect, that is, provided that the result can stand up in court, resisting challenges of contamination or manipulation.

Then there is the class of crime that forms the bulk of an investigators workload. Far from the interesting, intellectually challenging cases our TV investigators are working on, most real-life crimes are very mundane. This is because most criminals are not very bright. In fact, some are downright stupid or else, overcome by guilt, they confess to the crimes and we can all go home after the day's work. The majority of crimes are not well planned or thought through properly. They are carried out with the perpetrator seemingly oblivious to the chances of being caught and convicted. This, of course, doesn't make for very interesting viewing, so our public has a very skewed view of the world of crime and the people who commit it.

Criminal investigators do not spend large amounts of time gathered around whiteboards covered in obscure markings whilst someone operates the laser pointer. It is an unusual case that requires us to get together to compare notes and discuss our findings. The forensic pathology, crime scene investigation and specimen analysis all proceed independently, and the people involved all have well-defined roles in an investigation. There is not a lot of crossover. A forensic pathologist avoids contact with victims' relatives and possible perpetrators during the initial phases of an investigation, as we must be impartial when considering our findings. We play no part in the actual physical arrest of an offender, unlike our television counterparts, some of whom even carry guns. Similarly, police officers are far too busy to spend time wandering around our laboratories and offices, waiting for us to turn up that vital clue. We let them know, of course, when we find it, but it's just not all that dramatic. The reason underlying this is that we simply don't have the time to watch each other working. Also, we are not working on one particular case. We don't have the luxury enjoyed by our fictional counterparts of devoting all our time and energy to one case. There are backlogs accumulating, other investigators wanting results and court matters (an enormous waste of time and resources) to attend to. In addition to all the paperwork, most of us have other obligations such as research and teaching, none of which makes for riveting viewing.

So much of a real criminal investigator's work is routine, the dotting of 'i's and the crossing of 't's. The results of the tests that are performed in the name of criminal investigation must be able to withstand the rigor of the court scrutiny. They must satisfy the rules of evidence. Courts are very wary of allowing novel scientific methods to be presented in the courtroom. The science of 'finger-printing', for example, took years to gain acceptance, not just by scientists but also by the courts. The same applies to DNA evidence. The reason for this caution is to prevent 'junk science' being given credence, just because someone is prepared to call themselves an 'expert' and give their evidence. Whilst not all new methods of scientific study are 'junk', some do not satisfy tests of reliability, reproducibility and acceptance by peer groups. The rules of evidence have evolved at common law and are based on actual cases. Modern disciplines such as forensic entomology (study of insects) and forensic palynology (study of pollens) are still making their way into the courtroom. Our ardent crime-show-viewing public generally are not aware of these issues. They don't understand why we can't just perform the same 'laser-beam-saliva-extracted-DNA-chewing-gum' analysis that they saw so successfully performed on TV last night. Even if we could, we know that our chewing-gum analysis is unlikely to be heard in the courtroom.

Another way in which we differ from the fictional investigators is that we forgo the adrenalin rush associated with danger. Most of us are reluctant to enter burning buildings, wander round isolated graveyards alone at night or confront angry gunmen. Those things are not in our job description. Our excitement comes from matching a microscopic slide appearance to a picture in a text book. The television viewer may not be quite so thrilled if that was all we did.

Last, but not least, are the people who work in criminal investigation. We are not all young glamorous individuals. We don't wear fabulous designer outfits. Why would we? Crime scenes, laboratories and mortuaries are not catwalks and there is nothing like a few bloodstains or other body fluids to ruin an outfit. We dress for comfort and protection. Sometimes we are old, tired, fat, have headaches, colds and appear downright scruffy. We tend not to form romantic relationships with our work colleagues. We don't have the time or inclination to exchange meaningful and intense gazes with law enforcement personnel over a dead body. There is nothing less romantic than the odour of decomposing remains. There is also nothing glamorous or exhilarating about climbing out of bed at 3am to drive along unfamiliar fog-enshrouded roads to assist in the retrieval of body parts from the crawl-space beneath a house. It is also difficult to look like a photographic model in these circumstances.

The above notwithstanding, criminal investigation is a fascinating area in which to work. The reason that most of us continue to turn up to work each day does not seem to be portrayed in the television shows. It is a strong personal commitment to one's science, a desire to put the knowledge and experience gained from many years and academic institutions, to good use. It involves a preoccupation with detail and the ability to focus on a very small piece of a puzzle. Much of the work is mundane, routine, even boring, but it is satisfying to be able to submit that piece of the puzzle and see the big picture emerge. We don't need the glamour, excitement, romance or danger. We are just doing our jobs.

:18:

INVESTIGATING '*CSI* TELEVISION FANDOM'

Fans' Textual Paths through the Franchise

MATT HILLS AND AMY LUTHER

CSI[1] has been explored academically in a variety of ways: different shows in the franchise have been compared via textual analysis (Turnbull 2005; Branston and Stafford 2006); aesthetics and special effects have been analysed (Tait 2006); and the specific seriality of *CSI* identified and classified (Ndalianis 2005). Rather than taking the texts of *CSI* as objects of a scholarly, forensic gaze, however, here we are interested in how fan audiences – and not just professional academic readers – navigate their way through the franchise. Is there such a thing as a general '*CSI* fan', who follows all three TV shows in the franchise with seemingly equal devotion, or does *CSI* fandom tend to fragment into different affiliations? Is *CSI: Crime Scene Investigation* especially valued by sections of this fan culture for its status as the 'original' show?

In what follows, we consider fan postings to a range of unofficial *CSI* message boards available in the public domain, including the predominantly US-based Talk CSI (part of csifiles.com[2]), and more European-oriented sites such as Crimelab.nl based in the Netherlands, and the Norwegian Csiforum.no. We have specified 'television fandom' in our title for the very simple reason that, although the fans we are analysing here are posting to Internet sites, these sites are predominantly based around discussion of the various *CSI* television shows. Some fans will certainly post about, and discuss, spin-off comic books or computer games, but our focus remains – along with the fans we study – on *CSI* as it has appeared on television.

We will contextualise our work by addressing its multiple backgrounds in cyberethnography, cultural studies, and fan studies, before then moving on to consider the 'popular aesthetics' displayed by CSI's fans (Bird 2003). Fan postings will be analysed first in relation to how fans distinguish between the different television shows in the franchise, and second with regard to fans' discussions of their favourite episodes.

The former gives us a way into fan debates over what makes for 'good CSI' inter-textually, across the different strands of the overall franchise. By contrast, the latter allows us to explore judgements that are made intra-textually by fans of specific CSI variants. Across each part of our analysis, the importance of character for fans is emphasised (see Amesley 1989; Gwenllian Jones 2000). This aspect of CSI's televisual and narrative structures has arguably been downplayed in scholarly visions of the franchise, where discussions of special effects and the forensic 'look' at the body have instead predominated (Doherty 2003; Tait 2006; Fuery and Fuery 2003: 19). In the next section we will consider how this preoccupation with CSI's representations of abject, spectacularised bodies (Tait 2006) can be re-oriented via the study of online fan audiences.

SCENE-SETTING: CYBERETHNOGRAPHY, CULTURAL STUDIES, FAN STUDIES

We are drawing on three strands of recent research, and it will help to ground our arguments and findings if we first contextualise them. From cyberethnography – the study of media audiences and consumers in cyberspace – we have drawn our basic method and form of data collection. This is a convenient way of gaining access to audiences' perspectives, though processing the vast range of available data can remain problematic, if not overwhelming.

Looking at publicly available fan sites on the web meant that we were able to access naturally occurring data without issues of privacy restricting or ethically challenging such access. In this case, fans are fully aware that their postings can be read by anyone with an Internet connection, and there is little sense of their postings being akin to private chats. Instead, postings are highly performative in nature. As Jonathan Gray observed in his study of the website Television Without Pity, 'much ... commentary itself belies an awareness of (or even a desire for) a considerable audience' (2005: 847). The sites we examined also sought to reach this 'considerable audience' by more or less explicitly advertising themselves as open to transnational participants. Though the message board Talk CSI tended to potentially limit itself to a US-based fan community by virtue of basing itself around US TV schedules, Csiforum.no's homepage proclaims: 'We welcome members from all over the world, but news articles and airdates are based on European interest.'[3] This forum is divided into 'general' as well as text-specific sections for the three *CSI* shows, and country-specific areas for a range of different European member-states.

Recent work in cyberethnography has stressed how online fan forums can 'become focused on critical but pleasurable analyses of ... television texts', with fans adopting scholar-like strategies of close reading and detailed textual exegesis, sometimes alongside more 'shallow' discussions of which actors they think are 'sexiest' or 'most beautiful' (Bird 2003: 127). Steve Bailey notes that online fan communities frequently serve 'as a forum for critical and exegetical discussions of the [favoured] program' (2005: 185). He goes on to argue: 'this is ... [a] feature which would have been much more difficult in conventional, pre-Web fan cultures, which relied upon paper fanzines and interpersonal contact ... for such discussions' (ibid.).

Whilst cyberethnography has sought to gather web-based data and address how fans' interpretive practices have been partly reconfigured by computer-mediated-communication, developments in cultural studies have stressed the need to consider 'how ... people interact not just with single texts, but with textual fields' (Couldry 2000: 73). This question of the 'textual environment' a reader navigates through is one which is powerfully begged by contemporary media-saturated societies, where it makes less sense to isolate out audiences for singular texts (Bird 2003). Nick Couldry challenges media researchers to address how people

> in actuality screen out the vast majority of images and texts
> around them ... One person's 'textual world' will only partially
> intersect with another's. Surely, therefore, we should know
> more about what individuals' 'textual fields' are like ... Yet this
> is an area where cultural studies has done very little research.
> (2000: 73)

It might fairly be said that these textual fields have been repeatedly examined in one subsection of cultural studies, namely fan studies. Seemingly by definition, fandom offers up a community which shares at least one overlapping element across its members' textual fields, since all are precisely fans of a given text. However, fans may in actuality share far more of their textual field than just one text. Media fandom can be analysed as a discursive logic that knits together interests across textual and generic boundaries. While some fans remain exclusively committed to a single show or star, many others use individual series as a point of entry into a broader fan community, linking to an inter-textual network composed of many programs, films, books, comics. (Jenkins 1992: 40)

In short, Henry Jenkins (1992) was already doing just what Couldry (2000) calls for: analysing the communally shared 'inter-textual network' – or 'textual field' in Couldry's terms – characteristic of cult film and TV fans. Strangely, Jenkins' focus on media fandom as something *not* always inherently based around a singular text gave way to a series of studies of text-specific fandoms. Scholarly work proliferated on *Star Trek* fans, *Doctor Who* fans, *Buffy* fans etc (see Hills 2002: xiv and 2). This drift towards assuming that fandom can be readily equated with textual singularity, and hence that singular fan cultures form coherent interest blocs around 'their' show, has been disrupted by a new wave of academic arguments (e.g., Hills 2002; Sandvoss 2005). Partly returning to Jenkins's work, and partly resonating with Couldry's take on cultural studies, this body of work focuses on the contradictions, conflicts, and tensions within any 'one' fan culture.

For example, Cornel Sandvoss asks where 'the text' actually is for any one fan. He suggests that fans define the boundaries around what they count as 'the text' (2005: 131–3). Despite identifying themselves as fans of the same TV show, such as *CSI: Crime Scene Investigation*, some fans may have stopped watching after a particular season, some may always watch the show avidly alongside *CSI: Miami* and *CSI: New York*, and others may include *CSI* computer games, comic books, DVD extras or even fan-created fiction within the boundaries of their *CSI*-related textual field. Yet others may only have started watching the 'original' show some way into its run, or may perhaps love *CSI: Crime Scene Investigation* while heavily criticising and/or not watching *CSI: Miami* or *CSI: NY*, linking their fandom to an 'anti-fandom' of the spin-offs (Gray 2003). It is these issues which we will investigate, drawing on developments in fan studies and cultural studies, and using cyberethnography to access fans' textual fields.

SCENE-SHIFTING: NAVIGATING THE INTER-TEXTUAL ARRAY OF THE CSI FRANCHISE

The fact that a general or blanket 'CSI fandom' is rarely assumed by those who post to CSI-related sites is evident from the uncertainty of a number of posters when discussing the various shows which go to make up the franchise. On crimelab.nl, one poster asks, 'Is this about all the CSI shows? Since this is in General' (Fabian, May 10, 2005, 9:58pm, Re: All Time Fave episode...). Even where the architecture of the site seems to indicate that a particular 'General' area is reserved for discussion ranging across the franchise, there is still some hesitation as to whether a generalised fandom should be presumed. A very similar hesitancy occurs on the more US-centric site Talk CSI, where a thread asks 'What is your favourite CSI episode and character?' The first poster to respond again notes, 'I'm gonna add my favourite for all 3, so I'm hoping this is for all 3 series' (ThumpyG42, 22 August 2005, 1:49am).

Contrary to previous scholarly work, which has sometimes assumed that a singular 'fan identity' can be isolated out for specific shows or franchises, e.g. 'the *Star Trek* fan' (Bacon-Smith 1992), these fans appear to be highly conscious of the fact that they cannot take for granted that other participants in the online community will have appreciated, or even seen, the same range of *CSI*-related texts. There is a recurring sense, within the various sites we studied, that 'the original' – frequently referred to as *CSI: Las Vegas* or *CSI: LV* – is the superior show, meaning that fans usually assume others' familiarity with this, as if it is a 'core' text, before then branching out in different ways in terms of whether or not they appreciate the two 'spin-offs'. As csivegasnmiami puts it on Talk CSI:

> The Original is always the best
> CSI
> Then the next cut off
> CSI: Miami
> But if ur getting any farther than that ur just pushin it
> CSI: ny
> (18 August 2005, 0:38pm, re: what is your favourite CSI episode and character?)

On the same message board, Rookie articulates what appears to count as fan-cultural common sense, by posting that 'It's a given if you like CSI, you love Vegas' (28 March 2006, 11:04am). This comment occurs as part of a thread which asks 'Do you like CSI Miamy and CSI New York?' Of course, the question itself, which frames this particular debate, is already constructed in such a way as to resonate with these comments. Whether or not a 'CSI fan' would like *CSI: LV* is not even questioned. Fans who navigate their way through the franchise by favouring *CSI: Miami* and/or

CSI: NY, whilst perhaps not liking CSI: LV, are thus semiotically and fan-culturally marginalised within this community:

> I think I'm the only one that doesn't like Vegas. IMO it is way too dark
> (AlyssaluvsDanny, 10 April 2006 3:41am, Re: Least Favourite CSI Series, Talk CSI).

> Everyone is gonna throw stones at me but I dislike Vegas. I've seen a few NY, and almost all the Miami episodes ... Vegas is blah to me
> (Whit, 22 February 2006 1:38am, Re: Least Favourite CSI Series, Talk CSI).

These posters demonstrate an awareness that their views are out of alignment with the fan-cultural norm, where communal assumptions are repeatedly articulated regarding the pre-eminence of the 'Original' CSI: LV – drawing heavily on a romanticising discourse of 'authenticity' versus 'the derivative'. In contrast to the 'Original', posters sometimes positioned franchise-extending spin-offs as being closer to 'dumb cop shows' (Fogeltje, 30 May 2005, 12:01am, Re: CSI: NY – Your thoughts; crimelab.nl).

It is not always clearly the case that fans favour the symbolically subordinated spin-offs in order of their real-world broadcast chronology or inception. That is to say, CSI: Miami is not, contra csivegasnmiami's posting cited above, automatically favoured over the newer CSI: NY. Indeed, both within and without that fraction of fans following all three CSI shows, debate over the relative merits of CSI: Miami or CSI: NY dominates on these sites.

One way in which fans debate and discuss their preferences amongst these shows is by referring to their perceived characteristic colours and tones. 'Light' versus 'dark' (mapped on to CSI: Miami versus CSI: NY), and 'grey' versus 'colourful' (standing for CSI: NY versus CSI: LV) are key binaries here. Some fans value the 'darkness' of CSI: NY Season One, while others bemoan its general 'greyness' (tuesdaymorning, 17 October 2005 8:36pm Re: Miami vs. New York..., Talk CSI; sweetheart, 5 March 2006 11:03am Re: Least Favourite CSI Series, Talk CSI). The same binaries are reiterated but differently valued by fractions of fans navigating variant paths through the textual field of the franchise.

Perhaps surprisingly, it is not always apparent whether fans are discussing the literal lighting of a show's *mise-en-scène* or its thematic 'darkness' of subject matter. This blurring of form and content is, however, not wholly specific to fan debate, since it can be argued that the various *CSI* texts are marked by deliberate and brand-identifying differences in both their (relative) tone of subject matter and colouration:

> [C]haracteristically, in *CSI*, whole scenes may be post-produced and appear to be tinted green, blue, or as is frequently the case in the *CSI: Miami* series, orange. ... [T]he newest series in the ... franchise – *CSI: New York* – demonstrates a much greyer or bluer colour scheme and thus works against the fantastically heightened or 'comic-strip palette' of the earlier series (Lury 2005: 54–5).

This textual analysis certainly marries up with much online fan discussion. Fans may not write at such length – postings often becoming cryptic through their very brevity and lack of contextualisation – but their sentiments are not unrelated. Here, fans and scholars appear to share aesthetic concerns. This doesn't indicate that academic textual analysis is pointless (i.e. it just reproduces fan knowledge using longer words), nor that fans are making especially sophisticated readings (they aren't). Instead, this confluence points to the fact that these aesthetic and textual distinctions are based on industrial regularities of brand identification and differentiation, where all the entries in the *CSI* franchise are marked by strong use of signature colour schemes or restricted palettes, and where these have been coordinated to ensure maximum contrast, and thus differentiation, between *CSI*-branded series. Both professional textual analysts and fans alike are, here, recognising and reproducing the contemporary TV industry's strategies of branding (Johnson 2005: 110–14) which extend beyond TV texts to their merchandising, such as sell-through DVDs. Compare, for instance, the packaging colour schemes of the currently available Region 2 DVD box sets for *CSI: Crime Scene Investigation*, *CSI: Miami* and *CSI: NY*, and you find that their signature brand palettes of green/red/purple-blue, white/orange, and black/ice-blue are iterated.

Online fans' readings do not always converge with scholarly textual analysis. To take one example: a clearly identifiable group of fans, spanning across the sites we examined, attacks *CSI: Miami* in a variety of ways. What these fans appreciate and position as part of the innovative and distinctive value of *CSI: LV* is made clear when they suggest that

CSI: Miami 'just didn't seem very CSI to me' (bluebean, 1 June 2005, 8:20am, Re: CSI: NY – Your thoughts; crimelab.nl). One poster, Fogeltje, comments on being able to watch 'dumb German cop shows' if they want 'explosions and actions and shooting'. Fogeltje contrasts *CSI: LV* to this state of affairs, arguing that the show is instead about 'investigation and science and forensics'. *CSI: Miami* then comes in for specific censure:

> Most of the Miami episodes focus on explosions and gunfire, making it one of those dumb cop shows more than a CSI show. I guess all the funds that usually go to creative parts go to SFX here ... Yes, it's unavoidable to have gunfire every now and again or some explosion, but not ALL the time (30 May 2005, 12:01am, Re: CSI: NY – Your thoughts; crimelab.nl).

Like discussions of signature colour schemes, this is another example of what S. Elizabeth Bird has termed 'popular aesthetics' (2003: 125); i.e. it indicates how audience members enact aesthetic judgements and establish aesthetic criteria for distinguishing favoured shows. *CSI: LV* and/or *CSI: NY* fans, who nevertheless criticise *CSI: Miami* for not seeming 'very CSI', are seeking to defend and uphold what they have positioned as the 'cerebral' and scientific values of *CSI*, contrasting these to supposedly mindless action-adventure and gun-toting spectacle (see also Siegel 2003: 25). It may strike some textual-analytical scholars as odd for one *CSI* show to be distinguished from others in this way – and for a fan of *CSI: LV* to criticise spectacle when this show has itself been frequently analysed as having a highly spectacularised and almost fetishistic 'look' and style (Lury 2005: 56). But this fan-cultural distinction works via what Joke Hermes has identified as a kind of 'remarkable double code' (2005: 70). The doubling involves valorising a certain type of crime fiction as culturally acceptable, even educational and pedagogic, whilst simultaneously betraying an anxiety over the cultural status and content of more 'mainstream' crime fiction.

Hermes' identification of this 'double code' arose during her analysis of interviews with Dutch readers of crime novels, but its operation similarly marks out many of the online *CSI: LV* and/or *CSI: NY* fans' 'anti-fan' responses to *CSI: Miami*. However, attacks on this show are not just linked to its apparent failure to adopt a properly 'CSI-like' scientificity and cerebral tone. These critiques are also strongly linked to assessments of character. Put simply, many fans who dislike *CSI: Miami* also dislike the character of Horatio Caine.

There is a powerful linkage between fans (dis)liking a show, and (dis)liking its lead male protagonist, almost to the extent that character and TV show become entirely conflated. Criticism of *CSI: Miami* is, within the terms of debate on these fan sites, naturalised as criticism of Horatio Caine. Though examples of this process of character/programme conflation are legion, we shall offer a brief selection. In some cases, the 'popular aesthetic' already identified is linked to *CSI: Miami* and specifically read onto the character of Horatio, who is thus viewed as a gun-toting action hero. In other cases, Caine is described in irritated or apologetic terms which emphasise audiences' inability to 'get into' the character:

> I don't watch Miami, it never appealed to me. All the previews
> show Horatio with his gun out, never really doing anything
> useful. Miami just seemed too action for me. (Bluebean, 9 May
> 2005, 11:37pm, Re: CSI: NY - Your thoughts; crimelab.nl)

> Miami. I just never got into it. And, sorry for his fans, but I
> can't stand Horatio. (NikkiH, 20 February 2006, 3:56am, Re:
> Least Favoutite CSI series, Talk CSI)

> Urgh, the worst is absolutely Miami. Horatio is just so cliché.
> He always solves the crime and says really annoying one-liner
> jokes that aren't even funny and Urgh. He just annoys me so
> much. (Cat, 12 March 2006, 12:49am, Re: Least Favoutite CSI
> series, Talk CSI)

By marked contrast, the male lead character of *CSI: LV*, Gil Grissom, is rarely criticised, and the inverse of the Caine scenario holds: loving *CSI: LV* appears, first and foremost, to mean loving Grissom. The response to *CSI: NY*'s Mac Taylor is more ambivalent, with some fans finding him 'boring' but others favouring him (Cat, 12 March 2006 12:49am Re: Least Favoutite CSI series, Talk CSI). For these fans, comparing the *CSI* shows primarily appears to mean comparing their male leads:

> I like Mac too. I never liked Horatio (don't think that is that
> much of a secret) but Mac, well in time I might like him more
> than Grissom. Mac is no gunslinging cowboy like Horatio, but
> he can stand his ground, in contrast to Grissom. He is also far
> better with people. (Fogeltje, 9 May 2005, 9:50pm, Re: CSI: NY
> - Your thoughts; crimelab.nl).

Although there may well be some gendering and sexualisation of fan responses – a number of postings across these sites do indeed forsake critical exegesis in favour of recounting which male actors and 'ladies' the fans find 'hot' – character/show conflations appear, on the whole, to lack obviously gendered or sexualised components. It could be argued that the interpretive emphasis on male leads is indicative of a cultural masculinisation of these shows by fans, but this reading strategy nevertheless appears to generally hold true for the fan communities we surveyed. This indicates the significance of character in fans' readings. As Sara Gwenllian Jones has argued:

> Television ... industry merchandising ... reinforces the primacy of characters by capitalising upon the allure of characters rather than actors. ... [T]he series and commercial products associated with it are both dedicated to the circulation and perpetuation of fictional worlds for which characters function as metonyms and points of entry (2000: 11–12).

In 'How To Read *Star Trek*' (1989), Cassandra Amesley similarly demonstrates how character-based discourses have dominated fans' discussion of the programme. One alternative title for this chapter could well be 'How To Read *CSI*', for our analysis resonates with these earlier findings. However, character is not just a metonym for the different *CSI* series, it is also the primary semiotic and discursive ground on which fans' 'popular aesthetics', likes/dislikes, and inter-textual navigations, are played out and performed.

Navigating the inter-textual array of *CSI* texts, fans' comparisons and aesthetic evaluations of the franchise shows rarely refer to 'crossover' episodes combining different series' characters, such as 'Cross-Jurisdictions' (*CSI: Crime Scene Investigation*, 2:22), 'MIA/NYC – Nonstop' (*CSI: Miami*, 2:23), 'Felony Flight' (*CSI: Miami*, 4:7) and 'Manhattan Manhunt' (*CSI: NY*, 2:7). Instead, fans tend to discuss the three series as if they are self-contained and hermetically sealed entities. In a crimelab. nl thread (Who/What got you hooked onto CSI?, 17 November 2005 8:31pm), one poster, scorpii, recounts seeing the 'crossover epi' for *CSI: LV/Miami* and one for *Miami/NY*, indicating that she became a fan of the spin-offs as a result of these lead-ins (thereby corresponding, one might say, to the producers' preferred textual pathways). But very little commentary otherwise addresses these crossover episodes. The dominant interpretive framework is one where different *CSI* shows are treated as wholly separate, and as metonymically represented via male lead characters (in masculinising fan-cultural readings) and signature colour schemes (in fan and academic readings premised on brand-design strategies).

We will now move on to consider intra-textual rather than inter-textual evaluations, analysing fans' identifications of their favourite episodes. These again indicate how fans value and interpret *CSI*, giving us further access to their textual paths through the franchise.

SCENE-STEALING: FANS' ALL-TIME FAVOURITE *CSI*S

The identification of favourite episodes is a recurrent feature of fans' online discussions. Again, the fragmentation of the fan community into different subsets who navigate pathways through 'the text' of the overall franchise is evident. Even where an 'all-time fave episode' is asked for (as on crimelab.nl), fans split their answers by shows, indicating which out of the three they follow: 'I don't watch all csi's on the first my fave is butterflied' (Ashley, 20 May 2005 2:53am). Fans sometimes further subdivide their lists of favourites by seasons, perhaps indicating if they are behind the US broadcasts, or haven't yet watched certain seasons on DVD (James, 23 May 2005, 11:17pm, crimelab.nl).

Abercrombie and Longhurst argue that 'consumers', as opposed to 'fans' and 'cultists', are less likely to engage in intra-textual comparisons (1998: 145). Consumers supposedly state their 'likes' and dislikes', but with lesser degrees of analytical argument and self-reflexivity than fans:

> The fan tends to mobilise analytical skills within the genre or, the corpus ... The cultist becomes immersed in comparisons within the genre and between shows themselves, and analytical skills become exceptionally developed. (Abercrombie and Longhurst 1998: 145; see also Tulloch and Jenkins 1995: 136)

This development is, of course, evident in fans' postings which list series of favourites by *CSI* show and season (as in the case of James on crimelab. nl) , but it is less clear in relation to supposed fans like Ashley cited above, who simply profess to really like one episode without stating any reasons. It may partly be a product of the type of data we are analysing – sometimes very brief and decontextualised online postings – but we would argue that, despite the fact that these are messages occurring on supposed *CSI* fan sites, some 'fan' postings are actually closer to the 'consumer' mode identified by Abercrombie and Longhurst. In fact, assumed distinctions between 'fans' and 'consumers' seem to partly break down in these online venues and threads.

There are, however, specific episodes, especially of CSI: LV, which are repeatedly listed as fan favourites across the different sites we looked at. These include the show's 'Pilot' episode (1:0), Season Two's 'Alter Boys' (2:6), Season Four's 'Butterflied' (4:12), and the end-of-Season-Five two-part finale 'Grave Danger' (5.24 and 25). There is also evidence of some communal favourites for CSI: Miami, such as 'Dispo Day' (1:18), 'Big Brother' (2:8) and 'Wannabe' (2:18), and 'On the Job' (1:21) for CSI: NY. Crossover episodes introducing the spin-offs, or interconnecting them, are less frequently referred to, and episodes of CSI: LV which have dealt with fan cultures such as 'furry' fandom and Sherlock Holmes fans (see Mikulak 1998; Pearson 1997), namely 'Fur and Loathing' (4:5) and 'Who Shot Sherlock?' (5.11) respectively, also rate occasional mentions.

Episodes of CSI: LV also tended to be discussed in more detail, reflecting the fact that for these online fan communities, the 'original' show is the linchpin of their fandom, and so most commonly acts as a linking thread between fans who may either watch all three CSI shows, or different combinations of the two spin-offs and the 'original', but very rarely fail to display CSI: LV fandom. 'Butterflied' is appreciated by fans for the light it sheds on Grissom's relationship with Sara Sidle, indicating the focus of the fans on character and relationships (Kaylee, 26 August 2005 7:41pm, Talk CSI; GreyWillFade, 24 September 2005 2:43am, Talk CSI), while 'Alter Boys' is partly valued for the disruptive alteration it introduces into the show's basic format:

> Alter Boys will always be my favourite as it was kinda scary to see that the evidence can in fact lie. (jazzfan 216, 14 June 2005 6:53pm, crimelab.nl)

> Yes, Alter Boys will always be on of my favourites. I just love the episode, it's pretty intense. (Fabian, 15 June 2005 6:54pm, crimelab.nl)

Though format-stretching may be appreciated by fans using their analytical skills to nominate episodes as 'out of the ordinary', fans also favour episodes which establish franchise formats, such as the 'Pilot' and its follow-up, 'Cool Change' (1:12). One specific scene or moment from the 'Pilot' is especially validated and celebrated by fans, and thus can be taken to indicate what fans value about CSI:

Don't forget the pilot episode where Grissom said 'you asshole!' to that dead corpse!! Haha so funny I watched it over and over again. (Szmanda_Togo_Fan, 22 August 2005 5:11am, Talk CSI)

The Pilot was cute too. I liked the scene between Grissom and the new CSI girl when she got creeped out. He was such a gentleman. It was an awesome start to the series. (themusicalpoet, 18 July 2005 5:54am, crimelab.nl)

This scene and moment are rarely reflected on in academic textual analyses, which favour discussion of the 'CSI-shot' – that 'snap-zoom ... special effect' (Lury 2005: 53) which moves into an extreme, magnified close-up on a piece of forensic evidence, or which seems to enter and pull back out of characters' bodies. For these fans, though, it is not the 'CSI-shot' which secures the show's originality or distinction. It is rather Grissom's odd, humorous characterisation as leader of the Crime Scene Investigation 'nerd squad' that again appears to stand in metonymically for the 'distinctiveness' of the show; that is, positioning it as 'not just a dumb cop show', and demarcating it as especially witty, quirky and out-of-the-ordinary.

By far the most frequently identified and discussed favourite episode on these sites, surpassing even the *CSI: LV* 'Pilot', is 'Grave Danger' (5.24 and 25), the two-parter directed by Quentin Tarantino, and marketed as 'event' cinematic-style television. The Region 2 sell-through DVD of this was, unusually, released as a single story rather than as part of a box set, and features Tarantino's name emblazoned across it like a banner headline, a marketing strategy which quite deliberately sets it apart from the 'ordinary' *CSI* release schedule and half-season or season box sets. The pre-eminence of 'Grave Danger' may be a result of its relatively recent transmission, and may also be linked to Tarantino's status as a popular *auteur*. However, fans discussed it in a series of ways, positioning it as 'a unique episode' (Moppig, 22 August 2005 2:54am, Talk CSI), and focusing on the peril that character Nick Stokes was placed in:

My fav episode is Grave Danger ... because i just love nick Stokes ... when I saw it for the fisrt time, I was so nervous, I was so sure that nick was going to be hurt and I was suffering with me ... I know it's kinda stupid but when I am watching CSI I kinda leave this world to enter their world (kou_seiya_girl, 27 October 2005 11:59pm, Talk CSI).

Tarantino is rarely mentioned by name in these online discussions. But the continued status of 'Grave Danger' as a favourite appears to indicate that fans nevertheless accept industry discourses of the story's 'event' status, as well as recognising that it significantly stretches the *CSI* format. It does this by incorporating a reflexive device which places the criminalist characters in the same position as the horrified audience – both are compelled to watch, on camera, Nick Stokes' imprisonment in a buried coffin:

> The construction of the television image within the series is seductive, and while it strives for legitimacy by suggesting that the image is to be read as evidence, it also betrays a rather disturbing fascination with what it means to look at and be fascinated by images in this way. (Lury 2005: 56)

Paralleling the Crime Scene team's voyeuristic situation with that of the real-life audience's gaze allows for heightened identification, as in the posting quoted above. Just as the CSI team are sadistically subjected to the ordeal of witnessing Nick's troubles, so too are the actual audience manipulated.

Throughout this chapter, we have sought to follow the evidence – albeit the evidence of online audience postings. We have argued that a general '*CSI* fan' cannot be assumed. Many fans on the message boards we examined did indeed follow all three franchise shows, sometimes grudgingly: 'If it wasn't for the fact that the first 3 letters in the name was CSI I would have stopped watching a long time ago' (Nina, 11 August 2005 9:29am, csiforum.no). And though *CSI: LV* tended to most commonly unite fans, *CSI: Miami* and *CSI: NY* divided and fragmented the fan community. Both came in for 'anti-fan' criticism, *Miami* especially so, even though *CSI: NY* also had its detractors: 'It seems that New York just isn't your cup of tea then. I wouldn't force myself to watch it just because it's got CSI in front of it' (Nicola, 11 August 2005 12:39pm, csiforum.no). As cultural studies and fan studies writers such as Couldry (2000) and Sandvoss (2005) have argued, audiences trace varied pathways through media franchises, or 'textual fields'. What is counted as 'the text' varies for different audiences, with format, character, and brand identity all remaining important points of entry for these fans' interpretations and online debates.

:19:

THE *CSI* PHENOMENON

DAVID BIANCULLI

The question has been put before me, and begged to be answered from an American perspective: what is it about *CSI: Miami* in particular, and the *CSI* forensics franchise in general, that makes it such a hot international television phenomenon?

Why is David Caruso's stoic character of Horatio Caine – he of the clipped cadences, stiff posture and eye-obscuring sunglasses – such a popular TV icon, even though his personality, for the most part, is as hidden from view as his baby blue eyes?

Not to turn it right back to a British perspective – but as Marcellus says in the opening scene of 'Hamlet':

> Horatio says 'tis but our fantasy.

The ingrained appeal of the heroes populating the *CSI* universe – *CSI: Miami*, the subsequent *CSI: NY* and the original mother ship, *CSI: Crime Scene Investigation* – is that they do, indeed, fulfil a fantasy. With their state-of-the-art equipment, their individual specialties and their leaps of logic that seem unfettered by either logic or gravity, they always get their man, or their woman.

Always. No matter how little trace evidence is available, they find something. They not only get justice, they get closure. And in a TV world where more and more of the most compelling stories are serialised, there's something comforting, and certainly accessible, in that.

In the USA, where the combined forces of all its intelligence agencies have been unable to locate Osama bin Laden five years after 9/11, there's a longing for the miss-no-detail, extract-all-confessions, solve-all-cases approach of the likes of *CSI: Miami*. But that doesn't truly explain the franchise's popularity, because the original *CSI: Crime Scene Investigation*, the one set in the desert gambling mecca of Las Vegas, predated 9/11 by nearly a year.

When the original *CSI* was launched by CBS in October 2000, it was paired with, and preceded by, another new crime series, a remake of the old David Janssen series *The Fugitive*. That series, not *CSI*, was the one on which CBS was pinning its hopes that autumn – a fact that was driven home to me when someone from the network phoned me to complain, the day of their premieres, that I had missed the boat by dismissing *The Fugitive* and raving about *CSI*.

The new *Fugitive*, starring Timothy Daly, was gone by June. *CSI*, starring William Petersen as dogged forensics investigator Gil Grissom, isn't going anywhere any time soon.

The appeal of the original series, to me, wasn't so much the flashy visuals – zooming inside aortas and chest cavities, recreating gunshot trajectories from a bullet's-eye view – as the sparkling acting. Petersen, a favourite performer since his little-seen 1987 HBO baseball telemovie *Long Gone* (a precursor to *Bull Durham*), got everything right, from his obsession to detail (and for insects) to his uncomfortable but undeniable attraction to Lady Heather, the dominatrix played by Melinda Clarke in three episodes, and counting, of *CSI*. And Petersen's co-star, Marg Helgenberger (from ABC's *China Beach*) as Catherine Willows, had her own determined demeanour and personal quirks, including a past as a stripper.

When CBS and executive producer Jerry Bruckheimer conspired to spin *CSI* off into a second series, *CSI: Miami*, in 2002, Petersen made no secret of his dislike of the move. The elements of his show, especially the actors, weren't so easily replaceable, he argued. He was right, at least qualitatively. But the protected Monday-night time slot in which CBS launched the show, as well as the popularity of the episode on *CSI* which introduced Caruso's Caine character, made it the season's most popular new drama. In 2004, *CSI: NY*, starring Gary Sinise – like Caruso and Petersen, an actor gifted at brooding – followed, and also caught on big in the States.

Franchise fever, in the USA, is an undeniable and temporarily unavoidable phenomenon, driven by three different levels of network greed

– making it a sort of perfect storm of spread-the-wealth TV scheduling. In the 1990s, the broadcast networks had cloned news magazines with abandon, and, for a few years, with success. For a while, there were two editions of *60 Minutes* each week, three editions of *Dateline*, and so on.

And when ABC replicated the instant success of Britain's *Who Wants to Be a Millionaire* with its own version, it went crazy with franchise fever. Three different weekly editions were scheduled in the autumn of 1999, and ended up being that year's three most popular series. The following season, ABC, in a spasm of undiluted greed, scheduled four hours of *Millionaire* each week, and killed the brand, and the primetime version of the show, through overexposure. Network executives, without and within ABC, likened its reliance on *Millionaire* to a dependence on crack cocaine.

In the area of scripted television, that same type of franchise fever was driven by Dick Wolf's *Law & Order* series: the original article, as well as *L&O: Special Victims Unit*, *L&O: Criminal Intent* and others. In the autumn of 2002, all three of those *Law & Order* shows were in the season's top twenty in the USA. Their hold on the American imagination seemed unassailable – but that same season, *CSI: Crime Scene Investigation* was the most popular series of all, and its new spin-off, *CSI: Miami*, ended its freshman year tied for tenth.

So that's the first element of the network's greedy perfect storm: the shows are immensely popular.

The second element is that, being variations on a familiar brand, new entries are easily and instantly promoted. A brand new series on an autumn schedule usually has to be sold from scratch: here's the star, here's the premise, here's the tone, here's what to expect and why you should sample it.

When you say *CSI: NY*, you know exactly what you're getting. You're getting forensic specialists solving grisly crimes, and doing it in the country's biggest TV market. (That's why you'll never see a 'CSI: Boise'. Not enough home-town viewers to give it an instant push, whereas Vegas, Miami and New York all are self-starters.) All you have to do is select a new theme song from The Who's musical catalogue, and you're in business – a very lucrative business.

And the final greedy element, the one that makes *CSI* and its offspring the most amazing television phenomenon around right now, is that the largely self-contained episodes of these *CSI* shows repeat well. Extremely well. Astoundingly well.

Wolf's *Law & Order* shows are known for attracting viewers to multiple plays, especially on cable, where in the States there seem to be entire networks devoted to one *Law & Order* rerun cycle or another. In general, this is an inverse of the viewing pattern of, say, ABC's *Lost* or Fox's *24*, shows that fans love to watch the first time around and go on the thrill ride of unravelling a season-long mystery week by week. When those shows are repeated – and these days, they generally aren't – they get very low ratings. Whoever cared, saw them the first time, or is waiting for the full-season set to be released on DVD.

But at the moment I'm writing this, a late-summer week in which every network but Fox is wallowing in reruns, three of the week's top ten shows are repeats of *CSI* (third), *CSI: Miami* (fourth) and *CSI: NY* (tenth). Popularity, expandability, repeatability – it's no wonder there are three *CSI* shows on CBS right now. It's surprising, in a way, there aren't more.

Why worldwide, though? And why does *CSI: Miami* eclipse even its parent programme in terms of global popularity?

About this, I have only a few guesses. Internationally, Miami is a glamorous place to imagine, if not to actually visit, and the city and region still are benefiting from the twenty-year-old buzz over a previous international TV smash, *Miami Vice*. Similarly, while Petersen and Sinise would have little recognisable worldwide clout, at least in terms of their TV roles, Caruso has that one shining season of *NYPD Blue* under his belt.

Though there are continuing storylines on the various *CSI* shows, from Catherine's issues with her father to Caine's dogged search to learn the truth about his brother, they never really get in the way of the case of the week. Internationally as well as domestically, an hour of *CSI* can be plugged into nearly any appropriate programming hole and do well, and stand alone as an easily digested treat.

Easily digested, that is, if it's not one of the shows zooming in, up close and way too personal, on flesh-eating maggots or water-bloating corpses.

But having gone this far in explaining the *CSI* phenomenon, I can no longer hold back my own critical response, which is aligned with that of *CSI* star Petersen: the subsequent spin-offs are diluted, less imaginative versions of the original.

It bothers me on *CSI: Miami*, for example, that Caruso's Horatio Caine can fall in love with Marisol (Alana de la Garza), the sister of his CSI colleague Eric Delko, marry her – and then not kiss her. The morning after they're married, when he's saying goodbye as she eats breakfast outdoors, no kiss. When she's shot, and he's riding with her in the ambulance, no kiss. At her hospital bedside, on her death bed, no kiss. That's not just stoic. That's frozen.

And every episode of *CSI: Miami*, much more so than the original

CSI, always seems to hinge on at least one scene – usually two – in which Horatio, or one of his tough-talking colleagues, isolates a perp or a witness and, with a few well-chosen threats and questions, gets the formerly uncooperative person to fold, and spill the information that leads to the next plot point. Fold, fold, fold. There's less folding, on a weekly basis, in an origami factory.

I also don't like the jokey opening-scene punchline that always precedes the credits, or the convoluted plot machinations that aren't just twists, but approach the complexity of double helixes. My favourite one in all of *CSI: Miami* to date had an ex-girlfriend of Delko's taking aim at his sister, Marisol, from the balcony of an apartment complex. They caught her afterwards with the rifle in her trunk, but her story – which turned out to be true – was that she lost her nerve at the last minute, and didn't fire the gun. Instead, we (and Horatio) soon learn, Marisol was shot by a sniper who had it in for Horatio, and wanted to punish him by killing his new bride.

And just happened to take aim, and fire, one floor above the wacky ex-girlfriend's balcony, a few seconds after she had the same woman in her sights but decided not to pull the trigger. Go ahead. Compute the odds on that one and get back to me. Meanwhile, I'll be watching the original *CSI: Crime Scene Investigation*.

At least there, the plot machinations tend to be a little less absurd. And about once a season, just to sweeten the pot, there's a visit to a dominatrix.

::
NOTES

CHAPTER 1. THE HOOK AND THE LOOK

1. This entry has since changed, and Mr Parker has changed his opinion.
2. The Australian Channel Nine experience echoes that of Five in the UK, described by Ian Goode in his unpublished paper delivered to the Quality American TV conference in 2004.
3. www.museum.tv.
4. *Dragnet*, BCI Eclipse, 2003.
5. Or so says the Internet Movie Database biography for Webb, www.imdb.com/name/nm0916131/bio, downloaded 24 February 2006.
6. All the episodes in the first series are entitled The Big Something – an ongoing homage to Raymond Chandler's *The Big Sleep* perhaps?
7. Caldwell (2005: 91) lists the research of Chris Anderson, Michele Hilmes, William Boddy and Tino Balio in this regard.
8. By coincidence, on the same day that I viewed this episode, I also watched a Season Six episode of *CSI* which also includes a long and similarly extreme close-up of a teenage girl confessing to the murder of her mother. Although the confessional close-up is now a very familiar camera strategy in the TV crime series, *CSI* often exaggerates it to almost grotesque effect.
9. 'The Vibe of Vice' Featurette. Season One DVD.
10. 'Evan' first aired on NBC 3 May 1985.
11. Comments made in an interview on Disc Three of the Season One DVDs. *Crime Scene Investigation*, 2000 and 2001, CBS Worldwide Inc.
12. As Cannon tells the viewer in his voiceover commentary to the episode.
13. As possible confirmation of this claim, the episode 'Fight Night' (3:7) won an Emmy for 'Outstanding Sound Editing in a Series' in 2003.
14. Featurette, Season One DVD.

15. These are points made by Ian Goode in his unpublished paper presented to the Quality American TV conference – and I thank him for introducing me to the work of Stafford which is extremely provocative in relation to these issues.

16. The success of this strategy might be gauged by the fact that Bruckheimer's other crime show, *Cold Case*, seems to be premised entirely on the use of flashbacks to delineate the crime in the past which must then be revisited and solved in the present.

17. The last section of this paper which addresses the use of CGI images and sound is a revised version of the argument mounted in a previous article by the author entitled 'Crime Scene Investigations (CSI): A Fluorescent Analysis', in *Metro* magazine and is reproduced here with kind permission from the editor. See www.metromagazine. com.au.

CHAPTER 3. ANATOMISING GILBERT GRISSOM

1. I should in fairness also mention Murray Smith's *Engaging Characters: Fiction, Emotion and the Cinema* (Oxford: Clarendon Press, 1995) although he is interested in developing a cognitive-based theory of spectators' emotional responses to characters, whereas I am interested in developing a narrative-based theory of character construction.

2. Lury suggests that this decor links Grissom to the cinematic serial killer John Doe in *Se7en* (David Fincher, 1995). While I agree with Lury that the design of Grissom's office plays up the mad scientist trope, I'm a bit sceptical about this further claim.

3. I am indebted to William Uricchio, one of my favourite white males, for this point.

CHAPTER 6. BODY MATTERS

1. This stylised effect was previously most memorably seen in a cinematic context in Gulf war movie *Three Kings* (Russell, 1999).

2. In *CSI: Miami* this notion of 'talking' to or with the victim is even more overt, where pathologist Alexx Woods often directly addresses the victim lying on the gurney. As the CBS website notes, 'People have been confused by her bedside manner with the dead, but to Woods they are her patients and they have come to her *because they still have a story to tell*' (emphasis added). See www.cbs.com/primetime/csi_miami/ bios/index.php?cast_me mber=kandi, accessed 28 March 2006.

3. *Fantastic Voyage* won the Special Effects Oscar in 1966 (as did *Innerspace* subsequently in 1988).

4. While 'CSI producers acknowledge that they take some liberties with fact and the capabilities of science... to keep their storylines moving' they are also at pains to employ real crime lab technicians as technical advisers on the programme (Willing 2004: 2) and often draw on real documented cases as source material.

CHAPTER 9. *CSI* AND SOUND

1. In *Se7en* – thus, I suspect, not coincidentally – the detective Somerset (played by Morgan Freeman) also listens to Bach (in the scene in the public library).

2. The effect and function of the 'sound cliff' is described by one of its superior exponents: see Walter Murch, 'Touch of Silence', in Larry Sider, Diane Freeman and Jerry Sider (eds.) *Soundscape: The school of sound lectures, 1998–2001*, Wallflower Press: London (2003), pp.83–103. See p.95 where he describes this effect in relation to *Apocalypse Now* (1979).

3. Indeed, as Weissmann and Boyle point out: 'It is notable... that even sound evidence is generally translated, via technology, into a series of increasingly spectacular images." op cit. p.98.

4. This is possibly another reference to *Se7en* which features Dante's *Purgatory* as one of the texts consulted by the detectives.

CHAPTER 13. 'THE BULLET CONFIRMS THE STORY TOLD BY THE POTATO'

1. Avcibas, Ismail, Sevinc Bayram, Nasir Memon, Mahalingam Ramkumar, Bulent Sankur, 'A Classifier Design for Detecting Image Manipulations', in *International Conference on Image Processing* (1-5), 2004: 2645-2648; Peterson, Gilbert L., 'Forensic Analysis of Digital Image Tampering', in *Advances in Digital Forensics* (194) 2006: 259-270; Popescu, Any C., Hany Farid, 'Exposing Digital Forgeries in Color Filter Array Interpolated Images', in *IEE Transactions on Signal Processing* (53: 10, Part 2), October 2005: 3948-3959; Popescu, Any C., Hany Farid, 'Exposing Digital Forgeries by Detecting Traces of Resampling', in *IEE Transactions on Signal Processing* (53: 2, Part 2), February 2005: 758-767; Lukas, Jan, Jessica Fridrich, and Miroslav Goljan, 'Determining Digital Image Origin Using Sensor Imperfections', in *Image and Video Communications and Processing* (Parts 1 and 2): 5685. *Proceedings of the Society of Photo-Optical Instrumentation Engineers* (SPIE), 2005: 249-260; Lukas, Jan and Goljan, Miroslav, 'Detecting Digital Image Forgeries Using Sensor Pattern Noise', in *Proceedings of SPIE Electronic Imaging*, Photonics West, January 2006.

CHAPTER 14. MAC'S MELANCHOLIA

1. Soon after the towers collapsed it became clear that the emergency operation was not about rescue but recovery, not about saving lives but retrieving bodies. More troubling still was those who died but left no trace, no visible remains. In the days immediately after, people headed down to Ground Zero to locate missing relatives and friends; and many brought photographs of loved ones to hold and/ or leave at the site in the hope someone would remember. With few reunited, these images tapped into a broader, more important need to utter in public the pain of loss and grief, a desire to transfer private bereavement into a collective

experience. Night vigils in various public New York spaces – in Union Square, Houston and Washington Square Park – assumed a spontaneity, allowing people to grieve publicly, mourn and meditate on loss. One year later and the desolate Ground Zero site officially memorialised those gone with a roll call of the dead. Each name read out achieving, as Marita Sturken puts it, 'a historical presence through absence' (1997: 59).

CHAPTER 15. FIVE'S FINEST

1. *Baywatch* is the most high-profile example of a cancelled US show being rescued by international syndication.

2. Unattributed quotations from Jeff Ford, Five's then Director of Acquisitions, derive from a personal interview with the author on 27 February 2006.

3. The American specificity of *CSI*, and how the show manages its 'cultural discount' (Hoskins and Mirus 1988), would also be interesting to explore further.

4. These would include the scheduling of *CSI*, which was moved from Fridays to Thursdays in the slot behind the successful *Survivor* franchise.

5. There is an interesting circular tension here, in that this selective approach actually increases the likelihood of output deals, as sellers can package fewer more desired programmes with a larger number of less desired shows. So, to the idea of 'invisible television' (i.e. unscreened fragments) needs to be added the idea of 'partially visible television', namely the 'baggage' that accompanies hit shows, which is frequently shunted into early morning or late-night slots. Within an increasingly multichannel environment, both fragmented and 'unwanted' US shows are likely to become more and more visible on British television as they represent a cost-effective way to fill broadcasting hours. For example, Channel 4 screened *The Fugitive*, while *Dark Angel* and Rob Lowe's *The Lyon's Den* have been shown on Five.

6. This six-month delay gave Five the chance to see how *CSI* was performing domestically, but it also meant that the show's price rose, as *CSI* was taking off in the USA. Although no details of Five's deal are available, *CSI* 'is averaging an estimated $650,000 per episode from its sales to foreign broadcasters.' (Guider and Tasca 2002)

7. By contrast, *CSI* and reality show *Survivor* have worked successfully together for CBS.

8. In June 2005, Five's next move was to use medical drama *House, M.D.*, whose casting of British actor Hugh Laurie would have curiosity value to British audiences, to move into Thursday evenings.

9. CBS was already using *CSI* to exploit this sense of an 'end of an era' to challenge NBC's long-standing dominance of Thursday night.

10. That it was time for Five to signal its turnaround is suggested by the proliferation of digital off-shoots such as E4, which would fragment the market further and increase

competition for US imports.

11. This is obviously complicated by the fact that CBS also uses the *CSI* franchise for its branding.

12. Sky Networks' Dawn Airey comments: 'It's nice not to be reliant on another country's decisions for your programming, however Sky One is known for having top shows from the US and we absolutely intend to keep that positioning' (quoted in Johnson 2003; see also Revoir 2003).

CHAPTER 18. INVESTIGATING '*CSI* TELEVISION FANDOM'

1. Where we use only the term *CSI*, given in italics, we are referring to the franchise or group of branded fictional TV texts as a whole.

2. Talk CSI had 8925 registered users as of 15 April 2006. The European-oriented *CSI* sites do not supply comparable data.

3. Rather than repeatedly inserting 'sic', or correcting spelling or grammar, we will simply reproduce website material and postings exactly as they are given online.

EPISODE GUIDE

CSI: CRIME SCENE INVESTIGATION (CSI: LAS VEGAS)
Original Air Date: 6 October 2000

SEASON ONE

1:1 Pilot
w: Anthony E. Zuiker
d: Danny Cannon

1:2 Cool Change
w: Anthony E. Zuiker
d: Michael W. Watkins

1:3 Crate 'n' Burial
w. Ann Donahue
d. Danny Cannon

1:4 Pledging Mr Johnson
w. Josh Berman, Anthony E. Zuiker
d. Richard J. Lewis

1:5 Friends and Lovers
w. Andrew Lipsitz, Eli Talbert
d. Lou Antonio

1:6 Who Are You?
w. Josh Berman, Carol Mendelsohn,
   Eli Talbert
d. Danny Cannon

1:7 Blood Drops
w. Ann Donahue, Tish McCarthy
   (story)
d. Kenneth Fink

1:8 Anonymous
w. Anthony E. Zuiker, Eli Talbert
d. Danny Cannon

1:9 Unfriendly Skies
w. Anthony E. Zuiker, Andrew
   Lipsitz, Carol Mendelsohn
d. Michael Shapiro

1:10 Sex, Lies and Larvae
w. Ann Donahue, Josh Berman
d. Thomas J. Wright

1:11 I-15 Murders
w. Carol Mendelsohn
d. Oz Scott

1:12 Fahrenheit 932
w. Jacqueline Zambrano
d. Danny Cannon

1:13 Boom
w. Josh Berman, Ann Donahue,
   Carol Mendelsohn
d. Kenneth Fink

1:14 To Halve and to Hold
w. Andrew Lipsitz, Ann Donahue
d. Lou Antonio

1:15 Table Stakes
w. Anthony E. Zuiker, Carol
   Mendelsohn, Elizabeth Devine
   (story)
d. Danny Cannon

1:16 Too Tough To Die
w. Elizabeth Devine
d. Richard J. Lewis

1:17 Face Lift
w. Josh Berman
d. Lou Antonio

1:18 $35K O.B.O.
w. Eli Talbert
d. Roy H. Wagner

1:19 Gentle, Gentle
w. Ann Donahue
d. Danny Cannon

1:20 Sounds of Silence
w. Josh Berman, Andrew Lipsitz
d. Peter Markle

1:21 Justice is Served
w. Jerry Stahl
d. Thomas J. Wright

1:22 Evaluation Day
w. Anthony E. Zuiker
d. Kenneth Fink

1:23 The Strip Strangler
w. Ann Donahue
d. Danny Cannon

SEASON TWO

2:1 Burked
w. Carol Mendelsohn, Anthony E.
   Zuiker
d. Danny Cannon

2:2 Chaos Theory
w. Josh Berman, Eli Talbert
d. Kenneth Fink

2:3 Overload
w. Josh Berman
d. Richard J. Lewis

2:4 Bully For You
w. Ann Donahue
d. Thomas J. Wright

2:5 Scuba Doobie Doo
w. Andrew Lipsitz, Elizabeth Devine
d. Jefery Levy

2:6 Alter Boys
w. Ann Donahue
d. Danny Cannon

2:7 Caged
w. Carol Mendelsohn, Elizabeth
   Devine
d. Richard J. Lewis

2:8 Slaves of Las Vegas
w. Jerry Stahl
d. Peter Markle

2:9 And Then There Were None
w. Eli Talbert, Carol Mendelsohn,
   Josh Berman (story)
d. John Patterson

2:10 Ellie
w. Anthony E. Zuiker
d. Charles Correll

2:11 Organ Grinder
w. Ann Donahue, Elizabeth Devine
d. Allison Liddi

2:12 You've Got Male
w. Marc Dube, Corey D. Miller
d. Charles Correll

2:13 Identity Crisis
w. Anthony E. Zuiker, Ann Donahue
d. Kenneth Fink

2:14 The Finger
w. Danny Cannon, Carol
   Mendelsohn
d. Richard J. Lewis

2:15 Burden of Proof
w. Ann Donahue
d. Kenneth Fink

2:16 Primum Non Nocere
w. Andrew Lipsitz
d. Danny Cannon

2:17 Felonious Monk
w. Jerry Stahl
d. Kenneth Fink

2:18 Chasing the Bus
w. Eli Talbert
d. Richard J. Lewis

2:19 Stalker
w. Anthony E. Zuiker, Danny Cannon
d. Peter Markle

2:20 Cats in the Cradle
w. Kristy Dobkin
d. Richard J. Lewis

2:21 Anatomy of a Lye
w. Josh Berman, Andrew Lipsitz
d. Kenneth Fink

2:22 Cross-Jurisdictions
w. Anthony E. Zuiker, Ann Donahue,
   Carol Mendelsohn
d. Danny Cannon

2:23 The Hunger Artist
w. Jerry Stahl
d. Richard J. Lewis

SEASON THREE
3:1 Revenge is Best Served Cold
w. Anthony E. Zuiker, Carol
   Mendelsohn
d. Danny Cannon

3:2 The Accused is Entitled
w. Ann Donahue, Elizabeth Devine
d. Kenneth Fink

3:3 Let the Seller Beware
w. Andrew Lipsitz, Anthony E. Zuiker
d. Richard J. Lewis

3:4 A Little Murder
w. Naren Shankar, Ann Donahue
d. Tucker Gates

3:5 Abra Cadaver
w. Anthony E. Zuiker, Danny Cannon
d. Danny Cannon

3:6 The Execution of Catherine Willows
w. Carol Mendelsohn, Elizabeth Devine
d. Kenneth Fink

3:7 Fight Night
w. Andrew Lipsitz, Naren Shankar
d. Richard J. Lewis

3:8 Snuff
w. Ann Donahue, Bob Harris
d. Kenneth Fink

3:9 Blood Lust
w. Josh Berman, Carol Mendelsohn
d. Charles Correll

3:10 High and Low
w. Eli Talbert, Naren Shankar
d. Richard J. Lewis

3:11 Recipe for Murder
w. Anthony E. Zuiker, Ann Donahue
d. Richard J. Lewis and J. Miller Tobin

3:12 Got Murder?
w. Sarah Goldfinger
d. Kenneth Fink

3:13 Random Acts of Violence
w. Danny Cannon, Naren Shankar
d. Danny Cannon

3:14 One Hit Wonder
w. Corey D. Miller
d. Felix Enriquez Alcala

3:15 Lady Heather's Box
w. Carol Mendelsohn, Andrew Lipsitz, Eli Talbert, Naren Shankar
d. Richard J. Lewis

3:16 Lucky Strike
w. Eli Talbert, Anthony E. Zuiker
d. Kenneth Fink

3:17 Crash and Burn
w. Josh Berman
d. Richard J. Lewis

3:18 Precious Metal
w. Naren Shankar, Andrew Lipsitz
d. Deran Sarafian

3:19 A Night at the Movies
w. Anthony E. Zuiker, Danny Cannon, Carol Mendelsohn (story)
d. Matt Earl Beesley

3:20 Last Laugh
w. Bob Harris, Anthony E. Zuiker
d. Richard J. Lewis

3:21 Forever
w. Sarah Goldfinger
d. David Grossman

3:22 Play With Fire
w. Naren Shankar, Andrew Lipsitz
d. Kenneth Fink

3:23 Inside the Box
w. Carol Mendelsohn, Anthony E. Zuiker
d. Danny Cannon

SEASON FOUR

4:1 Assume Nothing
w. Anthony E. Zuiker, Danny Cannon
d. Richard J. Lewis

4:2 All For Our Country
w. Andrew Lipsitz, Carol Mendelsohn
d. Richard J. Lewis

4:3 Homebodies
w. Sarah Goldfinger, Naren Shankar
d. Kenneth Fink

4:4 Feeling the Heat
w. Anthony E. Zuiker, Eli Talbert
d. Kenneth Fink

4:5 Fur and Loathing
w. Jerry Stahl
d. Richard J. Lewis

4:6 Jackpot
w. Carol Mendelsohn, Naren Shankar
d. Danny Cannon

4:7 Invisible Evidence
w. Josh Berman, Kathleen Butler
d. Danny Cannon

4:8 After the Show
w. Andrew Lipsitz, Elizabeth Devine
d. Kenneth Fink

4:9 Grissom Versus the Volcano
w. Anthony E. Zuiker, Carol
    Mendelsohn
d. Richard J. Lewis

4:10 Coming of Rage
w. Sarah Goldfinger

d. Nelson McCormick

4:11 Eleven Angry Jurors
w. Josh Berman, Andrew Lipsitz
d. Matt Earl Beesley

4:12 Butterflied
w. David Rambo
d. Richard J. Lewis

4:13 Suckers
w. Danny Cannon, Josh Berman
d. Danny Cannon

4:14 Paper or Plastic?
w. Naren Shankar
d. Kenneth Fink

4:15 Early Rollout
w. Anthony E. Zuiker, Carol
    Mendelsohn
d. Duane Clark

4:16 Getting Off
w. Jerry Stahl
d. Kenneth Fink

4:17 XX
w. Ethlie Ann Vare
d. Deran Sarafian

4:18 Bad to the Bone
w. Eli Talbert
d. David Grossman

4:19 Bad Words
w. Sarah Goldfinger
d. Rob Bailey

4:20 Dead Ringer

w. Elizabeth Devine
d. Kenneth Fink

4:21 Turn of the Screws
w. Josh Berman
d. Deran Serafian

4:22 No More Bets
w. Naren Shankar, Carol
   Mendelsohn, Judith McCreary
d. Richard J. Lewis

4:23 Bloodlines
w. Carol Mendelsohn, Naren Shankar
d. Kenneth Fink

SEASON FIVE
5:1 Viva Las Vegas
w. Danny Cannon, Carol
   Mendelsohn
d. Danny Cannon

5:2 Down the Drain
w. Naren Shankar
d. Kenneth Fink

5:3 Harvest
w. Judith McCreary
d. David Grossman

5:4 Crow's Feet
w. Josh Berman
d. Richard J. Lewis

5:5 Swap Meet
w. David Rambo, Naren Shankar,
   Carol Mendelsohn
d. Danny Cannon

5:6 What's Eating Gilbert Grissom?
w. Sarah Goldfinger
d. Kenneth Fink

5:7 Formalities
w. Naren Shankar, Dustin Lee
   Abraham
d. Bill Eagles

5:8 Ch-Ch-Changes
w. Jerry Stahl
d. Richard J. Lewis

5:9 Mea Culpa
w. Josh Berman
d. David Grossman

5:10 No Humans Involved
w. Judith McCreary
d. Rob Bailey

5:11 Who Shot Sherlock?
w. David Rambo, Richard Catalani
d. Kenneth Fink

5:12 Snakes
w. Dustin Lee Abraham
d. Richard J. Lewis

5:13 Nesting Dolls
w. Sarah Goldfinger
d. Bill Eagles

5:14 Unbearable
w. Carol Mendelsohn, Josh Berman
d. Kenneth Fink

5:15 King Baby
w. Jerry Stahl
d. Richard J. Lewis

5:16 Big Middle
w. Naren Shankar, Judith McCreary
d. Bill Eagles

5:17 Compulsion
w. Josh Berman, Richard Catalani
d. Duane Clark

5:18 Spark of Life
w. Allen MacDonald
d. Kenneth Fink

5:19 4x4
w. Dustin Lee Abraham, David
    Rambo
d. Terrence O'Hara

5:20 Hollywood Brass
w. Carol Mendelsohn, Sarah
    Goldfinger
d. Bill Eagles

5:21 Committed
w. Sarah Goldfinger, Richard J. Lewis
    & Uttam Narsu
d. Richard J. Lewis

5:22 Weeping Willows
w. Areanne Lloyd
d. Kenneth Fink

5:23 Iced
w. Josh Berman
d. Richard J. Lewis

5:24 Grave Danger: Part 1
w. Anthony E. Zuiker, Carol
    Mendelsohn, Naren Shankar
d. Quentin Tarantino

5:25 Grave Danger: Part 2
w. Anthony E. Zuiker, Carol
    Mendelsohn, Naren Shankar
d. Quentin Tarantino

SEASON SIX
6:1 Bodies in Motion
w. Carol Mendelsohn, Naren
    Shankar
d. Richard J. Lewis

6:2 Room Service
w. Dustin Lee Abrahams, Henry
    Alonso Myers
d. Kenneth Fink

6:3 Bite Me
w. Josh Berman
d. Jeffrey G. Hunt

6:4 Shooting Stars
w. Danny Cannon
d. Danny Cannon

6:5 Gum Drops
w. Sarah Goldfinger
d. Rchard J. Lewis

6:6 Secrets and Flies
w. Josh Berman
d. Terrence O'Hara

6:7 A Bullet Runs Through It,
    Part 1
w. Richard Catalani, Carol
    Mendelsohn
d. Danny Cannon

6:8 A Bullet Runs Through It,

Part 2
w. Richard Catalani, Carol
   Mendelsohn
d. Kenneth Fink

6:9 Dog Eat Dog
w. Dustin Lee Abraham, Allen
   MacDonald
d. Duane Clark

6:10 Still Life
w. David Rambo
d. Richard J. Lewis

6:11 Werewolves
w. Josh Berman
d. Kenneth Fink

6:12 Daddy's Little Girl
w. Sarah Goldfinger, Henry Alonso
   Myers
d. Terrence O'Hara

6:13 Kiss Kiss, Bye Bye
w. David Rambo
d. Danny Cannon

6:14 Killer
w. Dustin Lee Abraham. Naren
   Shankar
d. Kenneth Fink

6:15 Pirates of the Third Reich
w. Jerry Stahl
d. Richard J. Lewis

6:16 Up In Smoke
w. Josh Berman
d. Duane Clark

6:17 I Like to Watch
w. Richard Catalani, Henry Alonso
   Myers
d. Kenneth Fink

6:18 The Unusual Suspect
w. Allen MacDonald
d. Alec Smight

6:19 Spellbound
w. Jacqueline Hoyt
d. Jeffrey G. Hunt

6:20 Poppin' Tags
w. Dustin Lee Abraham
d. Bryan Spicer

6:21 Rashomama
w. Sarah Goldfinger
d. Kenneth Fink

6:22 Time of Your Death
w. Richard Catalani, David Rambo
d. Dean White

6:23 Bang-Bang
w. Naren Shankar, Anthony E. Zuiker
d. Terrence O'Hara

6:24 Way To Go
w. Jerry Stahl
d. Kenneth Fink

SEASON SEVEN
7:1 Built to Kill: Part 1
w. Sarah Goldfiner, David Rambo
d. Kenneth Fink

7:2 Built to Kill: Part 2

w. Sarah Goldfinger, David Rambo
d. Kenneth Fink

7:3 Toe Tags
w. Richard Catalani, Douglas Petrie
d. Jeffrey G. Hunt

7:4 Fannysmackin'
w. Dustin Lee Abraham
d. Richard J. Lewis

7:5 Double Cross
w. Marlene Meyer
d. Michael Slovis

7:6 Burnout
w. Jacqueline Hoyt
d. Alec Smight

7:7 Post Mortem
w. Dustin Lee Abraham, David Rambo
d. Richard J. Lewis

7:8 Happenstance
w. Sarah Goldfinger
d. Jean de Segonzac

7:9 Living Legend
w. Douglas Petrie
d. Martha Coolidge

7:10 Loco Motives
w. Evan Dunsky
d. Kenneth Fink

7:11 Leaving Las Vegas
w. Allen MacDonald
d. Richard J. Lewis

CSI: MIAMI
Original Air Date: 9 May 2002

SEASON ONE

1:0 Cross-Jurisdictions (Pilot)
w. Anthony E. Zuiker, Ann Donahue,
    Carol Mendelsohn
d. Danny Cannon

1:1 Golden Parachute
w. Steven Maeda
d. Joe Chappelle

1:2 Losing Face
w. Steven Maeda, Gwendolyn Parker
d. Joe Chappelle

1:3 Wet Foot/Dry Foot
w. Eddie Guerra

d. Tucker Gates
1:4 Just One Kiss
w. Laurie McCarthy, Matt Witten
d. Scott Brazil

1:5 Ashes to Ashes
w. Mark Israel
d. Bryan Spicer

1:6 Broken
w. Ildy Modrovich, Laurence Walsh
d. Deran Sarafian

1:7 Breathless
w. Steven Maeda, Gwendolyn Parker
d. Charles Correll

1:8 Slaughterhouse
w. Laurie McCarthy
d. Richard Pearce

1:9 Kill Zone
w. Lois Johnson, Mark Israel
d. Daniel Attias

1:10 A Horrible Mind
w. Ildy Modrovich, Laurence Walsh
d. Greg Yaitanes

1:11 Camp Fear
w. Steven Maeda, Eddie Guerra
d. Deran Sarafian

1:12 Entrance Wound
w. Laurie McCarthy, Gwendolyn
   Parker
d. David Grossman

1:13 Bunk
w. Elizabeth Devine
d. Charles Correll

1:14 Forced Entry
w. Mark Israel, Lois Johnson
d. Artie Mandelberg

1:15 Dead Woman Walking
w. Ildy Modrovich, Laurence Walsh
d. Jeannot Szwarc

1:16: Evidence of Things Unseen
w. David Black
d. Joe Chappelle

1:17 Simple Man
w. Steven Maeda
d. Greg Yaitanes

1:18 Dipso Day
w. Elizabeth Devine
d. David Grossman

1:19 Double Cap
w. Marc Dube
d. Joe Chappelle

1:20 Grave Young Men
w. Lois Johnson
d. Peter Markle

1:21 Spring Break
w. Steven Maeda
d. Deran Sarafian

1:22 Tinder Box
w. Corey D. Miller
d. Charles Correll

1:23 Freaks and Tweaks
w. Elizabeth Devine, John Haynes
d. Deran Sarafian

1:24 Body Count
w. Ildy Modrovich, Laurence Walsh
d. Joe Chappelle

SEASON TWO
2:1 Blood Brothers
w. Ann Donahue
d. Danny Cannon

2:2 Dead Zone
w. Michael Ostrowski
d. Joe Chappelle

2:3 Hard Time
w. Elizabeth Devine

d. Deran Safarian

2:4 Death Grip
w. Steven Maeda
d. David Grossman

2:5 The Best Defence
w. Shane Brennan
d. Scott Lautanen

2:6 Hurricane Anthony
w. Ildy Modrovich, Laurence Walsh
d. Joe Chappelle

2:7 Grand Prix
w. Michael Ostrowski, Steven Maeda
d. David Grossman

2:8 Big Brother
w. Ann Donahue, Jonathan Glassner
d. Joe Chappelle

2:9 Bait
w. Steven Maeda, Shane Brennan
d. Deran Sarafian

2:10 Extreme
w. Elizabeth Devine
d. Karen Gaviola

2:11 Complications
w. Sunil Nayar, Corey D. Miller
d. Scott Lautanen

2:12 Witness to Murder
w. Ildy Modrovich, Laurence Walsh
d. Duane Clark

2:13 Blood Moon
w. Jonathan Glassner, Marc Dube

d. Scott Lautanen

2:14 Slow Burn
w. Shane Brennan, Michael Ostrowski
d. Joe Chappelle

2:15 Stalkerazzi
w. Elizabeth Devine, Steven Maeda
d. Deran Sarafian

2:16 Invasion
w. Brian Davidson, Jonathan Glassner
d. Felix Enriquez Alcala

2:17 Money For Nothing
w. Marc Dube
d. Karen Gaviola

2.18 Wannabe
w. Elizabeth Devine, Steven Maeda
d. Frederick King Keller

2:19 Deadline
w. Ildy Modrovich, Laurence Walsh
d. Deran Sarafian

2:20 The Oath
w. Alison Lea Bingeman
d. Duane Clark

2:21 Not Landing
w. Shane Brennan, Marc Dube
d. Joe Chappelle

2:22 Rap Sheet
w. Ildy Modrovich, Corey D. Miller
d. David Grossman

2:23 MIA/NYC – Nonstop
w. Anthony E. Zuiker, Ann Donahue,

Carol Mendelsohn
d. Danny Cannon

2:24 Innocent
w. Steven Maeda, Sunil Nayar
d. Joe Chappelle

SEASON THREE
3:1 Lost Son
w. Ann Donahue, Elizabeth Devine
d. Duane Clark

3:2 Pro Per
w. Steven Maeda, John Haynes
d. Karen Gaviola

3:3 Under the Influence
w. Marc Dube, Corey D. Miller
d. Scott Lautanen

3:4 Murder in a Flash
w. Anne McGrail, Sunil Nayar
d. Frederick King Keller

3:5 Legal
w. Michael Ostrowski, Ildy Modrovich
d. Duane Clark
3:6 Hell Night
w. Steven Maeda, Corey D. Miller
d. Scott Lautanen

3:7 Crime Wave
w. Elizabeth Devine
d. Karen Gaviola

3:8 Speed Kills
w. Sunil Nayar, Marc Dube
d. Frederick King Keller

3:9 Pirated
w. Michael Ostrowski, Steven Maeda
d. Duane Clark

3:10 After the Fall
w. Ildy Modrovich, Marc Dube
d. Scott Lautanen

3:11 Addiction
w. Charles Holland
d. Steven DePaul

3:12 Shoot Out
w. Corey D. Miller, Sunil Nayar
d. Norberto Barba

3:13 Cop Killer
w. Steven Maeda, Krystal Houghten
d. Jonathan Glassner

3:14 One Night Stand
w. Michael Ostrowski, John Haynes
d. Greg Yaitanes

3:15 Identity
w. Ann Donahue, Ildy Modrovich
d. Gloria Muzio

3:16 Nothing to Lose
w. Elizabeth Devine, Marc Dube
d. Karen Gaviola

3:17 Money Plane
w. Steven Maeda, Sunil Nayar
d. Scott Lautenen

3:18 Game Over
w. Michal Ostrowski, Corey D. Miller
d. Jonathan Glassner

3:19 Sex and Taxes
w. Ildy Modrovich, Brian L. Davidson
d. Scott Shiffman

3:20 Killer Date
w. Elizabeth Devine, John Haynes
d. Karen Gaviola

3:21 Recoil
w. Steven Maeda, Marc Dube
d. Joe Chappelle

3:22 Vengence
w. Corey D. Miller, Sunil Nayar
d. Norberto Barba

3:23 Whacked
w. Ann Donahue, Elizabeth Devine
d. Scott Lautanen

3:24 10-7
w. Ann Donahue, Elizabeth Devine
d. Joe Chappelle

SEASON FOUR
4:1 From the Grave
w. Ann Donahue, Elizabeth Devine
d. Karen Gaviola

4:2 Blood in the Water
w. Sunil Nayar, Dean Widenmann
d. Duane Clark

4:3 Prey
w. Barry O'Brien, Corey D. Miller
d. Scott Lautanen

4:4 48 Hours to Life
w. Marc Dube, John Haynes

d. Norberto Barba

4:5 Three Way
w. Marc Guggenheim, Ildy Modrovich
d. Jonathan Glassner

4:6 Under Suspicion
w. Sunil Nayar, Barry O'Brien
d. Sam Hill

4:7 Felony Flight
w. Anthony E. Zuiker, Ann Donahue,
    Elizabeth Devine
d. Scott Lautanen

4:8 Nailed
w. Corey D. Miller, Barry O'Brien
d. Karen Gaviola

4:9 Urban Hellraisers
w. Marc Guggenheim, Dean
    Widenmann
d. Matt Earl Beesley

4:10 Shattered
w. Ildy Modrovich
d. Scott Lautanen

4:11 Payback
w. Marc Dube, Ildy Modrovich, Marc
    Guggenheim
d. Sam Hill

4:12 The Score
w. Barry O'Brien
d. Jonathan Glassner

4:13 Silencer
w. Sunil Nayar
d. Ernest Dickerson

4:14 Fade Out
w. Corey D. Miller
d. Scott Lautanen

4:15 Skeletons
w. Elizabeth Devine, John Haynes
d. Karen Gaviola

4:16 Deviant
w. Krystal Houghton
d. Scott Lautanen

4:17 Collision
w. Dean Widenmann
d. Sam Hill

4:18 Double Jeopardy
w. Brian Davidson
d. Scott Lautanen

4:19 Driven
w. Ildy Modrovich
d. Eagle Egilsson

4:20 Free Fall
w. Marc Dube
d. Scott Lautanen

4:21 Dead Air
w. John Haynes
d. Sam Hill

4:22 Open Water
w. Marc Dube, Ildy Modrovich
d. Scott Lauranen

4:23 Shock
w. Corey D. Miller, Brian Davidson
d. Karen Gaviola

4:24 Rampage
w. Sunil Nayar
d. Duane Clark

4:25 One of Our Own
w. Krystal Houghton, Barry O'Brien
d. Matt Earl Beesley

SEASON FIVE

5:1 Rio
w. Sunil Nayar
d. Joe Chappelle

5:2 Going Under
w. Marc Dube, John Haynes
d. Matt Earl Beesley

5:3 Death Pool 100
w. Ann Donahue, Elizabeth Devine
d. Sam Hill

5:4 If Looks Could Kill
w. Barry O'Brien, Ildy Modrovich
d. Scott Lautanen

5:5 Death Eminent
w. Corey D. Miller, Brian Davidson
d. Eagle Egilsson

5:6 Curse of the Coffin
w. Krystal Houghton, Sunil Nayar
d. Joe Chappelle

5:7 High Octane
w. Marc Dube
d. Sam Hill

5:8 Darkroom
w. John Haynes

d. Karen Gaviola

5:9 Going, Going, Gone
w. Elizabeth Devine
d. Matt Earl Beesley

5:10 Come as You Are
w. Brian Davidson
d. Joe Chappelle

CSI: NY
Original Air Date:

SEASON ONE

1:0 MIA/NYC - Nonstop
w. Anthony E. Zuiker, Ann Donahue,
   Carol Mendelsohn
d. Danny Cannon

1:1 Blink
w. Anthony E. Zuiker
d. Deran Sarafian

1:2 Creatures of the Night
w. Pam Veasey
d. Tim Hunter

1:3 American Dreamers
w. Eli Talbert
d. Rob Bailey

1:4 Grand Master
w. Zachery Reiter
d. Kevin Bray

1:5 A Man a Mile
w. Andrew Lipsitz
d. David Grossman

1:6 Outside Man
w. Timothy J. Lea
d. Rob Bailey

1:7 Rain
w. Pam Veasey
d. David Grossman

1:8 Three Generations Are Enough
w. Andrew Lipsitz
d. Alex Zakrzewski

1:9 Officer Blue
w. Anthony E. Zuiker
d. Deran Sarafian

1:10 Night, Mother
w. Janet Tamaro
d. Deran Sarafian

1:11 Tri-Borough
w. Andrew Lipsitz, Eli Talbert
d. Greg Yaitanes

1:12 Recycling
w. Timothy J. Lea, Zachary Reiter
d. Alex Zakrzewski

1:13 Tanglewood
w. Anthony E. Zuiker
d. Karen Gaviola

1:14 Blood, Sweat and Tears
w. Erica Shelton, Eli Talbert

d. Scott Lautanen

1:15 Til Death Do We Part
w. Pam Veasey
d. Nelson McCormick

1:16 Hush
w. Anthony E. Zuiker, Timothy J. Lea
d. Deran Sarafian

1:17 The Fall
w. Anne McGrail
d. Norberto Barba

1:18 The Dove Commission
w. Anthony E. Zuiker, Zachary Reiter
d. Emilio Estevez

1:19 Crime and Misdemeanour
w. Andrew Lipsitz, Eli Talbert
d. Rob Bailey

1:20 Supply and Demand
w. Erica Shelton, Anne McGrail
d. Joe Chappelle

1:21 On the Job
w. Timothy J. Lea
d. David von Ancken

1:22 The Closer
w. Pan Veasey, David T. Catapano
d. Emilio Estevez

1:23 What You See Is What You See
w. Andrew Lipsitz
d. Duane Clark

SEASON TWO

2:1 Summer in the City
w. Pam Veasey
d. David von Ancken

2:2 Grand Murder at Central Station
w. Zachary Reiter
d. Scott Lautanen

2:3 Zoo York
w. Peter M. Lenkov, Timothy J. Lea
d. Norberto Barba

2:4 Corporate Warriors
w. Andrew Lipsitz
d. Rob Bailey

2:5 Dancing With the Fishes
w. Eli Talbert
d. John Peters

2:6 YoungBlood
w. Timothy J. Lea
d. Steven DePaul

2:7 Manhattan Manhunt
w. Anthony E. Zuiker, Ann Donahue, Elizabeth Devine
d. Rob Bailey

2:8 Bad Beat
w. Zachary Reiter
d. Duane Clark

2:9 City of the Dolls
w. Pam Veasey
d. Norberto Barba

2:10 Jamalot
w. Andrew Lipsitz

d. Jonathan Glassner

2:11 Trapped
w. Peter M. Lenkov
d. James Whitmore Jr.

2:12 Wasted
w. Bill Haynes, Pan Veasey
d. Jeff Thomas

2:13 Risk
w. John Dove
d. Rob Bailey

2:14 Stuck on You
w. Timothy J. Lea, Eli Talbert
d. Jonathan Glassner

2:15 Fare Game
w. Peter M. Lenkov, Zachary Reiter
d. Kevin Dowling

2:16 Cool Hunter
w. Daniele Nathanson
d. Norberto Barba

2:17 Necrophilia Americana
w. Andrew Lipsitz
d. Steven DePaul

2:18 Live or Let Die
w. Pam Veasey
d. Michael Daly

2:19 Super Men
w. Peter M. Lenkov, Pam Veasey
d. Steven DePaul

2:20 Run Silent, Run Deep
w. Anthony E. Zuiker

d. Rob Bailey

2:21 All Access
w. Timothy J. Lea, Anthony E. Zuiker
d. Norberto Barba

2:22 Stealing Home
w. Zachary Reiter
d. Oz Scott

2:23 Heroes
w. Eli Talbert
d. Anthony Hemingway

2:24 Charge of This Post
w. Timothy J. Lea
d. Rob Bailey

SEASON THREE
3:1 People With Money
w. Peter M. Lenkov, Pam Veasey
d. Rob Bailey

3:2 Not What It Looks Like
w. Peter M. Lenkov, Pam Veasey
d. Duane Clark

3:3 Love Run Cold
w. Timothy J. Lea
d. Tim Iacofano

3:4 Hung Out to Dry
w. Zachary Reiter
d. Anthony Hemingway

3:5 Oedipus Hex
w. Ken Solarz, Anthony E. Zuiker
d. Scott Lautanen

3:6 Open and Shut
w. Wendy Battles
d. Joe Ann Fogle

3:7 Murder Sings the Blues
w. Sam Humphrey
d. Oz Scott

3:8 Consequences
w. Pam Veasey
d. Rob Bailey

3:9 And Here's to You, Mrs. Azrael
w. Peter M. Lenkov
d. David von Ancken

3:10 Sweet 16
w. Ken Solarz
d. David Jackson

3:11 Raising Shane
w. Zachary Reiter, Pam Veasey
d. Christine Moore

FILM AND TV GUIDE

FILMS

Apollo 13 (Ron Howard, 1995)
Bad Boys II (Michael Bay, 2003)
Beverley Hills Cop (Martin Brest, 1984)
Black Hawk Down (Tony Scott, 2001)
Blues Brothers, The (John Landis, 1980)
Cool Hand Luke (Stuart Rosenberg, 1967)
Day After Tomorrow, The (Roland Emmerich, 2004)
Detective, The (Gordon Douglas, 1980)
Die Hard (John McTiernan, 1988)
Die Hard 2: Die Harder (Renny Harlin, 1990)
Enemy of the State (Tony Scott, 1998)
Evil Dead, The (Sam Raimi, 1981)
eXistenZ (David Cronenberg, 1999)
Fantastic Voyage (Richard Fleischer, 1966)
Flashdance (Adrian Lyne, 1983)
Forrest Gump (Robert Zemeckis, 1994)
Fort Apache the Bronx (Daniel Petrie, 1981)
From Here to Eternity (Fred Zimmerman, 1953)
Green Mile, The (Frank Darabont, 1999)
Innerspace (Joe Dante, 1987)
He Walked By Night (Alfred L.Werker, 1948)
In the Company of Men (Neil La Bute, 1997)
I Still Know What You Did Last Summer (Danny Cannon, 1998)
Judge Dredd (Danny Cannon, 1995)
Kiss of Death (Barbet Shroeder, 1995)
Lethal Weapon (Richard Donner, 1987)
Manhunter (Michael Mann, 1986)
Now Voyager (Irving Rapper, 1942)
Of Men and Mice (Gary Sinise, 1992)
Pearl Harbour (Michael Bay, 2001)

Pirates of the Caribbean: The Curse of the Black Pearl (Gore Verbinski, 2003)

Platoon (Oliver Stone, 1986)

Police Tapes, The (Alan Raymond and Susan Raymond, 1976)

Proof of Life (Taylor Hackford, 2000)

Psycho (Alfred Hitchcock, 1960)

Rock, The (Michael Bay, 1996)

Runner, The (Anthony E. Zuiker, 1999)

Se7en (David Fincher, 1995)

Silence of the Lambs, The (Jonathan Demme, 1991)

Single White Female (Barbet Schroeder, 1992)

Sin City (Frank Miller, Robert Rodriguez and Quentin Tarantino, 2005)

Solaris (Steven Soderbergh, 2002)

Towering Inferno, The (John Guillermin and Irwin Allen, 1974)

Thief (Michael Mann, 1981)

Three Kings (David O. Russell, 1999)

Top Gun (Tony Scott, 1986)

Vertigo (Alfred Hitchcock, 1958)

TV

Afterlife (Clerkenwell Films/ Independent Television 2005–)

Amazing Race, The (Jerry Bruckheimer Television/Touchstone Television/CBS, 2001–)

Arrested Development (Imagine Entertainment/20th Century Fox Television, 2003–)

Bad Girls (Shed Productions/ITV, 1999–2006)

Battlestar Galactica (British Sky Broadcasting/The Sci-Fi Channel/Sky One, 2004–)

Blackpool (BBC, 2004)

Boomtown (DreamWorks Television/National Broadcasting Company, 2002–2003)

Boston Public (David E. Kelley Productions/Fox Film Corporation, 2000–2004)

Buffy the Vampire Slayer (20th Century Fox Television/Mutant Enemy/ Kuzui Enterprises/Sandollar Television, 1999–2003)

Cannon (Quinn Martin Productions/CBS, 1971–1976)

Charmed (Spelling Television/WB Television Network, 1998–2006)

Chicago Hope (David E. Kelley Productions/20th Century Fox Television, 1994–2000)

China Beach (Warner Brothers Television/American Broadcasting

Company, 1988–1991)

Cold Case (Jerry Bruckheimer Television/CBS Productions/Warner Bros. Television, 2003–)

Columbo (Universal TV/NBC/ABC, 1968–2003)

Cop Rock (Steven Bochco Productions/20th Century Fox Television, 1990)

Cops, The (BBC, 1998–2000)

Cracker (A&E TV Network Inc/Granada/ITV, 1993–2006)

Crime Story (Michael Mann Productions/New World Television 1986–1988)

Dark Angel (20th Century Fox Television/Fox Network, 2000–2002)

Dateline (NBC News, 1992–)

Deadline (Studios USA Television/Wolf Films/NBC, 2000–2001)

Desperate Housewives (Touchstone Television/Cherry Productions/ABC, 2004–)

Doctor Who (BBC, 1963–1989; BBC/Canadian Broadcasting Corporation, 2005–)

Dragnet (Mark VII Productions/NBC, 1951–1959)

Due South (Alliance Altantis/Paul Haggis Productions/CTV Television Network Ltd/CBS, 1994–1996)

Dynasty (Aaron Spelling/ABC, 1981–1989)

ER (Constant Productions/Amblin Entertainment/WB Television Network/NBC, 1994–)

Frasier (Paramount/NBC, 1993–2004)

Freedom (Warner Bros. Television/UPN, 2000–2001)

Friends (NBC, 1994–2004)

Fugitive, The (Warner Bros. Television/CBS, 2000–2001)

Gordon Ramsay's Kitchen Nightmares (Channel 4, 2004–)

Hercules: The Legendary Journeys (Universal TV/MCA Television, 1995–1999)

Hill Street Blues (MTM Enterprises Inc/20th Century Fox, 1981–1987)

Home and Away (7 Network, 1988–)

Homicide: Life on the Street (Baltimore Pictures/NBC, 1993–1999)

House M.D. (Heel & Toe Films/Bad Hat Harry Productions/NBC Universal Television, 2004–)

Ironside (Universal TV/NBC, 1967–1975)

Joey (Silver and Gold Productions/Bright-San Productions/Warner Bros. Television, 2004–)

Jonathan Creek (BBC, 1997–2004)

Kojak (Universal TV/CBS Television/MCA Universal Pictures, 1973–

1978)

L.A. Law (20th Century Fox Television/NBC, 1986–1994)

Law & Order (Wolf Films/NBC, 1990–)

Law & Order: Special Victims Unit (Wolf Films/NBC, 1999–)

Law & Order: Criminal Intent (Wolf Films/NBC, 2001–)

Law & Order: Trial by Jury (Wolf Films/NBC Universal Television, 2005)

Lone Gunmen, The (20th Century Fox Television/Fox Network, 2001)

Lost (Touchstone Television/ABC, 2004–)

Lyon's Den, The (20th Century Fox Television/NBC, 2003–2004)

Madigan Men (Touchstone Television/ABC, 2000)

Magnum P.I. (Belisarius Productions/Glen A. Larson Productions/ Universal TV, 1980–1988)

Medium (CBS Paramount Network Television/NBC. 2005–)

Melrose Place (Darren Starr Productions /Fox, 1992–1999)

Miami Vice (Michael Mann Productions/Universal TV, 1984–1989)

Northern Exposure (Universal TV/CBS, 1990–1995).

NYPD Blue (20th Century Fox/Steven Bochco Productions/ABC, 1993–2005).

Police Story (David Gerber Productions/Columbia Pictures Television, 1973–1977)

Police Woman (David Gerber Productions/Columbia Pictures Television, 1974–1978)

Prime Suspect (Granada Television, 1991–2006)

Prison Break (Rat Entertainment/20th Century Fox Television, 2005–)

Quincy M.E. (Glen A. Larson Productions/Universal TV, 1976–1983)

Red Cap (Stormy Pictures Ltd/BBC, 2003–2004)

Sex and the City (Darren Star Productions/HBO, 1998–2004)

Shield, The (20th Century Fox/Columbia TriStar/fX, 2002–)

Silent Witness (BBC, 1996–)

Simpsons, The (Gracie Films/Film Roman Productions/20th Centruy Fox Television, 1989–)

Six Feet Under (The Greenblatt Janollari Studio/HBO, 2001–2005)

Sixty Minutes (BBC, 1983–1984)

Sopranos, The (Brad Grey Television/Chase Films/HBO, 1999–2007)

Special Unit 2 (Paramount Television/UPN, 2001–2002)

Spooks (BBC, 2002)

Star Trek (Desilu Productions (1966–1967) Paramount (1968–1969)/ NBC, 1966–1969)

Star Trek: The Next Generation (Paramount/CBS, 1987–1994)

Star Trek: Deep Space Nine (Paramount/CBS, 1993–1999)

Star Trek: Voyager (Paramount/United Paramount Network, 1995–2001)
Starsky and Hutch (Spelling-Goldberg Productions/ABC/Columbia
  Pictures Television, 1975–1979)
$treet, The (Columbia TriStar Television Inc./Fox, 2000–2001)
Survivor (Mark Burnett Productions/Castaway Television Productions/
  CBS, 2000–)
Titans (Spelling Television/NBC, 2000)
Tru Calling ('Oh That Gus!' Inc./Fox Television, 2003–2005)
24 (Imagine Entertainment/20th Century Fox Television, 2001–)
Untouchables, The (Desilu Productions/Langford Productions/ABC,
  1959–1963)
Vice, The (Carlton Television/ITV, 1999–2003)
Waking the Dead (BBC, 2000–)
West Wing, The (John Wells Production/ NBC, 1999–2006)
Wife Swap (Channel 4, 2003–)
Xena: Warrior Princess (MCA Television/Universal TV, 1995–2001)
Z Cars (BBC, 1962–1978)

RADIO

Jeff Regan – Investigator

VIDEO GAME

Resident Evil (Capcom Company, 1996)

::
BIBLIOGRAPHY

Abercrombie, Nicholas and Brian Longhurst. *Audiences.* London: Sage, 1998

Abbot, H. Porter. *The Cambridge Introduction to Narrative.* Cambridge: Cambridge University Press, 2002

Abbott, Stacey. 'Final Frontiers: Computer-Generated Imagery and the Science Fiction Film'. *Science Fiction Studies.* 33: 1. March 2006: 89–108

Amesley, Cassandra. 'How to Watch *Star Trek*'. *Cultural Studies.* 3:3. 1989: 323–39

Arnold, Eugene A. 'Autopsy: The Final Diagnosis'. Elizabeth Klaver, ed. *Images of the Corpse: From the Renaissance to Cyberspace.* Wisconsin: University of Wisconsin Press/Popular Press, 2004: 3–15

Bacon-Smith, Camille. *Enterprising Women.* Philadelphia: University of Pennsylvania Press, 1992

Bailey, Steve. *Media Audiences and Identity: Self-Construction in the Fan Experience.* London: Palgrave-Macmillan, 2005

Barthes, Roland. *Mythologies*, trans. Annette Lavers. New York: Hill and Wang, 1972

Bazin, Andrè. *What Is Cinema? Volume 1.* Berkeley: University of California Press, 1967

Bazin, Andrè. *What Is Cinema? Volume 2.* Berkeley: University of California Press, 1971

Bazin, Andrè. 'Science Film: Accidental Beauty (1947)'. Andy Masaki Bellows, Marina McDougall, Brigitte Berg, eds. *Science is Fiction. The Films of Jean Painlevé.* Cambridge, Massachusetts and London: The MIT Press. San Francisco: Brico Press, 2000: 144–7

Bignell, Jonathan. 'Seeing and knowing: reflexivity and quality'. Janet McCabe and Kim Akass, eds. *Reading Quality TV: American TV and Beyond.* London: I.B. Tauris, forthcoming

Bird, S. Elizabeth. *The Audience in Everyday Life.* New York and London: Routledge, 2003

Bishop, Claire. 'Antagonism and Relational Aesthetics'. *October.* 110. Fall 2004: 51–79

Black, Joe. *The Reality Effect: Film Culture and the Graphic Imperative.* London: Routledge, 2002

Bordwell, David. *Narration in the Fiction Film*. London: Methuen, 1985

Boyle, Karen. *Media and Violence: Gendering the Debates*. London: Sage, 2005

Branston, Gill and Roy Stafford. *The Media Student's Book: Fourth Edition*. London and New York: Routledge, 2006

Bronfen, Elisabeth. *Over Her Dead Body. Death, Femininity and the Aesthetic*. Manchester: Manchester University Press, 1992

Buren, Daniel. 'The Function of the Studio'. Claire Doherty, ed. *From Studio to Situation*. London: Black Dog Publishing, 2004: 16-23

Buxton, David. 'The Police Series'. *From the Avengers to Miami Vice. Form and Ideology in Television Series*. Manchester and New York: Manchester University Press, 1990: 120-60

Caldwell, John Thornton. *Televisuality: Style, Crisis and Authority in American Television*, New Brunswick, New Jersey: Rutgers University Press, 1995

Caldwell, John Thornton. 'Welcome to the Viral Future of Cinema (Television)'. *Cinema Journal*. 45:1. Fall 2005: 90-7

Cannon, Danny. 'The *CSI* Shot: Making it Real'. *CSI: Crime Scene Investigation* 3:13-3:23, DVD commentary, Momentum Pictures, 2004a

Cannon, Danny. DVD commentary to 'Alter Boys'. *CSI: Crime Scene Investigation* 2:-2:12. Momentum Pictures, 2004b

Carroll, Noël. 'Prospects for Film Theory'. David Bordwell and Noël Carroll, eds. *Post-Theory. Reconstructing Film-Studies*. Madison, Wisconsin: University of Wisconsin Press, 1996: 37-70

Carter, Bill. 'Hey, You Want Forensics? We Got Forensics'. *New York Times*. 16 May 2004: S13, 4-5

Casey, Neil, Bernadette Casey, Justin Lewis, Ben Calvert, Liam French, eds. *Television: The Key Concepts*. London: Routledge, 2001

Clover, Carol. 'Her Body, Himself: Gender in the Slasher Film'. *Representations* 20. Fall 1987: 187-228

Clover, Carol J. *Men, Women and Chain Saws: Gender in the Modern Horror Film*. London: bfi Publishing, 1992

Clover, Carol. Crime Scene Investigation and social anatomy'. *European Journal of Cultural Studies*, 8:4. November 2005, 445-63

Collins, Max Allan. *Cold Burn*. London: Pocket Books, 2003

Collins, Max Allan, Rodriguez, Gabriel and Wood, Ashley. *Bad Rap. CSI: Crime Scene Investigation* graphic novel. London: Titan Books, 2004

Comte, August. *Introduction to Positive Philosophy*. Indianapolis: Hackett Publishing, 1988

Connor, Steven. *Dumbstruck: a Cultural History of Ventriloquism*. Oxford: Oxford University Press, 2000

Cooke, Lez. 'Hill Street Blues'. Glen Creeber, ed. *The Television Genre Book*. London: bfi Publishing, 2001

Couldry, Nick. *Inside Culture* London: Sage, 2000

Crary, Jonathan. *Techniques of the Observer*. Cambridge: MIT Press, 1990

Creeber, Glen. *Serial Television. Big Drama on the Small Screen*. London: bfi Publishing, 2004

Debord, Guy. *The Society of Spectacle*. Detroit: Black and Red, 1983

Deleuze, Gilles. *Cinema 2: The Time-Image*. London: The Athlone Press, 1989

Derrida, Jacques. 'Signature, Event, Context', Montreal, August 1971. *Margins of Philosophy*. Trans. Alan Bass/ London and New York: Prentice Hall, 1982: 307-30

Derrida, Jacques. *Of Grammatology*. Baltimore: The John Hopkins University Press, 1974

Derrida, Jacques. *Éperon: Spurs Nietzsche's Styles*. Chicago and London: University of Chicago Press, 1979

Derrida, Jacques. *Limited Inc*, Evanston, Illinois: Northwestern University Press, 1988

Derrida, Jacques. 'La danse des fantômes/The Ghost Dance, interview with Andrew Payne and Mark Lewis'. *Public*. 2. 1989: 61-8

Derrida, Jacques. *Acts of Literature*. London and New York: Routledge, 1992.

Derrida, Jacques. *Specters of Marx: the State of the Debt, the Work of Mourning, and the New International*. New York and London: Routledge, 1994

Derrida, Jacques. *Acts of Religion*. New York: Routledge, 2002a

Derrida, Jacques. *Negotiations*. Stanford: Stanford University Press, 2002b

Derrida, Jacques and Bernard Stiegler. *Echographies of Television*. Cambridge: Polity Press, 2002

Detwiller, Lary. 'The CSI Shot: Making it Real'. *CSI: Crime Scene Investigation* 3:13-3:23. DVD commentary. Momentum Pictures, 2004

Doherty, Thomas. 'Cultural Studies and "Forensic Noir"'. *The Chronicle of Higher Education*. 50: 3. 24 October 2003: B15-16

Dyer, Richard. 'Male Gay Porn: Coming to Terms'. *Jump Cut*. 30. 1985: 27-9

Dyer, Richard. *Seven*, BFI Modern Classics Series. London: bfi Publishing, 1999

Eden, Jenny. 'Caruso Control.' *Radio Times*, 5-11 August 2006: 10-12

Ellis, John. 'Scheduling: the Last Creative Act in Television?' *Media, Culture & Society*. 22: 1. 2000: 25-38

Elsaesser, Thomas. *Fassbinder's Germany: History, Identity, Subject*. Amsterdam: Amsterdam University Press, 1996

Elsaesser, Thomas. 'Subject Positions, Speaking Positions: From *Holocaust*, Our *Hitler* and *Heimat* to *Shoah* and *Schindler's List*'. Vivian Sobchack, ed. *The Persistence of History*. New York: Routledge, 1996: 145-83

Elsaesser, Thomas. 'Postmodernism as Mourning Work'. *Screen*. 42: 2. Summer 2001: 193-201

Fletcher, James E. 'Syndication'. Horace Newcomb, ed. *Museum of Broadcast Communications Encyclopedia of Television VOL 4 S-Z*. New York: Fitzroy Dearborn, 2004. 2247-8

Ford, Jeff. Interview with Simone Knox, 27 February 2006.

Foucault, Michel. *Discipline and Punish: The Birth of the Prison*. London: Penguin, 1991

Foucault, Michel. *The Will To Knowledge. The History of Sexuality. Volume 1*. London: Penguin, 1998

Fuery, Patrick and Kelli Fuery. *Visual Cultures and Critical Theory*. London: Arnold, 2003

Gardner Conklin, Barbara and Robert Gardner, Dennis Shortelle, eds. 'Trace Evidence'. *Encyclopedia of Forensic Science*. Westport: Oryx Press, 2002

Gever, Martha. 'The Spectacle of Crime, Digitized: CSI: *Crime Scene Investigation* and Social Anatomy'. *European Journal of Cultural Studies*. 8: 4. 2005: 445–63

Goode, Ian. 'Channel 5, Quality and the Forensic Surface of C.S.I. Crime Scene Investigation'. Paper presented to the *Quality American TV: International Conference*. Trinity College, Dublin. April 2004

Grainge, Paul. Ed. *Memory and Popular Film*. Manchester: Manchester University Press, 2003

Gray, Jonathan. 'New audiences, New Textualities: Anti-fans and non-fans'. *International Journal of Cultural Studies*. 6:1. 2003: 64–81

Gray, Jonathan. 'Antifandom and the Moral Text'. *American Behavioral Scientist*. 48:7. 2005: 840–58

Gripsrud, Jostein. *The Dynasty Years: Hollywood Television and Critical Media Studies*. London: Routledge, 1995

Gunning, Tom. 'The Cinema of Attractions: Early Film, Its Spectator and the Avant Garde'. Thomas Elsaesser, ed. *Early Cinema: Space, Frame, Narrative*, London: bfi Publishing, 1990: 56–62

Guzman, Isaac. 'Third "CSI"'. *Daily News* (NY). 22 April 2004: 36–7.

Gwenllian Jones, Sara. 'Starring Lucy Lawless?' *Continuum*. 14:1. 2000: 9–22

Hatton, Josh. 'The CSI Shot: Making it Real'. *CSI: Crime Scene Investigation*. 3:13–3:23. DVD commentary. Momentum Pictures, 2004

Hayes, Jonathan. 'Exquisite Corpses.' *New York*. 27 September 2004: 36, 38–9

Healy, Patrick, D. 'New York Is Noir Again: In Dark Times, TV Sings of the Dark City', *The New York Times*. 21 February 2005: E1, E7

Helbig, Bob. 'Brain waves; Didn't They Used to Call it the Idiot Box? Not Anymore.' *Milwaukee Journal Sentinel* (Wisconsin). Section: 'E Cue'. 15 February 2006: 1

Hermes, Joke. *Re-reading Popular Culture*. Oxford: Blackwell Publishing, 2005

Hills, Matt. *Fan Cultures*. London and New York: Routledge, 2002

Holloway, Diane. 'Plot means a Lot. For *Law & Order*, CSI and other Procedural Dramas, the Story Plays the Starring Role'. *Austin American-Statesman* (Texas). 22 August 2003

Holston, Noel. 'The Science of Being No.1', *Newsday*, D12, D13, D14

Hoskins, Colin and Rolf Mirus. 'Reasons for the US Dominance of the International Trade in Television Programmes'. *Media, Culture & Society*. 10: 4. 1988: 499–515

Houseman, John. 'Today's Hero: A Review,' *Hollywood Quarterly*, 2: 2. 1946–1947: 161–3

Jacobs, Jason. *The Intimate Screen. Early British Television Drama*. Oxford: Clarendon Press, 2000

Jacobs, Jason. *Body Trauma TV. The New Hospital Dramas*. London: bfi Publishing, 2003

Jacobus, Mary, Evelyn Fox Keller and Sally Shuttleworth. 'Introduction'. Jacobus, Mary, Evelyn Fox Keller and Sally Shuttleworth, eds. *Body/Politics: Women and the Discourses of Science*. London: Routledge, 1990: 1–10

James, Caryn. 'How to Fight Lawlessness? Subdivide Crime Shows'. *New York Times*. 23 September 2002: E5

Jameson, Fredric. *The Political Unconscious: Narrative as a Socially Symbolic Act*. Ithaca: Cornell University Press, 1981

Jenkins, Henry. *Textual Poachers*. New York and London: Routledge, 1992

Jermyn, Deborah. 'Women with a Mission. Lynda La Plante, DCI Jane Tennison and the Reconfiguration of TV Crime Drama'. *International Journal of Cultural Studies*. 6: 1. 2003: 46–63

Johnson, Catherine. *Telefantasy*. London: bfi Publishing, 2005

Juul, Jesper. *Half-real: Video Games Between Real Rules and Fictional Worlds*. Cambridge Mass. and London: The MIT Press, 2005

Kaminsky, Stuart M. *Dead of Winter*. London: Pocket Books, 2005

Kaminsky, Stuart M. *Blood on the Sun*. London: Pocket Books, 2006

Kaplan, E. Ann. 'Melodrama, Cinema and Trauma'. *Screen*. 42: 2. Summer 2001: 102–205

Kristeva, Julia. *Powers of Horror. An Essay on Abjection*. New York: Columbia University Press, 1982

Krutnik, Frank. *In A Lonely Place: Film Noir, Genre, Masculinity*. London: Routledge, 2004

Lacan, Jacques. 'The Function and Field of Speech and Language in Psychoanalysis'. *Ecrits: A Selection*. London: Tavistock Publications, 1977. 30–113

Lacan, Jacques. *The Four Fundamental Concepts of Psycho-Analysis*. New York: Norton, 1978

Landsberg, Alison. *Prosthetic Memory: The Logic and Politics of Memory in Modern American Culture*. PhD dissertation, University of Chicago, 1996

Landsberg, Alison. 'America, the Holocaust, and the Mass Culture of Memory: Toward a Radical Politics of Empathy'. *New German Critique*. 71. Summer 1997: 63–86

Levin, David Michael. *The Listening Self: Personal Growth, Social Change and the Closure of Metaphysics*. London: Routledge, 1989

Levine, Robert. 'The Forensic Evidence Is In, And It Points to New York'. *New York Times* (Sunday). 16 May 2004: S2, 25

Lippit, Akira Mizuta. *'Phenomenologies of the Surface: Radiation – Body – Image'*

Jane Gaines and Michael Renov, eds. *Collecting Visual Evidence*, Minneapolis and London: University of Minnesota, 1999: 65–83

Lipscomb, Georgina. 'Lygo promises C5 will look after top series'. *Broadcast*. 19 October

2001: 1

Lury, Karen. 'Television Performance: Being, Acting and "Corpsing"'. *New Formations*. 27. Winter 1995–1996: 114–27

Lury, Karen. *Interpreting Television*. Hodder Arnold: London, 2005

MacCannell, Juliet Flower. *Figuring Lacan: Criticism and the Cultural Unconscious*. Lincoln: University of Nebraska Press, 1986

Marc, David. *Demographic Vistas: Television in American Culture*. Philadelphia: University of Pennsylvania Press, 1984

Marc, David and Robert J. Thompson. *Prime Time: Prime Movers*. Syracuse: Syracuse University Press, 1995

Mason, Dave. 'CSI vs. Reality, Experts say Real Labs Lack TV's Resources'. *Ventura County Star* (California). *Life*. 16 February 2003: K03

McCabe, Janet. 'Diagnosing the Alien: *Producing* Identities, American 'Quality' Drama and British Television Culture in the 1990s'. Bruce Carson and Margaret Llewellyn-Jones, eds. *Frames and Fictions on Television: The Politics of Identity Within Drama*. Exeter: Intellect, 2000. 141–54

McFadden, Kay. 'They're Hot! They're Sexy! They're Geeks!; TV catches up with Real Life: Left-brain Smarties Get Roles, and the Girl'. *The Seattle Times*. Section: Rop Zone; Northwest Life. 14 November 2005: E1

McGrath, Charles. 'The Blood-Splattered Triplets of CSI'. *New York Times*. 21 November 2004: 26, 32

Mikulak, Bill. 'Fans versus Time Warner'. Kevin S. Sandler, ed. *Reading the Rabbit*. New Brunswick: Rutgers University Press, 1998: 193–208

Mittell, Jason. *Genre and Television: From Cop Shows to Cartoons in American Culture*. London and New York: Routledge, 2005

Morris, Mark. 'Bored with ER? Try This'. *The Observer* (Review Section). 24 June 2001: 5

Mulvey, Laura. 'Visual Pleasure and Narrative Cinema'. Joanne Hollows, Peter Hutchings and Mark Jancovich, eds. *The Film Studies Reader*. London: Arnold, 2000. 238–48

Mulvey, Laura. 'Stillness in the Moving Image: Ways of Visualizing Time and Its Passing'. Tanya Leighton and Pavel Büchler, eds. *Saving the Image: Art after Film*. Glasgow: Centre for Contemporary Arts and Manchester: Manchester Metropolitan University, 2003: 78–89

Murch, Walter. 'Touch of Silence'. Larry Sider, Diane Freeman and Jerry Sider eds. *Soundscape: The School of Sound Lectures 1998–2001*. Wallflower Press: London, 2003:

Ndalianis, Angela. 'Television and the Neo-Baroque'. Michael Hammond and Lucy Mazdon, eds. *The Contemporary Television Series*. Edinburgh: Edinburgh University Press, 2005: 83–101

Newcombe, Horace and Alley, Robert S, eds. *The Producer's Medium: Conversations with*

Creators of American TV. New York: Oxford University Press, 1983

Palmer, Michelle. Interviewed in Stephanie Ogilvie, 'CSI: Roanoke; *CSI*: Pros Watch Show'. *The Roanoke Times* (Virginia). Metro Edition. 21 November 2003: 1

Parker, Cornelia. *The Turner Prize.* C4, 1997

Pearson, Roberta. '"It's Always 1985": Sherlock Holmes in Cyberspace'. Deborah Cartmell, I.Q. Hunter, Heidi Kaye and Imelda Whelehan, eds. *Trash Aesthetics.* London: Pluto Press, 1997: 143–61

Petersen, William. DVD commentary to Season One. *CSI: Crime Scene Investigation.* Momentum Pictures, 2002.

Peterson, Gilbert L. 'Forensic Analysis of Digital Image Tampering'. *Advances in Digital Forensics.* 194. 2006: 259–270

Pinedo, Isabel Christina. *Recreational Terror: Women and the Pleasures of Horror.* Albany, NY; State University of New York Press, 1997

Purse, Lisa. 'The New Spatial Dynamics of the Bullet-Time Effect'. Geoff King, ed *The Spectacle of the Real. From Hollywood to Reality TV and Beyond.* Bristol: Intellect Books, 2005: 151–60

Radstone, Susannah. 'Working With Memory: An Introduction'. Susannah Radstone, ed. *Memory and Methodology.* Oxford: Berg, 2000: 1–22

Revoir, Paul. 'Who needs American TV?'. *Broadcast.* 12 September 2003: 19

Richmond, Roy. 'CSI 100th: To Live and Die in Las Vegas'. *The Hollywood Reporter.* Special Edition on 100th CSI Episode. 18 November 2004: 5.

Rimmon-Kenan, Shlomith. *Narrative Fiction: Contemporary Poetics.* London: Methuen, 1983

Rixon, Paul. 'The Changing Face of American Television Programmes on British Screens'. Mark Jancovich and James Lyons, eds. *Quality Popular Television: Cult TV, the Industry and Fans.* London: bfi Publishing, 2003: 48–61

Saenz, Michael. 'Programming'. Horace Newcomb, ed. *Museum of Broadcast Communications Encyclopedia of Television VOL 3 M-R.* New York: Fitzroy Dearborn, 2004:1833–42

Sandvoss, Cornel. *Fans.* Cambridge: Polity Press, 2005

Sawday, Jonathan. *The Body Emblazoned: Dissection and the Human Body in Renaissance Culture.* London and New York: Routledge, 1995

Schmidt, Leigh Eric. *Hearing Things: Religion, Illusion and the American Enlightenment.* Cambridge: Harvard University Press, 2002

Schneider, Michael and Adalian, Josef. 'Mouse Won't Touch CBS Hourlong'. *Variety.* 14 August 2000: 13, 37

Sehlinger, Bob. *The Unofficial Guide to Walt Disney World 2004,* Hoboken, NJ: John Wiley and Sons, Inc, 2003

Sheridan, Alan. 'Translator's Note'. Jacques Lacan. *Ecrits: A Selection.* London: Tavistock Publications, 1977. vii-xii

Siegel, Lee. 'Crime scenes – why cop shows are eternal'. *The New Republic.* 31 March 2003: 25

Signer, Roman. *Audio Arts Magazine.* Vol. 22, No.1. London, 2004

Silver, Alian and Elizabeth Ward. *Film Noir: An Encyclopedic Reference Guide.* London: Bloomsbury, 1980

Sitchon, Myra L. and Hoppa, Robert D. 'Assessing age-related morphology of the pubic symphysis from digital images versus direct observation'. *Journal of Forensic Sciences.* 50: 4. July 2005: 791-5

Smith, Christine. 'Elstein slams C4 £60m show deal'. *Broadcast.* 13 December 1996: 3

Sontag, Susan. *Against Interpretation and Other Essays,* New York: Picador USA, 2001

Stafford, Barbara, Maria. *Body Criticism: Imagining the Unseen in Enlightenment Art and Medicine,* Cambridge, Massachusetts, MIT Press, 1991

Stafford, Barbara Maria. *Good Looking: Essays on the Virtue of Images.* Cambridge, Massachusetts: MIT Press, 1996

Stanley, Alessandra. 'CSI Moves To Gotham But Is Still From Mars'. *New York Times.* 22 September 2004: E1, E10

Sterne, Jonathan. *The Audible Past: the cultural origins of sound reproduction.* Duke University Press: Durham, 2003

Sternberg, Meir. *Expositional Modes and Temporal Ordering in Fiction.* Baltimore: John Hopkins University Press, 1978

Stiegler, Bernhard.'The Discrete Image'. Jacques Derrida and Bernard Stiegler, eds *Echographies of Television. Filmed Interviews.* Cambridge: Polity Press, 2002: 147-63

Sturken, Marita. *Tangled Memories: The Vietnam War, the AIDS Epidemic and the Politics of Remembering.* Berkeley: University of California Press, 1997

Sumser, John. *Morality and Social Order in Television Crime Drama.* Jefferson, North Carolina, and London: McFarland & Company Publishers, 1996

Tait, Sue. 'Autopic Vsion and the Necrophilic Imaginary in CSI'. *International Journal of Cultural Studies.* 9: 1. 2006: 45-62

Thornham, Sue. '"A Good Body": The Case of/for Feminist Media Studies'. *European Journal of Cultural Studies.* 6:1. 2003: 75-94

Todorov, Tzvetan. *The Poetics of Prose.* Oxford: Basil Backwell, 1977

Todorov, Tzvetan. 'Reading as Construction'. Michael J. Hoffman and Patrick D. Murphy, eds. *Essentials of the Theory of Fiction.* Durham: Duke University Press, 1988: 413; quoted in Genie Babb. 'Where the Bodies are Buried: Cartesian Dispositions in Narrative Theories of Character'. *Narrative.* 10: 3. October 2002: 196

Tomasulo, Frank P. '"I'll See It When I Believe It": Rodney King and the Prison-House of Video'. Vivian Sobchack, ed. *The Persistence of History: Cinema, Television, and the Modern Event.* London: Routledge, 1996: 69-88

Tulloch, John and Henry Jenkins. *Science Fiction Audiences: Watching Doctor Who and Star*

Trek. London and New York: Routledge, 1995

Turnbull, Sue. 'Bodies of Knowledge: Pleasure and Anxiety in the Detective Fiction of Patricia D. Cornwell'. *Australian Journal of Law and Society*. 9. 1993: 19–41

Turnbull, Sue. 'Crime Scene Investigations (CSI): A Fluorescent Analysis'. *Metro*. 143. 2004: 126–33

Turnbull, Sue. '*CSI*: A fluorescent analysis'. *Metro*. 143. 2005: 126–8

Wade, Gavin, ed. *Curating in the 21ˢᵗ Century*. Manchester: Cornerhouse Publications, 2000

Walton, Priscilla L. and Manina Jones. *Detective Agency: Women Rewriting the Hard-Boiled Tradition*. Berkeley, Los Angeles, London: University of California Press, 1999

Weeks, Janet. '*CSI* Confidential'. *TV Guide*. 23 February 2002: 16–20, 22,

Weissmann, Elke. *Crime, the Truth and the Body: The Move towards Forensics in the Representation of Crime on Television*, Unpublished PhD thesis, University of Glasgow, 2006

White, Hayden. *Tropics of Discourse: Essays in Cultural Criticism*. Baltimore: Johns Hopkins University Press, 1978

White, Hayden. 'Method and Ideology in Intellectual History'. Dominick LaCapra and Steven L. Kaplan, eds. *Modern European Intellectual History: Reappraisals and New Perspectives*. Ithaca: Cornell University Press, 1982: 280–310

White, Hayden. 'The Modernist Event'. Vivian Sobchack, eds. *The Persistence of History*. New York: Routledge, 1996: 17–38

Williams, Linda. *Hard Core: Power, Pleasure and the 'Frenzy of the Visible'*, London: Pandora Books, 1990

Williams, Linda. 'Film Bodies: Gender, Genre and Excess', *Film Quarterly*. 44: 4. Summer 1991: 2–13

Willing, Richard. '"CSI Effect" Has Juries Wanting More Evidence'. *USA Today*. 5 August 2004: 1–2

Wolf, Mark J. P., 'Subjunctive Documentary: Computer Imaging and Simulation' Jane Gaines and Michael Renov, eds. *Collecting Visual Evidence*. Minneapolis and London: University of Minnesota, 1999: 274–91

Wootton, Adrian. email interview with Kim Akass. 26 September 2006

Wootton, Adrian. email interview with Kim Akass. 17 October 2006

Wright Wiley, Kim. *Walt Disney World With Kids 2006*, NY: Fodor's, 2006

Zizek, Slavoj. 'The Undergrowth of Enjoyment: How Popular Culture can Serve as an Introduction to Lacan'. Elizabeth Wright and Edmond Wright, eds. *The Zizek Reader*. Oxford: Blackwell Publishers, 1999: 11–36

WEBSITES

Anon. 'Cast/Characters', *CSI: Miami* official web-site (Accessed: 31 March 2006) http://www.cbs.com/primetime/csi_miami/

Anon. 'CSI show 'most popular in the world'. 31 July 2006: http://news.bbc.co.uk/1/
hi/entertainment/5231334.stm

Anon. 'CSI Horatio Caine Sunglasses'. Accessed: 31 March 2006: www.CelebrityGlasses.
com

Anderson, Christopher. 'At Last, TV For People Just Like Me'. *Flow*. 1: 10. 20 February
2005: http://jot.communication.utexas.edu/flow/?jot=view&id=560

Binfield, Marnie. 'A Strange Parallel'. *Flow*. Comments. 1: 10. 20 February 2005: http://
jot.communication.utexas.edu/flow/?jot=view&id=541

Careless, James. Article on James Fowler. *Millimeter*. 2 October 2002: http://millimeter.
com

Carolina. 'Anthony Zuiker Weighs In On Procedural vs Serial Debate'. Posted 8 June
2006: http://www.csifiles.com/news/080606_01.shtml

Corner, John. 'Television and the Practice of "Criticism"'. *Flow*. 4: 12. September 2006:
http://jot.communication.utexas.edu/flow/?jot=view&id=1962

Crime Scene 2005. 21 June 2005: http://forums.booktrade.info/showthread.php?t=284

Dzenis, Anna. 'Michael Mann'. *senses of cinema*. 2002: http://www.sensesofcinema.
com/contents/directors/D2/Mann.html

Elsaesser, Thomas. 'One Train May be Hiding Another: Private History, Memory,
and National Identity,' *Screening the Past*. May 1992: http://www.latrobe.edu.
au/screeningthepast/reruns/rr0499/terr6b.htm

Fowler, Mick. Interview by James Careless for *Millimeter*. 2 October 2002. Accessed 9 July
2003: http://millimeter.com

Franses, Rico. 'In the Picture, But Out of Place: The Lacanian Gaze, Again'. *Fort Da*. 7:
2. Fall 2001: http://www.fortda.org/fall_01/picture.html

Gonzales, Vince. 'Prosecutors Feel The "CSI Effect"'. *CBS News Online*.10 February
2005. http://www.cbsnews.com/stories/2005/02/10/eveningnews/main673060.
shtml

Guider, Elizabeth. 'Pic Chic May Lure Foreign TV buyers'. *Variety International*. 19 May
2000: http://www.variety.com/article/VR1117781898?categoryid=19&cs=1

Guider, Elizabeth and Eileen Tasca. 'CSI: Miami Heating Up Screenings'. *Variety*. 20
May 2002: http://www.variety.com/article/VR1117867278?categoryid=14&cs=1

Jenkins, Henry. 'Transmedia Storytelling: Moving characters from books to films to
video games can make them stronger and more compelling'. *Technology Review*. 15
January 2003: http://www.technologyreview.com/read_article.aspx?id=13052&c
h=biotech&s

Johnson, Debra. 'BSkyB checks out L.A. Screenings'. *Variety*. 15 May 2003: http://www.
variety.com/article/VR1117886280?categoryid=1616&cs=1

Johnson, Heather. 'The Men Behind the Audio of US Drama, CSI: Crime Scene
Investigation'. *Audio Media Online*. Accessed 9 September 2003: http://www.
audiomedia.com

Johnson, Heather. 'The Men Behind the Audio of US Drama, 'CSI:Crime Scene Investigation'. *Audio Media Online*. Accessed 9 September 2003: http://www.audiomedia.com

Juul, Jesper. 'A Clash between Game and Narrative'. Paper presented at the Digital Arts and Culture Conference, Bergen, Norway. November 1998: http://www.jesperjuul.net/text/clash_between_game_and_narrative.html

Keane, John M. Interview for Garritan Orchestral Libraries and Northern Sounds. Accessed 28 October 2005: http://northernsounds.com/

Kushman, Rick. 'Procedural vs. Serial: The Great Debate'. *Variety*. 31 May 2006: http://www.variety.com/awardcentral_article/VR1117944332.html?nav=news&category id=1985&cs=1

Mittell, Jason. 'The Best of Television: The Inaugural Flow Critics' Poll'. *Flow*. 4: 12, September 2006: http://jot.communication.utexas.edu/flow/?issue=2006/09/22

Morris, Mark. 'Bored with ER? Try this'. *The Observer*. 24 June 2001: http://observer.guardian.co.uk/print/0,3858,4209234-102281,00.html

Ott, Brian L. 'Contemporary Television Criticism: State of the Art or Stuck in the Past?' *Flow*. 1: 2. October 2004: http://jot.communication.utexas.edu/flow/?jot=view&id=444

Ott, Brian L. 'Set Your Cathode Rays to Stun(ning)', *Flow*. 1: 10. February 2005: http://jot.communication.utexas.edu/flow/?jot=view&id=541

Ryan, Marie-Laure. 'Immersion vs. Interactivity: Virtual Reality and Literary Theory'. *Postmodern Culture*. 5: 1. 1994: http://www.humanities.uci.edu/mposter/syllabi/readings/ryan.html

Ryan, Maureen. 'Solving the mystery of the CSI finale shocker'. *The Watcher* A Chicago Tribune Web log, originally posted: May 25, 2006, http://featuresblogs.chicagotribune.com/entertainment_tv/2006/05/solving_the_mys.html

Santo, Avi and Lucas, Christopher. 'Welcome to Flow'. *Flow*. 1: 1. October 2004: http://jot.communication.utexas.edu/flow/?jot=view&id=372

Schaefer, Eric. Dragnet, www.musem.tv/archives/etv/D/htmlD/dragnet/dragnet/htm

Smith, Rupert. 'American Beauty'. *The Guardian*. 3 February 2003: http://www.guardian.co.uk/print/0,,4597175-103689,00.html

Westcott, Tim. 'Brit Buyers Bring More Cautious Mood'. *Variety*. 6 October 2002: http://www.variety.com/article/VR1117873788?categoryid=1407&cs=1

INDEX